Dementia Studies

Dementia Studies

A Social Science Perspective

Anthea Innes

Los Angeles • London • New Delhi • Singapore • Washington DC

© Anthea Innes 2009

First published 2009

SAGE Publications Ltd
1 Oliver's Yard
55 City Road
London EC1Y 1SP

SAGE Publications Inc.
2455 Teller Road
Thousand Oaks, California 91320

SAGE Publications India Pvt Ltd
B 1/I 1 Mohan Cooperative Industrial Area
Mathura Road
New Delhi 110 044

SAGE Publications Asia-Pacific Pte Ltd
33 Pekin Street #02-01
Far East Square
Singapore 048763

Library of Congress Control Number: 2008932230

British Library Cataloguing in Publication data

A catalogue record for this book is available
from the British Library

ISBN 978-1-4129-2163-3
ISBN 978-1-4129-2164-0 (pbk)

Typeset by C&M Digitals (P) Ltd., Chennai, India
Printed in India at Replika Press Pvt Ltd
Printed on paper from sustainable resources

CONTENTS

List of Figures   vi
Acknowledgements   vii

1 What is dementia? Unpicking what is 'known'   1

2 The context of dementia studies: political, economic
   and social issues   27

3 Caring for people with dementia: utopian ideals?   45

4 Dementia studies within cultural contexts   72

5 Researching dementia and dementia care: implications
   of the generation of research knowledge for policy,
   practice and approaches to research   102

6 A model for dementia studies: knowledge generation
   and development   133

References   165

Index   189

LIST OF FIGURES

6.1 A learning cycle – adapted from Kolb, 1984   138
6.2 Applying the notion of a cyclical process for the
study of dementia   139
6.3 A model for studying dementia   140
6.4 A web of understanding about dementia – from
a medical viewpoint   146

ACKNOWLEDGEMENTS

I wish to thank Alan Chapman, Fiona Kelly, Roxann Johnson, Kathryn Mackay and Jane Robertson for their comments on early chapter drafts. I am very grateful to Eileen Richardson for sourcing materials I cited in the book and for her careful checking and preparation of the manuscript. And thank you to my daughter for understanding that I needed to spend time writing rather than playing and thank you to my parents for doing the playing while I wrote.

1

WHAT IS DEMENTIA? UNPICKING
WHAT IS 'KNOWN'

■ ■ Chapter summary ■

- This chapter begins by charting the academic study of dementia from a social science perspective, highlighting biomedical, social-psychological and social-gerontological contributions to a subject that has gained rapid momentum in the last decade.
- Biomedical approaches tend to adopt stage theories of dementia, focusing on a general progressive decline consisting of increases in cognitive impairment and decreasing ability to complete tasks of daily living.
- Social-psychological, or psycho-social approaches (Kitwood, 1997; Sabat and Harré, 1992), provide an opportunity to refocus on the personhood or self of each individual with dementia, and provide the theoretical basis for person-centred approaches to dementia care. The difficulty of defining and ultimately attaining person-centred care has been documented (Brooker, 2004; McCormack, 2004), highlighting the limitations of achieving this in day-to-day care practices.
- Wider issues highlighted by social-gerontological work of the lack of consideration of the implications of the biomedicalization of ageing (Kaufman et al., 2004) and the low status of older people despite their heterogeneity (Dressel et al., 1997) also provide context to the study of dementia. Social gerontology has done much to contribute to the deconstruction of dementia (Harding and Palfrey, 1997; Lyman, 1989; Bond, 1992) and to help question what is 'known' about dementia and thus has implications for the delivery of dementia care services, a topic we will revisit throughout this book.
- This chapter presents an overview and critique of these three approaches, and as such provides a framework and the theoretical foundations underpinning the subsequent chapters in the book.

Introduction

This book approaches the subject of dementia studies from a social science perspective. Two conceptual frameworks underpin the discussion of what 'dementia studies' entails: the sociology of health and illness and the sociology of knowledge. As the book progresses, the contradictions, paradoxes and multiple interpretations and representations surrounding dementia and dementia care provision will be demonstrated. This all occurs within a specific social context, or what Gubrium (1986) has termed the 'cultural space' of dementia at any given moment in time. Holstein has argued that a worthwhile pursuit for the twenty-first century is to reflect on the relationship between culture and understandings of disease and how understandings of disease tell us about culture and how cultures can provide insights into constructions of disease (Holstein, 2000: 177). This reflects the concern of Harding and Palfrey (1997) in thinking about a 'sociology of dementia' as one whereby the 'facts' of dementia are critiqued and challenged to enable the current dominance of biomedically informed care regimes to be examined and explored.

The following questions have been used as heuristic devices and guide this book:

- What do we know about dementia?
- How do we know what we know about dementia?
- Where does the knowledge we have come from?
- What do we do with the knowledge in policy/practice/research situations?

This chapter does not present a 'theory of dementia' or a 'theory of dementia care', rather it explores and critiques issues and concepts that have emerged from biomedical, social-psychological and social-gerontological thinking. As such, this chapter offers the reader an opportunity to reflect on the underlying assumptions surrounding dementia and dementia care.

Starting points for social science

A concern with concepts of social justice, equality, citizenship and equity has long been the preserve of social science, arrived at from methodologically diverse starting points. Going back to Becker's (1967) classic question 'Whose side are we on?' is an interesting place to begin this chapter, even if it is a slightly simplistic one, where theoretical groundings of our knowledge about dementia are questioned, and their implications for dementia care practice, policy and research explored in later chapters.

Dementia could be understood as a chronic illness and as such the dominant approaches within sociology to understand illness are relevant. Two approaches are evident in the sociology of health and illness; socio-structural approaches which come under the umbrella of structural functionalists (who look at the impact of an illness for the individual, their family and their day-to-day lives); or interactionist perspectives (which look at the meanings the illness has for the individual and their family and the impact on their identity and sense of self) (Kelly and Field, 1998).

What is similar in sociological approaches to understanding health and illness is the assumption that illness is the antithesis of the norm and ideal of a healthy mind and body and brings with it associations of dysfunction and deviance. When studying health and illness, a popular approach has been to explore how behaviours have been defined as medical problems, thereby giving the medical profession authority to control such behaviour through medical treatments. This is known as the medicalization of illness in the sociology of health and illness literature and first gained popularity in the 1970s and 1980s (for examples see Zola, 1972; Conrad, 1975; Estes and Binney, 1989).

Another common theme identified within the sociology of health and illness literature in the last two decades is the emergence of the 'knowledgeable patient' (Prior, 2003: 41) who can contribute to challenging medical knowledge about disease and illness (as well as confirm it by focusing on experienced symptoms). Thus, the dementia field can be seen to reflect broader health and illness concerns where the views of the patient have become more apparent, reflecting a concern to see the person with dementia in research (Downs, 1997) and care practice (Kitwood, 1997).

So how can these selective social science concerns be applied to unpacking popular knowledge about dementia? We will begin by looking at the medicalization of dementia and the challenges to this medical discourse by social scientists and others who have demonstrated that the construction of dementia symptoms as a 'disease' was a way to make understandable the symptoms of dementia which challenge the social order of acceptable and understandable 'normal' behaviour.

3

The medicalization of dementia – a brief history

Dementia is a condition, or more accurately an umbrella term for a range of conditions, which has attracted much attention in the 100 years since the work of Alois Alzheimer, leading to the label 'Alzheimer's disease' being applied to individuals. Commonly cited definitions of dementia highlight its construction as a biomedical disease and the accompanying degeneration and loss of abilities over time:

> Alzheimer's disease is a degenerative brain syndrome characterized by a progressive decline in memory, thinking, comprehension, calculation, language, learning capacity and judgement. (World Health Organization, 2001)

> The term 'dementia' is used to describe the symptoms that occur when the brain is affected by specific diseases and conditions, including Alzheimer's disease, stroke and many other rarer conditions. Symptoms of dementia include loss of memory, confusion and problems with speech and understanding. (Alzheimer's Society, 2006)

Such definitions succinctly capture generations of health professionals, families and the person with dementia's experiences of cognitive difficulties and decline. What such definitions hide is the knowledge generation process that underpins such statements, which is arguably partial, flawed and incomplete.

A brief 'dig' into the history of one particular form of dementia, Alzheimer's disease, gives an early indication that knowledge about dementia is not as straightforward, nor as consensual, as such definitions may first appear; and that this has been the case since the time of Alois Alzheimer, a century ago.

Histories of the development of Alzheimer's disease highlight the change in focus over time of those concerned with dementia. Holstein (1997) charts the progression of understandings about Alzheimer's disease and senile dementia between 1885 and 1920, and thus includes the 20 years prior to the time when Alzheimer described a patient whose symptoms began with memory loss and disorientation. Through this history, Holstein (1997: 2) provides a direct challenge to what is commonly believed or 'known' about dementia and Alzheimer's disease; highlighting that the language used and symptoms described do not necessarily date back to the origins of the disease label, as may often be assumed. Thus, since the beginning of the twentieth century, it can be demonstrated that Alzheimer's disease, senility and senile dementia have attracted different degrees of attention over time (Dillman, 2000), and that various factors have influenced the direction that knowledge about dementia has taken. For example, Dillman (2000) highlights various phases in the generation of knowledge, beginning with Kraepelin's concepts of disease, psychiatry and Alzheimer's disease, through to specific pathogenetic theories, leading eventually to the introduction of cholinergic drugs to treat those with Alzheimer's disease. Thus, the production of knowledge and its resultant usage in practice will influence the treatments that those with dementia will be offered.

What Dillman successfully alerts us to is that elements of what is known and believed in contemporary times can be traced back to the early twentieth century, despite Alzheimer himself expressing doubts about the way in which others were using his description of his patient 'Mrs Auguste D' to describe and categorize others with similar symptoms (Dillman, 2000: 135–6). As Holstein explains, by the 1920s, the dilemma of separating pathology from normalcy in old age had not been resolved (1997: 10), leaving a dilemma for those following in the footsteps of Alzheimer, including those working in contemporary times. This legacy has resulted in limiting the focus of enquiry to the neurobiology or neuropsychology of the person with dementia (Cotrell and Schultz, 1993) rather than to the influence of the wider psychosocial context where the individual with dementia is located.

In a convincing critique of the biomedical model and a strong advocacy for including social factors in the study of dementia, Lyman (1989) similarly demonstrates that medical sociologists and social gerontologists had little interest in dementia in the 1980s, with much literature accepting the medical dictates of stages of the disease, the inevitability of a 'social death' and using the medical model as a way to try to understand and control experiences that were often difficult to understand and control. Thus, the medical model was used to legitimize treatments and control of people with dementia through the use of physical or chemical restraints, despite the widespread acceptance that there was no cure (Lyman, 1989: 599). This, Lyman argues (1989: 598), is an example of the 'medicalization of deviance', where behaviour that is difficult to comprehend is 'explained by pathological conditions of somatic origin subject to treatment by medical authority'. Bond (1992), in his discussion of the medicalization of dementia, selects four unfavourable aspects of this process: expert control, social control, individualization of

5

behaviour and depoliticization of behaviour. Expert control of diagnosis and treatment has led dementia to be the preserve of the medical profession; while social control has been exercised through the use of diagnosis itself which categorizes a person as having a dementia and the resultant treatment and care they may receive. Seeing deviant behaviour in individualized terms keeps a firm focus on the individual diagnosed rather than considering the response of society to such behaviour. Finally, the depoliticization of behaviour involves defining behaviour and interactions through a medical lens rather than looking at the meanings the person with dementia attributes to their situation and their subsequent reaction (Bond, 1992: 400).

Recent histories of the Alzheimer movement (Fox, 1989; 2000) provide the cultural context for the growing public interest in Alzheimer's disease and the corresponding increase in funding made available to biomedical research to investigate causes and cures for dementia. However, Fox (2000) highlights that the very success of the Alzheimer movement in the US in attracting government attention, public interest and funding for biomedical research and thus in tackling the economic burden predicted to increase in the future (2000: 223), has also led to a paradox, in that interest in the ongoing care for people with dementia has not similarly blossomed. Thus, until biomedical research finds a 'cure' for the so-called 'disease of the century', so tantalizingly suggested by the introduction of the 'anti-dementia drugs' in the 1990s, the care for people with dementia is relegated to a second place by funders of research. This is not to suggest that policy makers and funders of research are not concerned about the care of people with dementia today but are constrained by the more politically gripping agenda of a cure for tomorrow.

It is interesting to note the continued dominance of medical knowledge when attempting to explain and understand health and illness. Dementia provides a specific example of a label applied to a set of symptoms resulting in the labelling of people with such symptoms as having an illness or disease, typified by the term 'Alzheimer's disease'. Ticehurst (2001), when addressing the question 'Is Dementia a mental illness?', concludes that dementia has seen a departure from a mental illness to a disease category, and with this move come changes in the way people with dementia will be cared for and by whom. Using psychiatry and mental health legislation to illustrate the changes that have occurred in conceptualizing dementia, Ticehurst demonstrates that this has an impact on specialisms within the medical profession. Thus, even within medicine and among those working within a broadly medical model of care, there are tensions around who should be providing the care to people with dementia, a tension argued to be a result of outdated mind/body, disease/illness conceptualization of dementia held within medicine (Ticehurst, 2001: 716). Szasz's assertion, 'I hold that psychiatric interventions are directed at moral, not medical problems' (1974: xi), clearly demonstrates the challenge that social scientists have raised to draw attention to the links between the 'objective facts' medicine would have us believe in, and the influence of cultural norms and beliefs and the need to uphold some kind of (moral) order when faced with behaviour that is not acceptable to the majority population.

Indeed, using insights from the sociology of the body, it has been argued that 'society needs dementia to be medicalized, as, if it is classified as a disease, it holds out the prospect of a cure for ageing and for death' (Harding and Palfrey, 1997: 139). While Lyman suggests that viewing dementia as a biomedical condition helps bring order to dementia care (1989: 599). Thus, viewing dementia as a disease brings a legitimacy to the care offered to people with dementia and offers those who are not diagnosed with dementia the opportunity to believe in a cure and that dementia will not be their own individual destiny. Charting developments in the sociology of health and illness between 1979 and 2002, Prior uses Alzheimer's disease as one example of a condition which has developed a lay expertise. She demonstrates that carers' and patients' knowledge of their condition is partial and restricted, with the surface symptoms of the condition being of primary concern to laypeople (2003: 49), reflecting back in much the same way that treatment of symptoms is the primary concern of medicine.

Thus, it is apparent that the dominant medical model is open to critique and challenge, yet despite such challenges this approach remains dominant in discourse surrounding dementia and dementia care. What then are the alternative ways that have been advanced to understand dementia?

The construction of dementia

Through the above discussion of the medical model of dementia I would argue that the greatest contribution social scientists

7

(Gubrium, 1986; Lyman, 1989; Bond, 1992) have made to the study of dementia is through their deconstruction of the previously held views about dementia which the medical profession offered, and thus that dementia has been socially constructed as a disease or illness to meet society's prevailing concern for order and control. This issue will be apparent throughout the book when we explore, for example, the way in which many people with dementia are removed from their communities and placed in institutional care (discussed in Chapters 3 and 4) and the opposition to hearing the views of people with dementia in research (discussed in Chapter 5).

In the 1980s, Gubrium (1986: 52) was among the first to begin questioning the medicalization of dementia; in particular, he took issue with the terms 'senile dementia' and 'Alzheimer's disease' and the assumption that dementia is a normal part of ageing. Taking an historical look at developments in knowledge about dementia, senility and Alzheimer's disease over time, he concluded that dementia is not an extreme form of normal ageing, but that those with dementia are experiencing a disease that is distinct from normal ageing. Anglo-Americans unified the terms senile dementia and Alzheimer's disease into a distinct disease category in the 1970s and 1980s (Fox, 1989), and as an illness category and policy issue in the 1980s (Lyman 1989). Turning the condition into a disease matters (Holstein, 2000: 171), as this implies that action can be taken, and that both cause and cure can be sought and, further, indirectly constructing a condition as a disease 'contributed to the construction of careers, the instruction of students and the politicization of AD' (Holstein, 2000: 172). Thus, when a person is labelled in a certain way, it impacts on the 'career' (Goffman, 1991) of the person so diagnosed.

The nature of the social construction of dementia has been aptly questioned (Harding and Palfrey, 1997), with Gubrium (1986) clearly setting out the context for commonly held beliefs about Alzheimer's disease which stem from the concerns and agendas of those contributing to what is known about dementia, and Alzheimer's disease in particular. Gubrium presents the backdrop of medical concerns between old age and senility which over time led to the development of diagnostic screening tests relying on the input from family experiences and the presentation of symptoms from the person who may eventually be labelled as having 'Alzheimer's disease'.

Gubrium (1986) charts the development of interest in Alzheimer's disease to the point that Alzheimer's disease is part of 'public culture', where well-known public figures are used to advocate on behalf of carers and those afflicted with the 'disease' to a point where alarm stories emerge, focusing on: demographics (more people having this disease); finances (the financial burden of caring for people with dementia); and personal implications (loss of abilities leading to the removal of the pre-dementia self replaced by the physical shell of a person).

In a text targeted at care professionals, Gubrium (1991) clearly highlights the different interpretations that can be placed on and by older people, with dementia a term that can be applied to those who do not conform to the norms expected by others. In the first chapter of his book, *The Mosaic of Care*, he draws attention to the different interpretations various individuals place on events and the difficulty for staff when a social worker collects conflicting accounts of a situation. The questions posed are: Can the man's actions be understood to be part of his dementia? Or could they be understood to be part of his strategy to challenge the control of the care setting exerted by the woman bathing him? Thus, behaviours can be understood as part of 'dementia' and thus contribute to the construction of understandings about dementia.

These later insights into the construction of dementia as a disease come from a position begun by the medical profession, a position where symptoms arising from neurological impairment were medicalized and problematized. Such labelling of problem behaviours is not just for professionals but used by other older people. For example, Gubrium (1991) describes situations where individual residents can be labelled as 'losing their marbles' (inaccurately) by other residents should the personal characteristics of individuals not be appreciated by others. Gubrium (1991) further highlights the complexity of interpreting the realities of those deemed to be in need of 'care', whether in institutions, in the community (at day care) or care within their own home. An interesting concept of the 'demented role' has been used to allude to Parsons's (1951) 'sick role' (Golander and Raz, 1996). The notion of those with dementia taking on a 'demented role' legitimizes their behaviours that have been labelled difficult in some way and complies with medical definitions of disease and the deviation from the healthy or non-demented role of others. Thus, individuals can be seen to comply with constructions of

9

roles and behaviours and the meaning that others attribute to actions that deviate from the expected norm. This is problematic, as it further strengthens the preserve of medical and health professionals by dismissing what may be attempts, for example, to communicate by the person with dementia. Rather than look below surface at service provision inadequacies or staffing issues, the 'blame' can be laid at the door of the person who has dementia.

Harding and Palfrey (1997) systematically challenge what is known about dementia through the theoretical framework of social constructionism. In common with Gubrium (1986), they demonstrate that dementia has been equated with old age. While Gubrium concludes that dementia is 'an entity distinct from ageing' (1986: 201), Harding and Palfrey, (1997) suggest that the conceptualization of dementia used within Western societies binds dementia to old age, and the fear of ageing, disease and death that is associated with an ageing body.

The contributions from social scientists to challenge what is known about dementia have yet to receive mainstream recognition, with due consideration about what this may mean for common care practices where people with dementia are institutionalized when a decision is reached that their behaviours are no longer manageable within the community. This is not to deny that people with dementia require long-term care if they decline physically and become unable to maintain activities of daily living, but to highlight that people with dementia may be institutionalized because their behaviours challenge the norms expected within their families and wider communities.

Yet, individuals with dementia and their families are a heterogeneous grouping linked by symptoms associated with dementia, and differences in backgrounds along the lines of class, race, ethnicity and gender (Hulko, 2004) are not always taken into account when providing care solutions to symptoms that are difficult to control. Interestingly, Vittoria (1998) suggests that institutional care can actually help people with dementia preserve their sense of well-being, as it can offer a safe and controlled environment where staff are equipped (some better than others) to help maintain and reinforce the preferred reality of an individual with dementia. McColgan (2001), by contrast, provides a shocking account of the lack of opportunities offered to those living in institutional settings, and thus demonstrates the order and control function of institutional living for those who are labelled as having dementia. Cultures of care in institutions is an issue we return to in Chapter 4.

Social psychology – the loss and preservation of self or personhood of people with dementia

Arguably, the most important contribution social psychologists have made to the study of dementia and the care offered to people with dementia is to place *the individual* with dementia at the centre of academic and practice discourses. Social psychologists have clearly demonstrated that biomedical views have overshadowed the individual who is given the diagnosis of a dementia (Kitwood, 1997; Sabat, 2001) and that this can, and does have, disastrous outcomes for the individual with dementia.

On both sides of the Atlantic at around about the same time, during the late 1980s and early 1990s, Tom Kitwood (UK) and Steven Sabat (US) both independently began advancing alternative understandings to the decline, decay and deficiency models of dementia commonly espoused by those working within a broadly biomedical approach where dementia was seen as a fate worse than death, and, indeed, texts with such sentiments in their titles were popular at that time (*Alzheimer's Disease: Coping with a Living Death*, Woods, 1989).

Kitwood and personhood

Kitwood (1990) began his challenge to the standard paradigm in 1990 when he first wrote about the dialectics of dementia, highlighting the damage carers could be inflicting on the person with dementia due to careless and thoughtless interactions. He then moved on to begin theorizing about the interpersonal processes involved in caregiving and the impact interactions with caregivers may have on the person with dementia (1993). His thesis on dementia culminated in his book *Dementia Reconsidered: the Person Comes First* (Kitwood, 1997), published shortly before his untimely death. His key contribution to understanding dementia, and in the process challenging the medical model of care, was his insistence that what he termed 'personhood', defined as 'a status or standing bestowed upon one human being, by others, in the context of social relationship and social being. It implies recognition, respect and trust.'

(1997: 8), should be preserved, even if a person received the diagnosis of dementia.

Much of Kitwood's early work was devoted to demonstrating how personhood was eroded by the actions of carers, even if the actions were not maliciously intended, they could still have an adverse impact on what he called the well-being of a person with dementia. 'Malignant Social Psychology' was the term Kitwood used to describe a range of interactions that could be experienced by a person with dementia which were detrimental to their well-being. He called such interactions 'Personal Detractions'; initially, 10 categories were indentified (Kitwood and Bredin, 1992b) but these were later developed into 17 categories of personal detractions (Kitwood, 1997). Such personal detractions could occur at varying levels of severity; mild, moderate, severe and very severe. Mild detractions occurred when no malice was intended, very severe detractions occurred when a caregiver was aware of their actions and the impact they may have on the person with dementia. The final 17 types of personal detractions identified by Kitwood (1997: 46–7) are:

1	Treachery	10	Objectification
2	Disempowerment	11	Ignoring
3	Infantilization	12	Imposition
4	Intimidation	13	Withholding
5	Labelling	14	Accusation
6	Stigmatization	15	Disruption
7	Outpacing	16	Mockery
8	Invalidation	17	Disparagement
9	Banishment		

The crucial point Kitwood made through these categories of Malignant Social Psychology (MSP) was that an individual would respond when experiencing, for example, a care worker moving them around without explaining what was happening to them, and instead having a conversation with another worker (objectification and ignoring, respectively) and that this could result in a decline in well-being, if not result in ill-being. A full account of how Kitwood operationalized his categories of MSP was one of his first papers challenging the dominant model of understanding dementia (1990), and since then many have used the various categories of personal detractions to illustrate examples of poor care practice observed during research in institutional care settings

(Williams and Rees, 1997; Innes and Surr, 2001; Thompson and Kingston, 2004; Innes and Kelly, 2007).

Kitwood's other primary contribution to the understanding of dementia and dementia care practice was his conceptualization of 'positive person work'. Twelve categories of positive person work are advanced by Kitwood (1997):

1 Recognition
2 Negotiation
3 Collaboration
4 Play
5 Timalation
6 Celebration
7 Relaxation
8 Validation
9 Holding
10 Facilitation
11 Creation
12 Giving (119–20)

This framework provided care workers with the opportunity to aim for well-being enhancing interactions in their day-to-day work. Through the use of three specific healing arts therapy techniques used in dementia care, music, dance and art, Kasayka and colleagues (2001: 115–20) demonstrate that there are simple steps a worker can take to achieve positive person work and therefore enhance the well-being of people with dementia. For example, to operationalize negotiation in art therapy, a choice of materials can be provided to the person with dementia. For 'creation', that is the opportunity to be creative, to occur during music, singing and group improvisation can be used. Thus, positive person work provided a welcome addition to Kitwood's person-centred care approach; rather than stressing what was wrong with care interactions, he offered caregivers a way to enhance their caregiving skills and thus enhance the personhood of individuals with dementia they worked with.

Sabat and the self

Sabat's work also focuses on the individual with dementia. The central concern of his work is to stress that aspects of self remain, even for those who are labelled as having 'severe' or 'advanced' dementia. He initially proposed a twofold approach to the self of individuals with dementia (Sabat and Harré, 1992), and later developed this into a threefold categorization of self (Sabat and Collins, 1999; Sabat, 2002). Thus, Sabat argues that there are three forms of self; the attributes of each form of self can be summarized as follows:

13

- Self 1: this is the singular self and uses the indexicals of I, me, mine to describe personal attributes. For example, I like that, those belong to me, those are mine.
- Self 2: these aspects of self are the characteristics held by an individual, mental, physical and emotional, and the beliefs the individual holds about these characteristics or attributes. For example, I am good at cooking; or, conversely, I am hopeless at cooking.
- Self 3: this is the publicly presented persona that requires the cooperation of others. For example, the roles and relationships an individual holds; worker, parent and friend.

Using detailed case histories, Sabat has demonstrated that Self 1 can remain even when dementia is considered to be advanced. Self 2 can be enhanced or put down, depending on the situation in which a person with dementia may find themselves. Sabat provides examples of individuals in day care choosing not to participate in activities they deem inappropriate to their previous abilities and interests and thus demonstrating a clear sense of Self 2 and Self 3. Thus, choosing not to engage in certain activities may indicate a strong sense of self and not the lack of ability to perform a task or activity. The most vulnerable or fragile self Sabat suggests is Self 3 (2006), which he suggests requires skilled caregiving and interactions to uphold previous relationships and roles.

Sabat applies his concern for recognition of the self when he also questions the use of neuropsychological tests to reveal the incapacity or incompetence of a person with dementia, rather than observing and getting to know an individual to help ascertain the meaning-making behind behaviours attributed as symptoms of dementia (2005: 1031). He also highlights the legal implications of power of attorney and guardianship when tests 'conclude' that a person does not have the ability to construct meaning (2005: 1033). Sabat thus continues to challenge the way in which medical discourse dominates dementia studies and applies his theoretical conceptualizations of self to practice situations.

Kitwood and Sabat – some interesting parallels

Interestingly, Sabat (1994) applied Kitwood's Malignant Social Psychology (MSP) to case studies of individuals with Alzheimer's disease. By following this approach, he highlighted that the excess disability attributed to people with dementia combined with the malignant social psychology that can be experienced by those with dementia by those who provide care (as well as non-carers who do not have dementia) can exacerbate dementia symptoms. It could also be assumed that MSP can encourage professionals to perceive dementia as a progressively disabling disease, as is often observed and recounted by researchers and practitioners (Fontana and Smith, 1989). For example, in common with Fontana and Smith's discussion of the victim of Alzheimer's disease and the 'unbecoming of self' that accompanies the diagnosis of dementia, O'Connor speaks of the two 'victims' of Alzheimer's disease, the person with the diagnosis and their spouse (1993: 113). She argues that the distress experienced by the spouse brought about through observed loss of self in the person with dementia can help to explain the behaviour of spouse caregivers. In making this argument she implicitly accepts that there will be loss of self and that care interactions need to take account of this fact.

In a further application of Kitwood's concepts, this time well-being, to observations of people with dementia, Sabat and Collins (1999) developed Mrs F as a case study. They noted that Kitwood and Bredin's (1992a, b) notions of well-being can be used to recognize intact abilities, feelings and beliefs. Even though initial observations showed that staff found Mrs F very difficult to understand, careful observations over time highlighted remaining social, cognitive and emotional abilities, as well as indicators of the well-being proposed by Kitwood. The intact manifestations of self are also demonstrated through this case study, thus providing an example of a synergy between the ideas of two key contributors to the social psychology of dementia, Kitwood and Sabat.

What does person-centred care mean for practice?

Kitwood is not without his critics. Davis (2004), for example, although supporting the call for more humane approaches to people with dementia, suggests that 'while ostensibly advocating a personalized and relational approach, he is offering an idea of unimpeachable personhood which sanitizes the dying process (Lawton, 2000)' (2004: 377). Therefore, the pseudo-scientific framework Kitwood operates within, whereby the cause of loss of personhood is brought about by the effect of MSP, implies that changing the interactions and relationships with people with dementia will change experiences of dementia and

15

in so doing detracts from the challenges that face caregivers to make this a reality for individuals with dementia. Thus, an ideology that is widely accepted and promoted has yet to be tested in reality, and, as Davis has noted, it has not yet been possible to prove or refute Kitwood's hypothesis, but if it is true, then guilt and despair is a possible outcome for carers who cannot achieve the ideal of maintaining personhood.

This may account for the initial reaction of carers to Kitwood's ideas. Capstick has documented (2003) the initial reluctance of carers to accept Kitwood's challenge to the view of dementia prevalent at the time of his first writings about dementia; the language he chose to use was seen to be an attack on the care decisions and care interactions offered to people with dementia. Throughout the 1990s, care interventions became more popular with journals such as the UK-based *Journal of Dementia Care* providing practitioner accounts of success stories when they adopted an approach that could be described as 'person-centred'. The problem with such anecdotal accounts is that they are not based on empirical research; a recognized problem, addressed by an array of psycho-social intervention studies, suggesting, perhaps unsurprisingly, that when an intervention such as music, dance, or art is introduced to people with dementia, then visible signs of well-being increase. Tools to measure the impact of care interventions have also been popular. One devised by Kitwood and Bredin in 1992 (1992b), 'Dementia Care Mapping', aimed to measure the extent to which the principles of person-centred care, as advanced by Kitwood (1990), were a reality in care settings for people with dementia. This tool is currently in its eighth edition, a result of colleagues from the Bradford Dementia Group and their network of international trainers attempting to address problems with the tool and ensure that the tool could make greater claims to reliability and validity (Brooker and Surr, 2005).

The method, like the theory underlying the person-centred approach, is not without its problems, and a collection of edited papers from practitioners from various countries brings such issues to the fore (Innes, 2003a). For example, Müller-Hergl (2003) demonstrates the need for a certain belief system within an organization for Dementia Care Mapping to result in improvements to the care offered, while Scurfield-Walton (2003) provides an example of the need to provide training, mentoring and support to staff to enable them to act on the issues arising from using the Dementia Care

Mapping tool. Even relatively simple steps that could be taken by staff from Dementia Care Mapping, such as revising care plans (Innes, 2003b) may be difficult to achieve if the basics of a person-centred philosophy are not understood.

There are two writers who have tried to consolidate and develop what is meant by person-centred care. First, McCormack (2004), writing about person-centred gerontological nursing, argues that although the use of the term person-centred is commonplace, there are few research studies of person-centred practice and even fewer identifying the benefits of this approach to care practice (McCormack, 2004: 31). McCormack concludes that there are four concepts underpinning person-centred nursing: being in relation; being in a social world; being in place; and being with self. He thus brings together the ideas of Kitwood (1997) and Sabat (2001) but with a practice orientation. He argues that person-centred care principles require 'nurses to engage in authentic humanistic caring practices that embrace all forms of knowing and acting, in order to promote choice and partnership in care decision making' (McCormack, 2004: 36). Although McCormack concludes that personhood is a useful ideal to strive for and that person-centred models of care are worthwhile, he points out that care practice needs to be driven with a focus on the individual rather than a focus on theory and models for person-centred care to be a reality in practice. Thus, implicitly the ideas of searching for expressions of the self advocated by Sabat (Sabat and Harré, 1992, Sabat and Collins, 1999, Sabat, 2002, Sabat, 2006), are one way to help focus on the individual, rather than on person-centred principles which could lead to overlooking what, as Sabat has expressed it (2002), 'manifestations of the self remain'.

In a similar, if more pragmatic vein than McCormack (2004), Brooker suggests that person-centred care involves recognizing that 'dementia-ism' (2004: 217) exists in many care settings and that people with dementia are likely to be stigmatized and discriminated against, both strategically and individually. Building on the work of Kitwood, Brooker identifies person-centred care as a combination of four factors: valuing people with dementia and their carers (a theme we will revisit in Chapter 3); treating people as individuals; trying to look at the world from the perspective of the person with dementia; and a positive social environment to enable the person with dementia to experience relative well-being (Brooker, 2004: 216–19). Achieving the ideals of the theoretical approach to dementia set out by Kitwood is challenging. Brooker highlights that the term person-centred care 'has become a shorthand for encompassing a whole movement in the dementia field' (2004: 221). Thus, the theoretical concepts offered by social psychologists, Kitwood and Sabat in particular, are a beginning and provide a starting point for examining, challenging and changing dementia care practice.

Contributions of social psychology to understandings and conceptualisations of dementia

The last decade has seen a period of intense interest and support for person-centred approaches. Texts advocating care practice similar in perspective to Kitwood's approach have emerged from around the world. In America, for example, there has been a popular text, *The Best Friends Approach to Dementia Care* (Bell and Troxel, 2003). Kitwood's work now has widespread appeal, with person-centred care, person-hood and well-being phrases commonly used by practitioners in their day-to-day work. The impact, if any, of usage of such language on the care received and the lives of people with dementia is still relatively unknown.

Part of the problem in taking Kitwood's pioneering work forward stems from the lack of working definitions of the terms he uses, and the paradox between Kitwood's ideals and the underlying theory and models of research and disease influencing his work in the dementia field. Harding and Palfrey illustrate that it is difficult to dispute the hypothesis initially put forward by Kitwood and Bredin (1992a) that insensitive care serves to inhibit 'rementia' – which remains intact because it has neither been proved or disproved. It may therefore take its place alongside the biomedical 'theories', for in many respects it also adopts a positivist view of dementia as a condition, which in some individuals may be treated or even cured (Harding and Palfrey, 1997: 64). Thus, the problematic nature of dementia as a disease category is not fundamentally challenged by Kitwood. He takes issue with the narrow categorization, or 'standard paradigm' as he calls it (1997: 35), based on only neurological impairment and adds dimensions to what the experience of dementia entails, notably social psychology, physical health, life history and biography (Kitwood, 1996) but he does not take issue with the actual categorization of dementia as *a disease*. This can be seen in his belief that dementia can be treated in some way, although he advocates the need for skilled care practitioners and therapeutic interventions (Kitwood, 1997) rather than the use of psychotropic medications.

That said, symptoms associated with dementia are very real to those who experience them: the person with dementia and those who provide care or services. Advocating the use of sensitive care-giving which enhances life, rather than medications which can lead to individuals being in a semi-awake state and slipping in and out of lucidity, is arguably a more humane approach to the care for people with dementia.

An intriguing possibility has advanced that those with dementia are retreating from the realities of an ageing body; and as they do so, argue Harding and Palfrey, 'that with ageing comes a retreat from the body, and with this retreat comes a loss of sense of self' (1997: 140). Thus, the loss of self, or the difficulty in observing the three aspects of self developed by Sabat, may be compounded by the difficulty individuals with dementia may have in recognizing their ageing body and thus retreating to earlier memories of a healthy, youthful body and mind.

It can be seen that social psychology has contributed much to understanding the experience of dementia at an individual level and the impact dementia may have on the self or personhood of each person so diagnosed. How to operationalize conceptualizations of self and personhood is a challenge for individual care practitioners (we will explore this further in Chapter 3), yet the theoretical foundations are in place to build and develop further our understandings about dementia and dementia care. However, such individualized approaches need to be grounded in an understanding of wider structural forces that shape individuals' experiences for knowledge to develop beyond the individual level. The work of social gerontologists is useful to help achieve an understanding of dementia that takes into account wider social and structural factors that will shape the experience of an individual with dementia.

Applicability of wider social-gerontological understandings of being 'old' to the study of dementia

Old age is surrounded with perceptions which have been called the myths of old age (Sidell, 1995). Such myths include that older people are a homogenous group; that ill health can be expected in old age

(Sidell, 1995: xvi); in turn leading to a commonly held belief that older people are a burden, as they experience such ill health and physical decline. The homogenous grouping of older people together has been robustly challenged (Dressel et al., 1997), with differences along class, gender and race divisions now widely accepted to have an impact on an individual's experience of ageing. It was also commonly assumed that as people live longer, ageing will bring with it a 'burden of dependency' (Walker and Phillipson, 1986: 2). Challenging such a belief has proved problematic when writers describe what has been termed an 'apocalyptic demography' (Robertson, 1990), where the ever-growing number of older people need to be cared for by a shrinking working-age population who provide the tax payments to contribute to providing health and social care services.

This approach to demography has been applied to Alzheimer's disease (Robertson, 1990) and as such has acted as a disincentive to providing care for those with dementia as funders choose to finance research seeking a definitive cause and cure for the condition (Fox, 2000). Thus, beliefs about the burden that will be placed on society due to increasing numbers of people living into old age shape the social world experienced by older people. The interplay between society, image and place provides insights into the complexities and pervasiveness of ageism within Western societies (McHugh, 2003). Older people can be seen to have internalized such ageist messages when they state that they do not wish to be a burden (Hardy et al., 1999; Minichiello et al., 2000) when their views are actively sought.

An approach within social gerontology that is of particular relevance to understanding dementia is that of critical gerontology. Central to the approach of critical gerontology is that ageing is socially constructed (Vincent, 2003). Critical gerontology comes from key principles within four broad approaches concerned with the study of age, sociology, demography, anthropology and political economy (Baars et al., 2006: 5). In a review of the social construction of old age over time, Johnson (2005) demonstrates the variance in ways in which different societies at different moments in time perceive their older people, as such he effectively demonstrates the specificity of constructions of old age and how these reflect social and political concerns at particular points in time. In addition, critical gerontology does much to add to our understandings of the power differentials that older people encounter, for example the unequal distribution of resources said to prompt the emergence of critical gerontology (Powell, 2001: 120), an issue that has been argued to be of global importance and will influence gerontological theory in the future (Phillipson, 2003: 9). Furthermore, critical gerontology has argued for the need to explore the lives of older people (Walker, 2006), including their identities, and the way in which their experiences are represented (Cohen, 1994), in much the same way that the dementia field has begun to include the views of people with dementia, an issue we will explore in Chapter 5 of this book. This emphasis on the construction of old age parallels the arguments about the social construction of dementia discussed above, as such critical gerontology can be useful in helping to develop understanding about dementia.

Featherstone and Hepworth (1991) were among the first to apply the analogy of a 'mask' to describe the experience of ageing. The concept of a 'mask' has been used by others concerned with ageing experiences (Ballard et al., 2005) and has also been developed and applied to the experience of dementia (Golander and Raz, 1996). The use of the term 'mask of ageing' or 'mask of dementia' demonstrates that individuals who are experiencing old age and dementia are, figuratively speaking, wearing this experience on top of the self (younger, healthier) that the individual wishes to recognize.

Estes and Binney (1989) highlight the problems of the biomedicalization of old age. They describe how old age has been socially constructed as a process of decremental physical decline, 'fostering the tendency to view ageing negatively as a process of inevitable decline, disease and irreversible decay' (1989: 594), and how this has led ageing to be placed in the domain and control of biomedicine. Revisiting the concept of biomedicalization of old age, Kaufman et al. argue that, 'A major effect of biomedicalization today is that the aged body tends to be viewed now as simultaneously a disease entity, a site for restoration and a space for improvement' (2004: 736). They suggest that as increases in medical interventions to prolong life have become available, this places older people and their families under an obligation, rather than a choice, to accept treatments in their efforts to prolong life and avoid the images and reality of demise in old age.

This in turn places family members in a new cycle of caregiving, where care is tied up with medical interventions to prolong life. Kaufman et al. highlight that medical advances prolong life and as such redefine what is considered 'normal' or 'natural' about ageing, which has led to as yet unexplored sociocultural and ethical impacts of the biomedicalization of ageing (2004: 733). Thus, the biomedicalization of dementia reflects a wider trend in conceptualizations of age and ageing. The advent of anti-dementia drugs fuels the search for prolonging life in the hope that a cure will emerge, reflecting, as Kaufman et al. (2004) point out, the hope that scientific developments have brought to older people and their families.

Dementia also presents an interesting example of the anti-ageing science discussed by Vincent (2006a) where new scientific developments are often viewed as a panacea for ageing and a way to eradicate this final stage in the life course, a position Vincent takes issue with as it continues to see old age as a problem to be resolved rather than a stage of life to be embraced and accepted. The long-term ramifications for society – as attempts are made to grow older without ageing, and to extend life and postpone death – remain unknown, but Kaufman et al. argue (2004: 737) that it is likely that relationships and care provision will have to alter to meet the increased life expectancy of future generations.

Social gerontology, therefore, alerts us to the discrimination faced by older people in Western societies and highlights the cross-cutting interplay of gender, class and age (Dressel et al., 1997) on ageing experiences. Given the ageist social context people with dementia are located within, it is perhaps unsurprising to discover the push towards medicalizing this condition and the avoidance of engaging with the lived realities of people with dementia. Not until the time of Kitwood (1997) and Sabat (2001) was this approach challenged when they suggested alternative ways to conceptualize and then look at the experience of dementia, an experience where the self and personhood of individuals may remain intact in some way, despite the discourse propounding the progressive and irreversible nature of dementia.

What is known about dementia? A social science overview

Medical understandings of dementia have dominated dementia studies discourse for 100 years. Katz (2006) argues for critical gerontology to question the extent to which assessment of functionality as the dominant approach to understanding ageing, similarly those working in the dementia field need to question the conceptualizations of dementia that are based on lack of ability to function due to cognitive impairment. Yet, the foundations of such understandings, from lack of consensus over medical categorizations to treatments and the never-ending quest for a cause and cure, have perhaps been the key factors influencing social pyschologists and social scientists to challenge and contribute to shaping alternative discourses about dementia.

As has been noted:

> If medical researchers and practitioners were basing their judgments on firm theory resulting from an extensive body of empirical evidence then their inter-pretation of dementia as a disease ought to carry more weight. The positivist search for a cause-effect nexus has to be framed within a social and cultural context. This human quest to discern the first cause, to establish a predictable and natural social universe, creates for itself systems of rationality. These in turn produce categories to which experience is allocated: 'Our inheritance is a dichotomized world view in which we attempt from our idiosyncratic beliefs, to reconcile apparent opposites: good–bad; mad–sane; diseased–whole.' (Harding and Palfrey, 1997: 144)

Thus, it is somewhat inevitable that challenges to disease models of dementia would emerge, resulting in alternative ways to approach to care and treatment of people with dementia.

The key contribution of social psychologists and sociologists such as Sabat, Kitwood and Gubrium is that they offer alternative expla-nations of the lived experiences of dementia to the commonly held pseudo-medical interpretations of loss of self, abilities and meaning-ful lives. The conceptual difficulties surrounding the term 'demen-tia' are acknowledged by many but as Post highlights (1995; 2000a) there is a moral challenge that remains, no matter what the defini-tion used, and that is to enter the culture of dementia. Kitwood (1997) takes this position further and provides a detailed account of the damage that can be inflicted on a person with dementia should the individuality, or 'personhood', not be maintained. Should no attempts be made to engage with personhood, and should person-hood not be maintained, then the process Kitwood (1997) coined 'Malignant Social Psychology (MSP)' occurs where, as a direct result of the actions (even if they are unintentional) the person with dementia may experience, for example:

- Disempowerment
- Invalidation
- Infantilization
- Treachery
- Objectification

Kitwood (1998) and Post (1995) both engage with the 'moral' challenge of dementia, recognizing that dementia poses a challenge to what is desirable within Western cultures, with Post calling for 'moral solidarity' (1995) and Kitwood calling for 'relationship-centred care' which abandons the standard paradigm of understanding dementia and breaking down the barriers between 'us' (without dementia) and 'them' (who have dementia). This is reinforced by Sabat (2001: 340) when he argues that dementia is about us all and how we are as human beings. The fear dementia can promote, due to images of the loss of selfhood so prevalent in the literature, with compelling images conjured up in the titles to publications such as *Alzheimer's Disease: Coping with a Living Death* (Woods, 1989) and images of carers living through a '36-Hour Day' (Mace and Rabins, 2006) and 'The Loss of Self' (Cohen and Eisdorfer, 1986), contributes to statements of dementia being 'the disease of the century'. War analogies, where caregivers 'battle' against the disease and Alzheimer's movements 'fight' for government recognition of the consequences of dementia (Gubrium, 1986), have all contributed to a climate where dementia has been perceived negatively. It is not until later challenges have emerged clearly providing examples of the continuation of aspects of self (Sabat and Harré, 1992; Sabat, 2001, 2006) or 'personhood' (Kitwood and Bredin, 1992a; Kitwood, 1997) that conceptual debates can be circumnavigated to look at the experiences of those directly affected by dementia – the diagnosed and their caregivers.

Vittoria (1999) provides further insights into the lives of people with dementia, where the constructed reality of living in an institution can act as a buffer to the detrimental and degrading views of people with dementia. She aptly demonstrates that the lives of those in long-stay care will be perceived by different people in different ways, depending on the starting point or perspective of any individual, thus echoing Gubrium's position where he provides various scenarios of older people (not just those with dementia) and the interpretations that the individual, different staff members and family members can place on situations. Vittoria's (1999) position in particular challenges the often negative perceptions of dementia care based on other interpretations of institutional life (McColgan, 2004), alerting us to the need to revisit the challenges that have been made to the care of people with dementia, an issue we will return to in Chapter 3.

The dominant medical position is now argued to be that Senile Dementia of the Alzheimer's Type (SDAT) is a disease where exogenous and endogenous events cause pathological changes in the brain; these may be a result of age-related characteristics but not exclusively (Holstein, 2000: 171). Thus, as outlined above, it is now easy to find challenges to perspectives of dementia solely defined as a 'disease'. However, it should be noted that the above discussion is intended to offer a critique of the knowledge that prevails about dementia in the twenty-first century, a critique of 'what is known' being after all one of the key dimensions social science can bring to the study of dementia.

Conclusions

Drawing on conceptual frameworks stemming from the sociology of health and illness and sociology of knowledge, this chapter highlights that adopting a social science perspective (of which there are many) can help us to begin to challenge the knowledge and underlying assumptions about what is 'known' about dementia. The flaws inherent in our understandings of dementia can therefore emerge, helping to illuminate the rationale underlying care practices that continue to exist, despite critiques of the starting points of disease labels. The medical approach does, of course, have its place – dementia does, after all, often involve decline over time and causes distress to the person afflicted and their families. By placing too much emphasis on the need for future treatments (medical) and future cure (also medical), there is a regrettable shift away from responding to the care needs of those who have dementia in the here and now.

This chapter has begun to address the first question guiding this book, where does our knowledge about dementia come from? It highlights that assumptions underpinning 'dementia' that go back over a century have not necessarily been consensual concepts, nor have knowledge generation and theories of dementia emerged that encompass the perspectives of all players in the theory generation game. In some ways, developments in the dementia field reflect the further developed movements with in gerontology, where it has been argued that 'despite the valuable and often provocative insights generated by each of these perspectives … None of these approaches taken alone, provides an adequate paradigm or conceptual basis for theorizing aging' (Baars et al., 2006: 3). Rather, medical dominance remains through the language that is used to describe dementia and through the responses of society to those who have dementia (an issue we will return to in Chapter 3). However, the point made by Vincent (2006b: 268) in relation to gerontology also holds true for the study of dementia:

> Processes of social stratification mark some people out by age criteria and institutionalize a set of social positions within which they are required to live out their lives ... A critical analysis is required if we want to find out how such processes happen and how they might be changed.

We will now move forward to consider what we know about the context shaping our knowledge of dementia, and in the process address how we know what we know about the lived realities of people with dementia.

■ ■ Further reading ■

For a full account of the principles of person-centred care that are still very much in evidence at the time of writing, read Kitwood (1997); for a similar psychosocial approach but using the concept of self rather than personhood read Sabat (2001). The first critiques (Lyman, 1989; Bond, 1992) of the biomedical approach provide a useful starting point for thinking about what dementia is and the implications of conceptualizations for those with dementia.

2

THE CONTEXT OF DEMENTIA STUDIES:
POLITICAL, ECONOMIC AND SOCIAL ISSUES

■ ■ Chapter summary ■

- This chapter provides an overview of the global political, economic and social issues surrounding the study of dementia. Building on the previous chapter's exploration of what is known about dementia, this approach is developed to address the question of 'how we know what we know' about dementia. It achieves this by looking at the politicization of dementia, the economic costs of providing care and the social context of dementia that has received attention at individual, family, community and societal levels. By considering such contextual factors this chapter presents a stepping stone to then move forward to consider care principles and policies, the concern of Chapter 3.
- First then, this chapter considers the 'numbers' issue of dementia, which reflects demographic changes and the growing politicization of dementia, in particular Alzheimer's disease. Next, the chapter considers economic concerns relating to the financial costs of providing care, while remembering the personal costs of care provision borne by family and paid carers. The social context of dementia, including the institutionalization of people with dementia, the stigma relating to dementia and the marginalized position people with dementia and their families may occupy, is then outlined. This chapter therefore provides a contextual overview of the study of dementia required to explore the numerous challenges faced by those providing care to people with dementia and support for their carers.

The politicization of dementia: the concern with numbers

Worldwide it is estimated that there are 18 million people with dementia and this is expected to double to 37 million by 2025 (World Health Organization, 2006). There are differences in estimates of prevalence according to whether a country is classified as developed or developing, with developing countries estimated to have lower prevalence of dementia; this may be due to lower rates of survival with dementia, environmental factors, as well as higher levels of mortality earlier in life (Ferri et al., 2005). However, Hendrie (2006: 487) predicts that by 2050, 70 per cent of people with dementia worldwide will be living in developing countries. It is also predicted that social care needs will increase in developing countries due to social, medical and economic factors, leading to less availability of care through traditional family caregiving (Chandra, 1998). Although current and future figures about the number of people with dementia vary – for example, across all European countries the estimates for the number of people living with a form of dementia vary between 5.3 and 5.8 million people (Alzheimer Europe, 2007) – it is widely accepted that the number of people with dementia is expected to increase by the middle of the twenty-first century (Knapp et al., 2007b).

It is important to contextualize the study of dementia within issues relating to prevalence and demography as they shape the cost of dementia care and the services that can be delivered within finite monetary constraints. Knapp et al. (2007a) have explored such issues in relation to countries classified as 'high-income'. They demonstrate that for the eighteen countries examined, the ratio of people aged 65 and over to people aged 15 to 64 will increase. The prevalence of dementia also increases with age, thus the authors estimate that there will be significant increases in the number of people with dementia by the middle of the twenty-first century, for example in the UK alone, there is a projected 28 per cent increase by 2021 and 154 per cent increase by 2051 (Knapp et al., 2007b).

The UK provides an example of what appears to be a worldwide trend in increasing numbers of people with dementia, with corresponding increases in the financial burden of providing care to people with dementia and support for family and paid carers. The Alzheimer's Society in the UK commissioned a report into the prevalence and cost of dementia in the UK (Knapp et al., 2007b). The projected burgeoning numbers of people with dementia are used to great effect on the front page of this UK report, where it states that 'by 2025 one million people in the UK will have dementia', followed by 'dementia costs the UK over £17 billion per year'. This is a stark image of both the number of people affected by dementia and the substantial economic costs of this condition. Estimating the number of people with dementia has been difficult due to differences in epidemiological studies. The UK report attempts to rectify prior difficulties through the use of a consensus Delphi exercise where age (including younger people with dementia) and gender were considered, as was where people lived, in care homes and the community, enabling the authors to estimate the economic costs of dementia (Knapp et al., 2007b: 8). Key points from this report are that:

- The prevalence for dementia was higher for men for the 50–65 age range but higher for women for the over-65 age bands.
- Around 2.2 per cent of those with dementia are classed as younger people with dementia (age 50–65).
- Around two-thirds (63.5 per cent) of people with dementia live in the community and one-third in care homes (36.5 per cent).
- The proportion of people with dementia living in care homes rises with age, from 26.6 per cent for the 65–74 age range to 60.8 per cent of those 90 or over.
- The cost of providing care in the community increases with the severity of dementia but is still cheaper than providing care in care homes.

The projected increase in numbers gives rise to emotive language, such as 'the dementia epidemic' (Wilson and Fearnley, 2007), and calls for making dementia a national priority (Knapp et al., 2007b). This is in a sense a return to images promoted in the 1980s of a 'rising tide' of people with dementia (Ineichen, 1988), and could be interpreted as a ploy adopted by lobbyists to bring attention to dementia and in turn the need for funding and resources for research and care services; a ploy that has reported success elsewhere, for example in North America (Holstein, 2000).

The concern with growing numbers, and the resultant concern with how to provide care for the person with dementia and support to their carers may explain why dementia, in particular Alzheimer's disease, is viewed as the 'most publicized health problem in old age' (Robertson, 1990: 430).

Manthorpe and Adams (2003: 35) use three themes to discuss dementia care policy, suggesting ways to chart the developments in policy making over time. These can be summarised as follows: the place of people with dementia; dementia and decision making; dementia at the frontier.

- Where people with dementia should be cared for and the negative labelling applied to people with dementia, demonstrates the lowly status bestowed on people with dementia and the concerns of those wishing to influence policy to create more humane environments for people with dementia to live. The developments within community care policy locate people with dementia within their family network, again influencing particular policy developments.
- Dementia and decision making reflect a move towards looking at the individual with dementia and the legal and ethical debates surrounding their care and decisions made about their capacity or incapacity; this could be seen to reflect the theoretical developments calling for seeing the person with dementia.
- Dementia at the frontier reflects the move of countries to call for more attention, resources and interest in the condition and the development of standards of care to meet such objectives. (Manthorpe and Adams, 2003).

This 'legacies of the past' (Cantley, 2001: 202–3) approach to dementia care policy demonstrates the interplay between policies concerned not only with dementia, but also with older people, mental health and community care issues. As such, much dementia care policy can be seen to reflect long-standing policy issues of the role of the family and the state, how to control costs of care, particularly in institutions; managing health and social care boundaries; and concerns about equity and eligibility for service provision (Cantley, 2001: 219).

The growing convergence of dementia care policies across countries is demonstrated through developments in European Union countries. Despite the diverse political origins and cultural perspectives, as well as differences in economic developments, Alzheimer's disease movements across Europe are calling for similar care principles, namely, that people with dementia should be able to stay at home for as long as possible; carers need support to achieve this; people with dementia should have control over the support they receive; services should be coordinated at a local level; and institutional care should be as homely as possible (Warner and Furnish, 2002).

Longley and Warner (2002: 11) suggest that there are two driving forces behind different countries coming to broadly similar policy positions on dementia care; politico-economic and humanitarian. The politico-economic position reflects the growing number of older people, the prevalence of dementia in older people and the associated increased costs of providing care to more people with dementia. The humanitarian driving force reflects theoretical work, arguing for a focus on the person with dementia, and the maintenance of the self and personhood of individuals through the provision of quality care, discussed in Chapter 1. The growth in legislative frameworks promoting individual rights (the decision making issues discussed by Manthorpe and Adams, 2003) can all be seen to contribute to legal and policy frameworks promoting standards of care which arguably have an ethical (Gove, 2002) or moral position shaping their development and resulting policy frameworks.

The applied nature of much research on dementia has resulted in a plethora of recommendations for policy makers and practitioners, reflecting wider social concerns. Recommendations for care delivery are made because of the projections about the rising number of people with dementia. For example, based on international comparisons of 18 wealthy countries, similar issues requiring policy and practice consideration were evident, such as:

- A shortage of skilled staff in long-stay care working in poor conditions.
- Quality of care being questioned and a cause for concern.
- A shift in state provision of care to more voluntary and private sector care provision.
- Public sector bodies being largely responsible for coordinating and commissioning care services.
- Inter-agency working as a preferred option.
- High-level policy initiatives in individual countries being evident, bringing dementia to the fore as an issue requiring national attention. (Knapp et al., 2007a: 15–16).

An Organization for Economic Cooperation and Development (OECD) report (Moise et al., 2004) based on a study of nine countries, Australia, Canada, England, Wales, France, Japan, Spain, Sweden and the United States, all with diverse welfare and health care systems, provides broad objectives that those formulating dementia policies should consider. Thus, despite differences in the approach to health and social care provision, it was possible for the authors to arrive at common objectives in relation to dementia care provision. The need for common objectives is contextualized within the demographics of an ageing population where increased longevity is linked to projected increases in the number of people with dementia who will require health and social care. Resources and skilled staff will be required to meet these care needs. The advice of the OECD (Moise et al., 2004: 62–3) is for:

- The needs of older people over 75 to be targeted within dementia policies.
- Measures to be put in place to enable early detection and diagnosis of dementia.
- Education, including counselling, for carers of people with dementia.
- The use of anti-dementia drugs to be encouraged.
- People with dementia to remain in the community for as long as possible.
- Coordination of services to be given due consideration to enable agreement about responsibilities to be reached amongst the multiple service providers.
- More evidence about the benefits of dementia-specific services.

Two ways to support dementia caregivers are advanced (Moise et al., 2004: 63):

- A financial support package for carers to compensate for the loss of earnings and pension contributions which may help enable carers to continue caring for longer.
- The promotion of respite care.

By focusing on dementia as an individual pathology, policies focus on micro-level issues relating to the individual, for example there is a focus on service development and service needs. This occurs – when service solutions are designed to be acceptable to policy makers and care professionals, rather than addressing issues at the structural level – where the way disease and older people are conceptualized can be challenged (Robertson, 1990: 438–9). This would in turn enable policies to be formulated, which would address, for example, economic challenges of growing numbers of older people and social challenges of providing care in a way that is acceptable to older people and their families. However, the first challenge to policy influencers has been to bring the condition to the attention of the respective governments who require data on the numbers of people with the condition. Thus, early diagnosis is often perceived as the first issue requiring attention, to ensure that people can receive early medical interventions (Rimmer et al., 2005), as well as be counted in the numbers presented to governments setting out the need for government attention.

To achieve early diagnosis requires health professionals to recognize the signs of dementia and also for the general public to avoid accepting the early symptoms of dementia as part of old age and thus not requiring attention or resource. Yet physicians have been found to routinely under-diagnose dementia even when cognitive impairments have been documented (Callahan et al., 1995). By recognizing and diagnosing dementia early on, it is suggested that cost-effective therapies can be offered promptly and thus perhaps prevent the need for more costly interventions at a later date (Geldmarcher, 2002). It is evident that public health concerns and the influence of such concerns for policy making actively engage with economic issues, mainly how to finance dementia care and how to be cost effective in this process. We will now move on to consider economic issues that shape knowledge and understanding about dementia and dementia care practices.

Economic issues

Three aspects to economic concerns surrounding dementia and dementia care have been identified (Keen, 1993): the impact on national economies; the impact on individual finances; and the costs and benefits of different types of care. The first issue, impact on national economies, relates to the impact on government spending in particular and national economies in general. The concern with the growing number of people with dementia is thus related to economic concerns: what is the cost of dementia and how can society pay for dementia and dementia care? To estimate costs accurately it is important to know the expected prevalence and incidence of dementia; prevalence being the rate at which a condition occurs within a given population and incidence the number of new people with a particular condition within a given population within a given time frame. Thus, the political concerns discussed above giving rise to talk of a 'dementia epidemic' (Wilson and Fearnley, 2007) based on a projected worldwide increase in the number of people who will be affected by dementia (Knapp et al., 2007a) lead to concerns about how much the condition will cost and how it will be paid for.

The cost to society of the predicted increase in the number of people with dementia is hard to predict and the OECD recommends that better models for predicting costs be developed (Moise et al., 2004: 64). The exact cost of dementia is difficult to estimate, however, as Bloom et al. (2003) demonstrate, the estimated costs of Alzheimer's disease are hugely variable, making it difficult to work out the 'real' costs of the disease. Reasons for the difficulty in comparing costs relate to the variation in the resource items, for example staff costs, included in individual studies as well as differences in the approach, for example retrospective studies or studies which follow individuals prospectively (Jonsson and Berr, 2005). Compared with other conditions, Alzheimer's disease appears to be more expensive than stroke, heart disease and cancer (Lowin et al., 2001), with reported costs for dementia care higher than costs for caring for those who do not have dementia (Husaini et al., 2003), and institutionalization appearing to use up the highest amount of resources available for the care of people with dementia (Wolstenholme et al., 2002).

Given that economic considerations influence policy drives, and the use of numbers of people and the predicted costs by lobbying groups, it is at first glance surprising that the exact costs of dementia are not known. However, when the unpaid care provided by families is taken into account, alongside the variation in services offered and the way in which such services are financed, it is less surprising that it is difficult to estimate economic costs (Knapp et al., 2007a). Also, it appears that a universal finding is that costs increase along with the increased severity of the dementia (Jonsson and Berr, 2005: 51), with more hours of informal care required as the dementia advances (Langa et al., 2001) and institutional care costing more than care in the community, no matter what the degree of severity of the dementia (Knapp et al., 2007b). What is clear, however, is that the costs have been reported to be 'very high across European countries' (Jonsson and Berr, 2005: 52) and are expected to increase, given the projected increase in the number of older people with dementia and the expected decline in the ability of family members to provide 'free' care. However, difficulties in estimating costs due to demographic and economic factors have led to notes of caution against making 'apocalyptic judgments regarding the effects of ageing in general and dementia in particular on health-care expenditure' (McNamee et al., 2001: 265), but there is increasing pressure to define the costs of dementia to help improve resource allocation in the future (O'Shea and O'Reilly, 2000).

The second area of economic concern identified by Keen (1993) related to the costs of dementia is the impact of dementia on individual finances – this may be the finances of the person with dementia or their family members. Although it is often assumed that informal dementia care is cheaper than institutional care, one study has found that this is not necessarily the case, as the costs of informal care could be underestimated by 25 per cent for people living alone and 40 per cent for people with a co-resident carer (Schneider et al., 2003: 321). The same study also found that a high level of formal care inputs equated with high levels of informal care inputs, thus formal care supplemented rather than substituted for informal care-giving (Schneider et al., 2003).

The unpaid costs of caring are also considerable, with one study estimating that unpaid caring labour accounted for 71 per cent of the total cost of providing care to a person with dementia at home (Stommel et al., 1994). Although it is widely known and accepted that family members make great efforts to care for people with dementia, the total cost to society of family members' formal and informal work is unknown (Winblad et al., 1996). The model used by Wanless (2006: 283) suggests that informal carers account for half the required care input of older people. The impact on the well-being of carers as well as their finances is likely to be substantial. Although this model is about older people generally, rather than people with dementia per se, it is likely that there is a similar pattern of care provision for people with dementia. Further, the OECD (Moise et al., 2004: 64) predicts that there may be an under-supply of family carers in the future which will in turn put a strain on other resources. Although family care may be seen as 'free' it is important that some monetary value is attached to family caregiving to ensure that the hidden costs of caring can be included in overall estimates of the cost of dementia to society (O'Shea and O'Reilly, 2000), be it through the public or private purse.

The third area of economic concern relates to the economics of service delivery (Keen, 1993: 375). This means looking at the relationship between the costs of the services that an individual may require, and the anticipated benefits of such services. The World Health Report, *Global Burden of Disease* (Lopez et al., 2006) estimates that dementia contributed more years lived with a disability for those over 60 years than many other conditions; 11.2 per cent for dementia compared to, for example, 2.4 per cent for cancer and 9.5 per cent for stroke. Thus, the impact of dementia for individuals is considerable, the number of individuals who are likely to experience dementia is projected to increase, in turn increasing the projected economic costs society will bear. It is expected that the combination of increase in prevalence of dementia will put stress on health care systems in all countries, developed and developing (Wimo et al., 2006). How these costs are met varies from country to country with a mix of financing arrangements often used but broad finance arrangements have been grouped into four types:

- 'User charges' paid by the service user or their family.
- Private insurance.
- Tax-based support from direct and/or indirect taxes.
- Social insurance linked to employment. (Knapp et al., 2007a).

How care should be financed has been widely debated, for example in the UK, Wanless (2006) recommended that there should be increased finance for long-term care for older people and that there should be a non-means-tested entitlement to social care. In Scotland, free personal care has been introduced and appears to be having early success in its implementation, with fears that there would be an explosion in the number receiving care proving unfounded (Bell and Bowes, 2006; Bowes and Bell, 2007). However, different countries have different financing arrangements and crucially, as Wanless notes, 'the choice of funding arrangement affects who receives care, how much care they receive and what they pay' (2006: 287). Thus, debates about funding and decisions reached will have a direct impact on the lives of people with dementia and is therefore an important factor in the study of dementia.

The cost of providing care to a projected increasing number of people with dementia will incur a variety of costs. For example, the cost of providing care through staff costs is recognised by Wanless (2006: 282), who states that 'the pay rates needed to secure a suitable workforce are also a major factor'. The demand for long-term care in England alone is expected to increase by 88 per cent between 2002 and 2031, thus costs of providing long-term care services are predicted to be considerable in the future (Comas-Herrera et al., 2007). Yet, as Townsend (2007) notes, the conflicting messages in reports and the lack of obligation to implement recommendations means that the impact of such commissioned work is highly variable, a case in point being the implementation of free personal care in Scotland but not the rest of the UK after the Sutherland Report. A Swedish study found that providing care to someone with dementia in long-term institutional care involved more time costs than caring for someone in the same setting who does not have dementia, with more time required for increased severity of dementia (Nordberg et al., 2007). Thus, not only the presence of dementia but the severity of the condition impact on the time costs required to care for a person with dementia in long-stay care.

Long-stay care can be provided by the private or the public purse (O'Shea, 2004) so models of funding care provision are an important consideration in policy developments designed to respond to projected increase in demand for services. However, the debate, transcending national boundaries, on who should pay for long-term care, the relative contribution between public and private funds, whether family carers should receive any form of payment and whether public funds should be targeted at specific individuals is long running (Tester, 1999), with no real end in sight, despite recent proposals for radical shifts in financing arrangements of care provision (Wanless, 2006). A US study demonstrates that the value of the costs incurred for dementia care vary, depending on the perspective of different payers, the groups whose perspectives are explored are medical insurers, family carers or the service user themselves, and society (Murman et al., 2007). This study therefore demonstrates that different stakeholders will define need and costs differently and thus consensus on cost-effectiveness is difficult to determine.

Barriers to early diagnosis and treatment relate to the financial resources available within specific countries' health care systems (Waldemar et al., 2007), but also reflect differences in the availability and use of drug treatments and differences in physicians' ability to make the diagnosis. Thus, the economic context surrounding the study of dementia has some consensus, for example the need to estimate the costs of dementia and the cost-effectiveness of interventions and treatments. But there is also a lack of overall coherence in recommendations for policy makers – for example, what treatments and interventions should be funded and how they should be financed – as how to pay for care and the choice of what care to provide is based on value judgements reflecting social discourse surrounding dementia and dementia care.

Social context of dementia

Policy developments and economic decisions about, for example, the funding of long-term care reflect individual countries' views and expectations about caregiving: for example, whether care is provided by health or social care sectors; whether long-stay care is financed by the state or individuals; and the availability of informal carers and the expectation that they can provide care for 'free' (Wittenberg et al., 2007). Thus, policy and economic decisions will reflect social norms and expectations, and it is to the social context of dementia and dementia care that we will now give some attention and which will be developed in later chapters. Yet, dementia and dementia care have historically occupied a low position on the political agenda, with little specific government policy on caring for people with dementia (Sassi and McDaid, 1999). The underlying explanations for such a 'laissez-faire' approach can be explored by contextualizing the study of dementia within socially constructed marginalized positions, particularly relevant for the study of dementia care, old age and mental health and for dementia care and the gender of the care worker.

The social context surrounding the study of dementia is one where there are numerous socially-constructed categories where individuals may be placed. For example, race, gender, class, age, are socially constructed groupings, all of which will influence understandings about the experience of dementia. However, as Dressel et al. (1997) note, such categories are not mutually exclusive, and attempts to look at the connections between such groupings can be problematic. Attempts to be more inclusive incorporate a range of approaches that have limited success:

- 'Add and stir': where previously excluded groups are added to existing models or ways of thinking and knowing which may lead to atheoretical understandings of the very topics to be included in the analysis.
- Tokenism: when a group identified as being on the margins is selected as a special case to be studied.
- Looking at the social reality from the vantage point of those traditionally at the margins.

To do this requires acknowledgement of historical power differentials and questioning the taken-for-granted assumptions that underpin social organization and social policy (Dressel et al., 1997: 580–3). To understand the social discourse surrounding dementia and dementia care involves looking at how older people are perceived:

Perhaps ultimately, our pervasive concern with the meaning of Alzheimer's disease reflects our society's efforts to grapple with the nature of the relationship between those who are already old and the wider community of people who will yet become old in the future. (Herskovitz, 1995: 148)

Thus, studying dementia is a fraught process requiring an engagement with issues that may be uncomfortable to acknowledge.

The move towards a more inclusive viewpoint of dementia where those with dementia and their carers' experiences are actively sought (explored in Chapter 5) has itself a social context where user views movements have become more vocal and strive to counteract the negativity and stigma surrounding old age and mental health.

Dementia: negativity and stigma

Attitudes towards dementia can be seen to reflect negative views of old age and stigma surrounding mental health. For example, a study of six European countries (Bond et al., 2005) found that although policy makers recognized Alzheimer's disease as a serious condition they did not necessarily prioritize it as a serious condition as it did not affect the most productive members of society. The same study also found that there was variance in the way countries diagnosed dementia and then recommended treatments (Wilkinson et al., 2005); there was also a widely held view by carers that governments were not investing enough in Alzheimer's disease. The variance in time from symptoms to diagnosis across the countries ranges from 10 months in Germany to 32 months in the UK (Wilkinson et al., 2005: 28). While such variations can be explained according to cultural norms and expectations in treatment, the question arises about accuracy of diagnosis and the early availability of information and treatment offered to people with dementia and their families.

It is argued that to change practice, professionals must recognize and reflect on their own attitudes to mental health and old age for challenges to the status quo of service delivery to occur (Wilkinson et al., 2005: 27). Using the example of Ireland, O'Shea (2004) argues that in the absence of government support through investment in community care services the health of informal carers suffers. This arguably applies to countries worldwide where dementia care falls predominantly on family members for at least some time in the trajectory of the illness. Personal accounts of the desire to keep a relative with dementia at home, but being unable to do so due to a lack of support and personal exhaustion (Pointon and Keady, 2005), demonstrate a lack of care and support for family caregivers to enable them to care in the way they would prefer and a resulting institutionalization of the person with dementia, not through choice but out of necessity.

Although not specifically referring to dementia or dementia care, Dressel and colleagues' (1997) analysis of the interlocking categorizations individuals may be placed in is a sharp reminder that people with dementia are not a homogenous group but may experience multiple interlocking oppressions (or privileges). However, people with dementia have tended to be lumped together into a socially convenient grouping where decisions about care and treatment rely initially on the diagnosis of dementia. The issue of stigma is one we return to in Chapter 4.

Caring for people with dementia

There are two primary arenas where dementia care takes place, within the community in the person with dementia's own home, or the home of a family member, or in a form of institutional care, be it hospital, residential, nursing or care home. Where people with dementia live is of interest in two ways: first, where people live will have a marked impact on their experience of dementia; and, second, how society chooses to provide care reflects values and beliefs about caregiving, as well as political preferences and economic constraints and resources available for caregiving.

Informal caregiving

The majority of people with dementia today live within the community and are cared for by family members. This trend has remained relatively constant over time (Nolan et al., 1996). Understandings about caregiving resonate with stereotypical views about gender and what it means to care, with care being constructed as an issue for women (Dalley, 1988). However, the experience of caring has been reported as quite different for men and women, with women reporting greater stress and strain than male caregivers (Morris et al., 1991). The problems, burden and stress that accompany family or informal caregiving have been well documented (Black and Almeida, 2004), highlighting the human costs of caring for a person with dementia. The satisfactions that can accompany family caregiving have also received attention (Hellstrom et al., 2005) and demonstrate the importance of maintaining a relationship between the person with dementia and the caregiver. Thus, reinforcing and developing Kitwood's (1997) assertion that being in relationships was crucial to the person with dementia and that attempts to evaluate the quality of life of people with dementia must include reference to the importance of maintaining a relationship with the carer.

The ability to maintain relationships at the onset of dementia is of course called into question if a model of understanding where decline and loss are used. However, if a social-psychological approach is adopted where the personhood and self of the person with dementia remain, then it is possible to advocate relationship-centred care rather than stressing the burden of caregiving. Thus, beliefs and attitudes towards dementia caregiving reflect discourses surrounding what it means to have dementia and the impact this will have for the person and their life and the lives of those close to them. In Chapter 3, the discourse of informal caregiving is discussed further in relation to dementia caregiving, and for the purpose of this social context setting, the important message is that the majority of people with dementia are cared for at home rather than in an institution. Carers may experience stress and strain as well as satisfaction, and most importantly, the role of caregivers is vital in providing care and shaping the experience of living with dementia.

Paid care

There are interesting connotations attached to paid care work, with the assumption that women will enjoy paid care work and that they can do this fairly naturally and easily, as they extend their domestic duties into the public sphere of work (Lee-Treweek, 1997b: 48). However, care work is demanding, emotionally and physically, and may not be carried out through choice but from economic necessity. The remuneration for providing paid care is low, with policy-driven reports not seeking to challenge this status quo position (Royal Commission on Long-Term Care, 1999) through lobbying for higher than minimum wage payments for caring for members of society who require care, although the need for payment to reflect the requirements of the work has been more recently highlighted (Wanless, 2006).

A further example of the social context surrounding dementia care is long-stay care provision for people with dementia and the changes over time in the way care is provided. There are also some similarities in that people with dementia continue to be excluded from society and placed in institutions staffed by workers who are themselves often on the margins of society whose work is seen to be of low value. Ideas about dementia care today are shaped and influenced by the historic images of institutional care. The common perception of the old culture of care may be that described by Townsend (1962) where residents were dressed alike, with similar haircuts and housed in shared dormitories. The effects on old people living in residential homes, such as loss of occupation, loss of privacy, isolation from the community and loss of powers of self-determination (Townsend, 1962: 338–55) may be factors associated with residential home life. The 'new culture' of care espoused by Kitwood (1997) demands a recognition of the individual, and movements such as the Eden Project (Thomas, 1996) tried to go forward from such negative images of institutional care by changing the physical environment where people lived and also the way in which they spent their time, for example, by engaging in meaningful activities supported by caregivers who were expected to uphold individuality and meet individual needs.

The clash of private space and public working life creates an interesting dynamic for those living and working in institutional care. Following on from Goffman's (1961) seminal work on asylums, studies focusing on institutional care for older people remind us of the complex relationships that exist within institutions. For example, Tellis-Nayak and Tellis-Nayak (1989: 312) describe the care situation as one where residents and nursing aides come together as 'two parties, both powerless, little respected and hardly recognized by society'. While McColgan (2004: 169) reminds us that the labelling of people with dementia can occur merely by their presence in a setting designated as a setting where people with dementia live.

Although care staff may be perceived as powerless within the care setting, they can exert power over those in receipt of care, and the ways in which they do so will impact on the lived experiences of people with dementia (Vittoria, 1998). The world of paid carers and those living with dementia reflects an interest and recognition that care homes have a culture worth investigating (Henderson and Vesperi, 1995), and is explored further in Chapter 4. For the purposes of this chapter, where the context of the study of dementia is being reviewed, it is enough for now to acknowledge that the social world of care settings is a complex interplay of macro-level social factors where paid care is relatively undervalued as are those who receive care: two groups on the margins of society in some way coexisting in a socially constructed physical space designed to 'provide care' to those who can no longer remain in their own homes.

The closure of long-stay geriatric wards, the rise of voluntary and private sector care provision in residential and nursing homes and the emergence of care in the community (which includes residential and nursing homes) has contributed to a rise in the profile of both dementia and dementia care. Almost simultaneously, it would appear, there have been conceptual shifts in the discourse around dementia and care provision for those labelled with the condition 'dementia'.

Moving on to look at the finance of long-stay care for older people across Europe and the US, Wittenberg et al. (2007) suggest that the social contract surrounding the finance of such care proceeds from an assumption that society will pay (through taxes) for care for those who are most in need, with alternative financing arrangements for those who can afford to pay. Thus, a general expectation that society will look after those most in need is evident across the Western countries included in the analysis. However, the standards of care that might be expected and where care can be provided may reflect popular beliefs, fears and expectations about dementia often formed through very little knowledge about dementia. In addition, those paid to provide care for people with dementia may also begin this task from a position of relative ignorance about what dementia is and what dementia care should involve and be offered very little practical support or monetary recognition for the difficult work they perform.

Conclusions

The key issues from the political, economic and social issues and concerns which contextualize the study of dementia demonstrate that;

- Dementia is on the increase.
- Costs will rise.
- Informal care and institutional care provide, and are expected to continue to provide, the bedrock of care provision in the future.

Thus, any theoretical work (reviewed in Chapter 1) will be influenced by the context of a particular moment in time, as will policy and practice frameworks shaping the provision of care to people with dementia and support for those who provide care (discussed in Chapter 3).

To study dementia requires an understanding of the complexities and interconnections between theory, context and frameworks for care delivery, as the links between these factors shape the discourse surrounding dementia and dementia care and will impact on the experiences of individuals with dementia. Douthit (2006) argues that political and economic will is required to develop knowledge of dementia beyond medical agendas. While Lechner notes the wider macro level of care may appear to be at odds with the concern of practitioners who seek to provide individuals with quality care level (2003: 132); however, to understand the micro level of care experiences, whether they be conceptualized as quality of life or quality of care issues, demands an engagement with macro-level issues which shape the discourse of dementia care, including political, social and economic issues.

For people with dementia and their carers to be recognized, however, 'will require a revolution in our thinking and practices' (Callahan, 1991: 142). To truly appreciate the position people with dementia occupy requires an exploration of historical and contemporary movements where social values link with policy developments and economic considerations. Thus, what has been termed the 'political and moral economy of growing old' (Minkler and Estes, 1991) aptly describes the processes underpinning interpretations of dementia and dementia care and the resultant beliefs and attitudes those with dementia and their carers may encounter, shaping their experience of this condition, which is debilitating no matter what the theoretical approach adopted, biomedical or social. Although biomedical approaches will stress disease and decline aspects, social approaches uncover oppressions and prejudice. Taken together, a rather negative climate to exist with dementia prevails.

■ ■ Further reading ■

Cantley (2001) gives a useful overview of the policy context of dementia care. Knapp et al. (2007a) provide an international comparison of key issues shaping the context of dementia care. Wanless (2006) discusses the future of care of older people in the UK – the issues, however, are relevant to other countries in the Western world.

3

CARING FOR PEOPLE WITH DEMENTIA: UTOPIAN IDEALS?

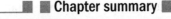

Chapter summary

- This chapter focuses on developments in the care of people with dementia since the 1980s. The 1980s is selected as the starting point as this is the time when Alzheimer's was recognized as a disease and the medicalization of dementia and its subsequent deconstruction began (Fox, 1989). The chapter begins by discussing expectations about dementia care. It includes a discussion about the implications such expectations have for the role of family carers and frontline workers in the promotion of high-quality support to people with dementia. The chapter highlights the difficulty in applying care ideals universally, using two examples of diversity amongst those with dementia arising through ethnic identity and geographical location.
- This chapter therefore builds on the guiding questions of 'what do we know about dementia?' and 'how do we know what we know about dementia?' discussed in Chapters 1 and 2, respectively. By remembering these questions and considering specifics of providing care for people with dementia, it becomes apparent that our knowledge about dementia care is wide and varied but far from comprehensive or complete.

Introduction

The subtitle of this chapter 'utopian ideals?' reflects my intention of questioning the expectations on which care policies, mission statements and legal frameworks surrounding dementia care are based. Three specific foci of this chapter are located within this contextual overview of expectations and the resulting implications for those who provide care. These are:

- The low status of those who are paid to care.
- The reliance on families to provide care.

- The lack of homogeneity in dementia care practice. Two examples are given: providing care for urban and rural dwellers; and providing care for minority and majority ethnic groups.

The expectations and ideals of care provision may be laudable but are they possible? Given the context of care provided in Chapter 2, demonstrating the worldwide projected increase in the number of people with dementia, the associated growing economic costs and the remaining stigma and marginalization of dementia and dementia care in the social world, it is heartening to find reports of good practices which promote quality of life for people with dementia, particularly when viewed through the conceptual lens of personhood and selfhood. However, can such ideals become the norm rather than the exception throughout the world of dementia care? The study of dementia from a social science perspective demonstrates the challenges, tensions and paradoxes faced by societies who do not value those who require care or those who provide care, thus posing a challenge to the ideals espoused by policy makers and theoreticians of dementia and dementia care.

Dementia care: expectations

The care that a person with dementia may expect to receive is largely dependent upon conceptualizations of dementia. The predominance of the medical model is apparent, although the influence of psychosocial approaches is also present. For example, the World Health Organization (WHO) states that:

There is currently no cure for Alzheimer's disease. The goals of care are to:

- Maintain the functioning of the individual;
- Reduce disability due to lost mental functions;
- Reorganize routines so as to maximize use of the retained functions;
- Minimize symptoms such as depression, agitation, suspiciousness;
- Provide support to families.

Psychosocial interventions, including education, support, counselling and respite care, are extremely important in Alzheimer's disease, both for patients and family caregivers. Some medicines have demonstrated usefulness in ameliorating cognitive dysfunction and improving attention, as well as reducing delusions. (WHO, 2001).

Despite the articulate and painful pictures presented by the Alzheimer's disease Movement members, it has been argued that the issue of caring has been overlooked. This may, in part, be explained by the caring of people with dementia emerging as a 'women's issue' within the Alzheimer's disease Movement (Fox, 2000: 222). Indeed, women provide most of the world's work of 'long-term care without financial remuneration' (Estes, 2006: 94). Yet, recent developments about the care relationships between the person with dementia and family caregivers demonstrate that the role of men in the caregiving and care receiving enterprise cannot be ignored (Askham et al., 2007), and thus although more women than men have dementia and more women than men tend to provide care, men cannot be 'edited' out of discussions about care giving and receiving. A useful reminder of the need to remember the relationships between family members and people with dementia has been highlighted in ongoing discussions about the importance of relationships in dementia care (Adams, 2008).

Post poses the question 'what pictures shall we draw of the person with dementia?' (2000a: 26). He states that if pictures are sketched which are achievement-orientated, socioeconomic and based on cognitive values, then harm will result to the person with dementia. He goes on to discuss harm as the absence of love and care, the absence of what Kitwood (1997: 8) describes as 'a status or standing bestowed on others', which describes the concept he termed personhood. Society, family members and health care professionals will all interpret the experience of dementia (Post, 2000b), and it follows that different individuals will interpret dementia in different ways according to, for example, their sociocultural background and personal knowledge of dementia. How we interpret and conceptualize dementia will shape the care that is offered and the expectations society, paid and family caregivers will have about the care experiences the person with dementia should expect.

A moral practice of care has been advanced where professionals should include, listen to and seek to act on the input from carers (Goldstein et al., 2007). Such an approach requires the changes in role and experiences of both the person with dementia and their family carer to be considered. However, the problem with many of these somewhat abstract ideas and principles is how to find a way for practitioners to do such things, and to carry them out routinely within the constraints of their paid work.

The challenge of implementing ideals, apparent through policy documents and mission statements of governments, organizations and institutions, is how those at the coalface respond and interpret such ideas. For example, a study found that staff in nursing homes who were encouraged to reflect on conflicting values (that of the organization mission statements and the demands placed on them by residents) did not find it difficult to choose between different values; rather they interpreted them subjectively and on a case-by-case pragmatic basis (Kalis et al., 2003). If this way of working is typical of care homes then it follows that person-centred ideals may be implemented some of the time for some of the people, but that for some of the time and some of the people they won't be. As Kalis et al. (2003: 41) argue, to progress from ideals articulated in policy documents and mission statements about quality of life, to a reality that reflects such ideals, is not easy and requires practitioners to be encouraged to reflect on the decisions they make about care delivery. The demands of care work are often such that there is not time to reflect on the job, but rather to act, and to act in a way that makes the task orientation of the work quick, easy and efficient.

There is an expectation that women will care, and the care they provide should be appreciated. However, Post argues that policy should not be geared to expecting women to take on this role, and that the traditional familial ethics of care, where women are expected to embrace the caring role, is damaging to women and is therefore unacceptable (2000a: 39). Policy should protect women from taking on too heavy a caring role, rather than assume that families will take on a large proportion of the caregiving required for older members of society. Yet, this is not the reality, as Knapp et al. (2007a) demonstrate that policy makers accept that family carers, in particular women, will provide care. Thus, women may often find themselves in a position where their family expects them to provide care to a relative with dementia as an extension to their family caring responsibilities, with this position backed up by the absence of care alternatives provided by health and social care services. Thus, policy making and family expectations perpetuate an ideology which can force women into taking on caregiving roles that may place them under considerable pressure, as they juggle paid work and existing family responsibilities with the new caregiving role.

New expectations have emerged in relation to the standards of care that will be offered by those providing care to people with dementia requiring formal care services, either in the home or in long-stay care facilities. In their review, Edvardsson et al. (2008) note that expectations for the care of people with dementia are based on upholding the personhood of the individual with dementia and prioritizing the relationship between the person and their carer over care tasks. It is worth remembering that these expectations are placed on workers who are predominantly female, who receive low pay (or no pay if family carers) and thus have low economic status within Western societies (Innes et al., 2006).

The approach to care that underpins changes in expectations of paid workers is that known as Person-Centred Care. As we have noted in Chapter 1, this is a term that has gained popular usage in the dementia field since the 1990s, with policy frameworks endorsing and giving credibility to the term. For example, one of the standards emerging from the UK Department of Health's National Service Framework for Older People is entitled 'Person-Centred Care' (Department of Health, 2001: 23). Recognition by policy makers of the widespread appeal of the notion of 'person-centred care' has been noted (Ryan et al., 2004), however, definitions of what this means for care practice have remained somewhat elusive. If taking a cynical stance, it could be argued that the humane and individualistic image of care that the term 'person- or patient-centred' provokes, is the image governments wish to project onto the care they promote for vulnerable groups. How to make this image a reality is challenging for governments (and practitioners); as is deciding how best to evaluate the impact of new care standards on care practices, particularly as governments have yet to produce conclusive evidence that changes have resulted from such positive mission statements in policy documentation.

To deliver person-centred care in the manner outlined by Kitwood (1997) places huge demands on family carers and paid care workers. Carers, paid and unpaid, are often expected to perform physically strenuous, often 'dirty' work, while engaging in a positive manner with the emotional needs and demands of the individual they are caring for. As Post reminds us, 'it is easy to point to cases of familial abuse of people with dementia', however, 'it is remarkable that spouses and adult children in the United States remain the center of caregiving' (2000a: 34).

The emotional demands of care work have been clearly described by Lee-Treweek (1997a, b) and Lopez (2006), with care worker strategies for distancing themselves from unpleasant emotional work part of the coping mechanisms used when 'caring' becomes too difficult. To achieve the 'warm' caring relationship described by Ungerson (2005) may not always be possible; this may simply be due to personalities but also to the nature of the physical, mental and emotional demands of the cared-for and the response of an individual carer. Brannelly suggests that nurses – although her ideas can be transposed to other professional care workers – can seek to help support people with dementia and their family carers and to maintain relationships throughout the person's dementia, that 'promote empowering rather than oppressive care' (2008: 257). Similarly, Woods et al. (2007) have argued for the need for the care of the person with dementia in care homes to be driven by good communications with care home staff and families to help promote good relationships with workers and families that will in turn promote high quality care for the person with dementia.

Communication has also been stressed as key in promoting care triads when people with dementia are living in the community (Adams and Gardiner, 2005) to promote high-quality support for the person with dementia and their caregiver. While these aims are laudable, the difficulties in managing what have been called 'health care triads' also need to be taken into account (Fortinsky, 2001), as there is the possibility that one set of views will be excluded and two voices collude to override the wishes or perspectives of the third triad member. Further, care triads assume one primary family caregiver, when in fact family care may be organized by a range of family members (Fortinsky, 2001; Adams and Gardiner, 2005). Thus, promoting a relationship-based approach to care decisions is complex.

A report on an intervention to promote care dyads in dementia care found that involving both the person with dementia and their family caregiver in a series of nine educational sessions was an effective way of exploring and meeting the needs of the person with dementia and their family member soon after the diagnosis of dementia was given (Whitlach et al., 2006). Fostering a partnership approach to the experience of dementia at diagnosis stage may thus be a key component to promoting a relationship-centred approach as the dementia progresses.

A senses framework has been proposed (Nolan et al., 2004) to help develop relationship-centred care for older people. This framework aims to promote shared understandings about the care relationship and argues for the need for a sense of security, continuity, belonging, purpose, achievement and significance. Each of these can be applied to the older person, staff and family carers to promote an overall sense of being in relation to one another. Working within a 'relationship-centred' framework requires recognizing the various ways relationships between carers and those with dementia may be preserved and adapt through the illness (Adams, 2008), and as such the senses framework does not fully engage with past relationships. In a paper arguing a move from person-centred care to relationship-centred care, Adams (2005) concludes that living with dementia should be seen as part of a lifelong trajectory of shared experiences. Thus, dementia needs to be located within relationships past and present, and if person-centred care is to be a reality for people with dementia, their relationship history cannot be ignored.

Government guidelines talk about person-centred care and the importance of recognizing the needs of carers, paid and unpaid, and providing support to carers to enable them to interact with the person with dementia and provide person-centred care (NICE-SCIE, 2006); thus the need to go beyond the individual with dementia and to look at the relationships between caregiver and care recipient is acknowledged. However, they have also been critiqued for polarizing the needs of the 'carer' and 'cared for' (Henderson and Forbat, 2002). Thus, although the need for support for the caregiver is also acknowledged, how to achieve this remains an open question. In a similar way to the ideals of person-centred care being articulated as specific care objectives, having the aim and seeing this as a reality for all people with dementia remains the challenge. Forbat has argued that policy makers need to consider the relationships between family carers and people with dementia as:

> for the family carer the relationship is often at the forefront of how, and indeed why, care is delivered. For family carers, then, there is a need not just to recognize that they play an integral part in providing assistance ... but to place relationships centrally within this understanding. (2008: 234).

Kitwood and Bredin (1992a: 281–2) describe a culture of care where it is possible to ascertain well-being in dementia as care situations where people with dementia can expect:

1 To assert will or desire.
2 To have the ability to express a range of emotions.
3 The initiation of social contact.
4 Affectional warmth.
5 Social sensitivity.

CARING FOR PEOPLE WITH DEMENTIA

6 Self-respect.
7 Acceptance of others with dementia.
8 Humour.
9 Creativity and self expression.
10 To be able to show pleasure.
11 Helpfulness.
12 Relaxation.

Thus, care which enables the above well-being indicators may be a sound basis for expectations of care that a person with dementia would receive. However, despite the appeal of the so-called 'person-centred' approach to care, putting such ideals into practice can prove problematic. When services attempting to maintain the personhood of people with dementia prove popular with carers and staff, commissioners may not necessarily agree, as their views on success may vary from those directly giving or receiving the service (Gladman et al., 2007), resulting in a decrease in funding and thus affecting the service's ability to continue. This reflects differences and misunderstandings about what can be achieved for people with dementia and also what it is perceived to be worth financing. Person-centred care cannot be seen as a cheap option, either financially or personally, as it requires a high level of input and commitment from carers, both paid and unpaid. Thus, sustaining services found to be popular is likely not only to require continued financial commitment from commissioners of services but also high levels of motivation and personal commitment from those individuals who are providing the service, as well as providing ongoing support to enable care workers to provide high-quality care.

Promoting a person-centred model is an ideal that has gained in popularity, even if there is a lack of clear consensus and definition about what this means in theory (Brooker, 2004; McCormack, 2004) and in practice (Gladman et al., 2007). However, the language of person-centred care is in evidence in texts originating from across the globe and also in attempts to influence policy. This could be seen as testament to the appeal and desirability of providing high-quality care to people with dementia and ensuring that people with dementia receive appropriate services that maintain their well-being through the recognition of each individual's personhood (Kitwood, 1997) and self (Sabat, 2001) and as such provides a discourse to locate service provision.

Operationalizing the concepts and meeting the expectations such language engenders is problematic. One way to analyse the extent to which care is occurring from the viewpoint of the person with dementia has been advanced by Brannelly (2006). Applying Tronto's (1993) ethic of care model to dementia care, Brannelly argues for an ethic of care where the impact of care decisions can be assessed according to four criteria:

- Attentiveness, when the needs of the person with dementia are upheld and the caregiver relinquishes control to empower and reaffirm the agency and citizenship of the person with dementia.
- Responsibility, where practitioners identify connections between themselves and the person with dementia.
- Competence, when the person with dementia is enabled to set the outcomes of care that would be good for them.
- Responsiveness, when the care provider understands the viewpoint of the person with dementia and provides the opportunity to change care to make it more suitable for the person.

Brannelly demonstrates that some decisions about care are not in fact 'care', and gives as an example of the decision to make a residential placement permanent for a man. Despite his expressed wish to go home, his dementia was blamed for his distress rather than the decision to move him to live in a place that he did not choose (Brannelly, 2006: 208–9).

Links between the moral or value base as well as personal and professional ethics and person-centred dementia care demonstrate that person-centred care requires a commitment beyond the language of empowerment, dignity, respect and choice, to an application of such concepts to each individual situation. That each individual finds themselves in a care situation reliant on the value base of individual practitioners who work within organizational as well as practical constraints is perhaps part of the reason why person-centred care does not appear to happen for everyone. Thus, person-centred care as an ideology may be popular, but to happen in practice proves problematic.

It is problematic for a number of underlying reasons relating to:

- Who provides care.
- Where care is provided.
- The lack of homogeneity in those who require care.

This places substantial demands on service commissioners and providers to be creative, innovative, enthusiastic and dynamic in their approach. Such demands occur within particular economic contexts where there are finite resources at practitioners' disposal, and within a social framework where older people and those with cognitive impairment are marginalized. As has been noted:

> People with dementia can also receive oppressive care, a kind of care that protects from all risks while ignoring capacities to make choices and live actively, so they are to a degree made more demented than they are ... Communities struggle to accept people with dementia in affirmative and creative ways. (Post, 2000a: 14)

Thus, providing care according to predefined ideals is not easy to achieve.

Who provides care to people with dementia?

As Gubrium highlighted (1986), Alzheimer's disease is a disease that is often deemed to require institutionalization. This position has not changed in the last two decades: as dementia progresses people with dementia are often unable to remain at home, or carers are no longer able to continue caring for the person with dementia at home, resulting in a move to institutional care. Such a move may not necessarily be what the person with dementia or their carer wants, but one of necessity, as appropriate care packages within the community are not available. Thus, the care of people with dementia falls to two primary groups of people: families and paid care workers. Often a person with dementia will begin their experiences of living with dementia at home with the support and perhaps a gradual increase in care over time from family members, most usually a spouse or daughter or daughter-in-law. A crisis situation or change in circumstances may then lead to institutionalization, with care primarily provided by paid care workers.

It has been estimated that around one-third of those with dementia live in institutional settings, and the proportion of those living in institutional care increases with age (Knapp et al., 2007a). Thus, a substantial number of older people with dementia in Western societies will find themselves living in long-stay care facilities. The size of such facilities varies across countries. In the UK and Scandanavian countries, for example, smaller group-living is promoted (although these 'small' facilities can house 40 beds, so are not 'small' in the sense of nuclear family living), whereas in the US 100-bed units are more common, with other European countries having similarly large institutions for older people.

The location of such establishments is also worthy of note, as positioning long-term care institutions in areas beyond the traditional community serves to exclude and marginalize those who live there (for example, hospital buildings on the periphery of communities or care facilities located in run-down inner-city areas which are not popular to live in). The size of a facility will have an impact on the care that is provided. Staffing ratios may differ, physical environments may promote or diminish physical freedom and may enhance or detract from the motivation and morale of those who work there. Thus, the physical size, ambience, state of repair and geographical location will have an impact on those who work there and the care they may then offer.

Post (2000b: 250) argues that whatever definition of dementia or Alzheimer's disease is used, the challenge for care providers is to 'enter the world of the severely demented, and respect the mystery of the person'. This echoes Kitwood's call for what he termed 'person-centred care', with the task for care givers being to enter into a relationship with the person with dementia. Indeed, he argues, 'If the first psychological task in dementia care is helping to generate interactions of a really positive kind, the second is that of enabling the interactions to continue' (1997: 96). Thus, it is not enough for a one-off interaction; individual caregivers need to build on these to develop a relationship with the individual with dementia.

Life history is a popular tool used by paid caregivers to remind themselves of what the person with dementia has achieved and was like before the onset of dementia. This type of care Post has termed 'Care based on loyal memory of what was' (2000a: 24). Approaches such as life history offer practical ways in which individual family members and care workers can seek to interact with an individual with dementia to build a relationship based on an understanding of what was and may continue to be important to the individual, despite the progression of their dementia. However, to carry out such positive interactions requires time, commitment and emotional reserves of energy which a hard-pressed care worker responsible for ten or more individuals, who may require extensive physical care during the work shift, or a family carer who is juggling multiple other roles, do not have at their disposal.

Askham et al. (2007) provide an interesting analysis of the difficulties in providing care at home that preserves home life and intimate relationships (that may or may not have been good) alongside the need to routinize life to meet the care demands arising from the dementia that are often accompanied by a need to monitor and control the movements of the person with dementia. By drawing attention to the similarities of providing care at home or in institutions, Askham et al. demonstrate that the need 'for surveillance clearly interfered with the intimate relationship and with their sense of the comfortable habitualisation of the home' (2007: 21). Thus, the ideals of promoting care at home for people with dementia may be as fraught with the difficulties of providing care within institutions where the goal is to promote well-being for the person with dementia. Providing care at homes may therefore engender similar difficulties in providing individualized care while promoting a sense of order and routine, with the further difficulty of preserving 'an intimate relationship alongside providing care and custody' (Askham et al., 2007: 21).

An emerging issue in Western countries is the use of migrant labour to fill the gaps in the employment market caring for older people, with reports indicating that the social and health care workforce is becoming more dependent on minority ethnic group workers and migrants to deliver care services (Social and Health Care Workforce Group, 2002). This has occurred for two primary reasons: labour shortages in developed countries, such as the UK, and restrictive immigration policies leading to informal recruitment practices by care organizations allowing work opportunities for migrants, but also for migrant-worker exploitation (McGregor, 2007: 803).

The ethics of the growing trend for employing migrant workers in the care sector has been discussed in relation to the nursing profession (McElmurry et al., 2006). This raises important broad questions about the potential for exploitation of such migrant workers to fill employment market gaps in countries that are predominantly classified as 'developed' nations, by workers from 'developing nations'. Points raised by McElmurry and her colleagues that are of particular note in the case of dementia care is that migrant workers often find themselves in posts where there are poor working conditions and low job satisfaction reported by non-migrant workers. Further, migrant workers may find themselves placed in inequitable work roles within a particular work setting. Thus, there is huge potential for the exploitation of migrant workers to occur. Given the lowly status of dementia care within the health professions it is possible that the least attractive jobs will be filled by workers who are arguably exploited by the host country (although the attraction of better pay may outweigh such concerns for workers). Further, finding people willing to work in posts which are generally unattractive will do nothing to address the underlying problems of stigma and the marginal place of those who work in the dementia field.

Yet, migrant workers may be perceived as a solution to fill posts that are marginal and low status by workers who are glad of the opportunity to earn money to support themselves and their families. However, potential practice problems may arise. For example, even if companies provide orientation to the country and basic training in dementia care, language barriers may prevent verbal interactions with people with dementia that are meaningful to either the carer or the person with dementia. Differences in conceptualizations of care or understandings of dementia may lead to potential problems in delivering the ethos of care that an organization or government may be promoting. Immigrant workers may find themselves marginalized within the workplace and find it difficult to integrate with other workers, perhaps due to prejudice from the host population. Although there is a growing body of work concerned with migrant worker experiences, this is beyond the focus of this book. Rather, the concern here is to look at the use of migrant labour in dementia care. As such, many of these issues I pose above are empirical questions, as at present research has not been carried out to look at the benefits and potential drawbacks of migrant workers providing dementia care.

An exception to this is Solari's (2006) study of immigrant workers from the former Soviet Union working in elderly care in the city of San Francisco in the United States. Solari provides an interesting analysis of perceptions of the care work that Russian Jews and Russian Orthodox Christians find themselves doing following their resettlement in the United States. She demonstrates that cultural understandings of care as well as the resettlement channels available to different groups of immigrants shape the views held about care work. Solari highlights the fact that immigrants employed in the care sector had experienced downward occupational mobility and that care work was generally seen as low status. In response to this, Solari found that immigrant care workers tended to adopt one of two discourses about their work, based on their religious grouping and the resultant work opportunities offered to groups of immigrants. For example, on the one hand, Russian Jews tended to professionalize their work and found the performance of 'dirty work' (bathing or toileting, for example) as degrading and shameful. On the other hand, Russian Orthodox Christians adopted a 'sainthood' approach to their work and would go over and above the tasks set to them, responding to the individual needs of those they served using their own time to perform tasks requested by their clients, who they renamed using familial expressions of father, grandmother, uncle. Thus, to adapt to the changes in their occupational standing, two patterns of approach to their work were apparent, which Solari terms professionals or saints.

Solari's study is an important addition to the literature on care work as it alerts us to the potential difficulties migrant workers face in adjusting to work roles that are perceived as lower status than their professional background in their country of origin. Such conceptualizations about care will impact on the care experience of the person receiving care, and this is an issue that requires further exploration in the future, for migrant and non-migrant workers. Indeed, it has already been noted that migrant workers may have very different perceptions of what care work involves (McGregor, 2007: 802). Given the projections of growing numbers of older people and those with dementia in the future, it is possible that migrant workers will be utilized to fill gaps in care delivery which may further marginalize care work and the position of those who give and receive care.

The issue of deskilling and working in lower status positions that Solari (2006) describes for migrants from the former Soviet Union has also been discussed in relation to Zimbabwean workers in the UK employed in the care sector (McGregor, 2007). McGregor (2007) suggests that the most common jobs taken on by Zimbabwean migrants are those of carer or cleaner and that when care work in homes for older people is taken on, as immigrants they find this 'new and shocking' (McGregor, 2007: 807). She also reports her respondents seeing care work as 'dirty', 'low' and 'shameful' (2007: 807–8), thus migrants are engaged in work for which they hold little respect. The work conditions migrant workers experienced varied according to their route into employment; personal introductions and recruitment agencies were both able to lead to jobs for unofficial migrants but this made it easier to exploit workers through very low payments (McGregor, 2007: 811).

The work of Solari (2006) and McGregor (2007) demonstrates the importance of support for migrant workers to enable them to deliver the type of care that they are employed to provide. However, given the generally low levels of support, training and resources offered to those who perform frontline care work (Innes et al., 2006), it appears unlikely that migrant workers will receive special attention and support to perform the work they are contracted to perform. They are also more vulnerable to exploitation given their entry routes into employment to jobs they were able to take on 'simply because they are available' (McGregor, 2007: 813) and may be given the most difficult tasks to perform and expected to work longer hours for less pay. This raises the question, how then can workers in such circumstances be expected to meet the ideals of person-centred care delivery which requires emotional and physical energy?

Migrant workers are not just seen as a way to fill gaps in the formal care sector but also for care at home traditionally provided by family members. This issue is discussed by Bettio et al. (2006) in relation to the use of migrant labour to fill the gaps in care traditionally provided by families in Italy. They highlight the preference for families to employ live-in migrant carers, as this is the closest form of paid care to the traditional model of care provided to older people in Italy, as well as being the cheapest form of care they can purchase (2006: 281). As Bettio et al. point out (2006: 282) the concern over the migrant workers' position in the economy and the lack of equity in their pay and conditions is not an issue that is of concern to families who wish cheap solutions to the problem of finding care alternatives in a time of changes in traditional family structures. Thus, the potential for exploitation of workers from less developed countries is very real but unexamined phenomenon.

Further, as Bettio et al. (2006: 283) suggest, if the sustainability of providing care to older people – currently met through the use of cheap migrant labour – is not explored, this may hinder attempts to address long-term care needs and find solutions that will work in the long term. The use of cheap migrant workers to fill current care gaps raises two primary issues: first, the exploitation of migrants who fill positions that the host population does not want and who receive low pay and little training and support; and, second, their use places a temporary avoidance of how to address projected long-term care needs across societies that address why care work is unpopular and continues to be low paid and low status. Finally, if migrant workers themselves are exploited, and also experience racial and gender discrimination, as reported by McGregor (2007), then it is likely that care practices will not meet the ideals espoused by policy makers. Rather, older people will experience poor care practices that will in turn result in low quality of life for those with dementia.

What are the implications for family care?

'Informal family caregivers are vital in the culture and practice of care' (Post, 2000a: 20). Post argues that family caregivers may be more attentive than others in looking for remaining aspects of self-hood and that they can continue to see the person when a detached outsider may decide that no abilities and thus no personhood remains.

However, recognizing the personhood of those diagnosed with dementia can result in a problem for carers experiencing a change in their relationships. Davis (2004) argues that 'he [Kitwood] must allow for a loss of personhood, for to deny this is to denounce the legitimacy of carers who no longer recognize a spark of their former relationship … . In postulating that personhood can ultimately be sustained, he prevents the initiation of a grieving process that should begin with the involution of the sufferer' (p. 377). Thus, by taking the person with dementia's 'side' one aspect of dementia is apparent; by taking the carer's 'side' (in Becker's terms) would result in a different response to dementia and the care offered to the person with dementia and their carer. Acknowledging that caregivers, usually women, often give up their own interests to provide care, Post cautions us to remember that many gain fulfilment from caregiving and not to always pursue a 'pedagogy of the oppressed' (2000a: 37). Thus, understanding the reasons for family caregiving and the satisfaction that a carer may experience by providing care, is as important as understanding the stress and strain experienced by caregivers, which may result in an eventual decision to stop providing care and to place a family member in a care facility.

Post asks, without family caregivers, would society move towards the 'easy abyss of non voluntary euthanasia? Would we decide that enough is enough …?' (2000a: 28). He argues that the family can create a value framework for the care of people with dementia where people with dementia are deemed to be worthy of well-being (2000a: 33). Post (2000a) concludes that family caregivers have an indispensable protective role for the person with dementia, as they protect people with dementia from potential harms of society; a society that fears deviance and disorder, and craves control and conformity to the cultural 'norms', a set of fears and values that dementia undermines. Thus, there are expectations surrounding family caregivers' roles that do not recognize the costs to carers, and these may be personal or financial. The personal costs have been documented in terms of physical stresses and strains and the constraints caregiving places on day-to-day living.

Financial costs have received less interest until more recently with loss of earnings, loss of contributions towards pensions, and the carer's own retirement and future quality of life provoking policy makers to look at the hitherto largely ignored financial losses and costs involved when providing care to a family member.

Payment for care provided by family members is an interesting policy development across developed welfare states where 'cash-for-care' schemes have been in operation since the 1990s. The tensions and paradoxes inherent in the origins of such schemes are discussed by Ungerson and Yeandle (2007). For example, the underlying rationale for such schemes relates to views that individuals would rather remain at home. Alongside this is the belief that it is cheaper to provide care at home, while passing on the responsibility for paying for care not only meets user empowerment agendas but also reduces associated costs that larger bodies would have to meet, such as recruitment, sickness and monitoring of quality.

The issue of cost containment underlying cash-for-care schemes can be illustrated in different ways. For example, in the UK, family carers were initially specifically excluded from cash-for-care schemes unless there were exceptional circumstances reflecting an ideology of free care provision by family carers. Meanwhile, in the Netherlands, the generosity of cash-for-care schemes has been critiqued for potentially leading to spiralling costs and thus defeating the agenda of cost containment (Ungerson and Yeandle, 2007: 196).

Thus, the intuitive appeal of cash-for-care schemes for service users and their families who would like greater control in their service use, most clearly articulated by the disability movement in the UK and US (Morris, 1993; Oliver, 1996), may hide the underlying agendas of cost containment and abdication of responsibility for the quality of provision of care to those in need. So the future of family caregiving remains uncertain, with changing patterns of female employment influenced by factors such as more women continuing to work after having children, or choosing not to have children and concentrating on building fulfilling careers, and as couples choose to have fewer children the reserve of unpaid family carers may diminish over time. This, coupled with the demographic factors of an ageing population, where, as people grow older, dementia has a greater chance of presenting itself, may lead to a crisis in the unregulated market of family caregiving which will have knock-on implications for the provision of formal care services.

Where is care provided?

As the majority of people with dementia (80 per cent) (Nolan et al., 1996) live within the community, family caregivers provide a significant amount of care and much has been written about family caregivers' coping strategies and stress (Ungerson, 1987; Morris et al., 1991). Yet, recent surveys in Scotland, England and Wales suggest that more than 20 per cent of people with dementia live in institutional care (Audit Commission, 2000; Gordon et al., 1997). It is important to acknowledge the context of paid care within the wider domain of care carried out in the private sphere, but it appears that a greater proportion of time has been spent exploring informal caregivers' experiences compared to those who perform the direct frontline care. It is of interest to note that researchers have paid similar attention to the experience of 'professional' paid carers' work, particularly nurses (Jacques and Innes, 1998). And, as I have noted previously (Innes, 1997), the experiences of frontline paid carers, such as care assistants and nursing auxiliaries, have been neglected or sidelined, with the exception of studies such as those by Lee-Treweek (1997a and b) and Hockey (1990). Even if more people are cared for within the community by informal caregivers this does not fully explain the lower levels of interest in low-status paid care workers.

The primary staff groups who will be involved in providing long-stay care for people with dementia are care assistants (also known as nursing aides) and nurses, with managers of homes/wards/institutions and middle management within organizations making decisions about the care that will be provided within a ward/care unit/care home. There is a wealth of literature exploring management and leadership of organizations and institutions (Goffman, 1961; Handy, 1993; Dawson, 1996; Hall, 1997), much is transferrable to the residential or nursing home, but these settings themselves have remained relatively unexplored. Nurses' experiences and coping strategies have been well documented (Boejie et al., 1997), with suggestions on 'sustaining' and recognizing the difference nurses can make to residents (Royal College of Nursing, 1995).

There has not been a similar swell of support for the care assistant. This can be partially explained by the low status care assistants have due to their lack of qualifications and low economic status. Popular beliefs about care and care as work also contribute to the low levels of support and recognition for care assistant work. As noted above with reference to family care, care has traditionally been perceived as women's work, carried out for low or no pay in the private sphere (Dalley, 1988; Graham, 1981). It is often assumed that women care out of obligation and/or love. This, however, hides the position of women within society and the expectation that women will care leading often to the identity of being a woman bound up with notions of care (Graham, 1991). It is of interest to note that the recent Royal Commission report *With Respect to Old Age* (1999) similarly undervalues the position of the care assistant by accepting that care assistants will be paid at the level of the minimum wage. There is no challenge to the assumptions surrounding the position of care assistants nor recommendations to improve the conditions of this work group. Thus, the gendered nature of care work at the very least influences the position of the care assistant and the lack of interest in their work and experiences of work.

A paradox is apparent in the world of paid dementia care work. Low-status workers (predominantly female) are caring for a client group that is undervalued and objectified rather than as individuals of value to society. However, the low-status workers are in a position to exert power and control over a similarly low-status client group. As Lee-Treweek (1997b: 61) has argued, 'there remains an underlying social expectation that women undertake paid care because they enjoy it and that it involves altruism and nurturance rather than choice and skill'. Such expectations around the gendered nature of care work means that the difficulties and challenges inherent in care work are not always recognized, nor is the potential for abuse to occur within the care environment. Arguably, it is vital that those who are paid to care are given support and training to equip them to care in the manner dictated by policy directives espousing ideals about what care recipients can expect of the care situation, to ensure that the worker is able to deliver the expected standards of care.

By focusing on expectations about care provision, who provides care and where, it is perhaps evident that those who are most affected by dementia (those with the diagnosis) are only beginning to be heard. Those who direct care provision (policy makers) are not those who actually provide the care (families and paid care workers). Those who receive the care have, to date, been the least consulted group involved in care situations (Chapter 5 goes on to discuss patterns in dementia care research and the growing emphasis on attaining service users' views and contextualizes such trends within research discourse). It is also apparent that there are marginal and unheard voices amongst carers, (paid and unpaid) and people with dementia. In Chapter 4 we specifically explore culture in terms of the values, beliefs and norms of groupings of people; differences across countries as well as cultures within individual care settings. For now, we will go on to discuss the heterogeneity of dementia with reference to geographical and ethnic differences, to illustrate the difficulty in encapsulating the needs of many diverse interests within the policy frameworks used to project care ideals of those making policy decisions relating to care practices.

People with dementia: a heterogeneous group

People with dementia tend to have marginal voices, with the voices of those people with dementia that are heard, through for example participation in research advisory groups, speaking at conferences and through written accounts of their personal experiences (Robinson, 2002), not necessarily reflecting the experiences and views of other people with dementia. Yet, people with dementia are self-aware in their experiences of dementia (Clare, 2003), and thus there is untapped potential to hear more about the diverse experiences of dementia.

Initial, lifelong and current issues in relation to biological, genetic, medical, psychosocial and environmental characteristics are discussed as a framework to understand the heterogeneity in dementia (Cohen-Mansfield, 2000). Such a model offers a way to explore the multi-faceted nature of the experience of dementia and serves as a reminder of the importance of the past and the current position of the person with dementia when exploring how best to care for an individual with dementia.

The impact of gender, ethnicity and social class on the experience of living with dementia is a somewhat under-researched issue. Hulko (2004) explicitly explores the intersection between gender, race and class and in doing so illustrates that a range of factors will impact on the experiences of people with dementia. The issue is not about race *or* gender *or* class but the interconnection between these social groupings and the multiple oppressions or multiple privileges an individual may experience. Thus, heterogeneity and diversity are complex phenomena and not necessarily easy to work with when trying to provide care that meets the expectations set out within policy documents which make certain assumptions about the role and ability of paid and unpaid carers to provide care.

For the purpose of this chapter, we will look at two examples of diversity which may pose particular challenges for those seeking to implement the care ideals postulated in policy, practice and legal frameworks surrounding the delivery of care.

Ethnic diversity

Work that looks at ethnicity and dementia reminds us that people with dementia may experience multiple jeopardy. That is, they have a stigmatized condition, are old and are from a minority group (Bowes and Wilkinson, 2002). Thus, there are a multitude of factors researchers must be sensitive to, in addition to the cultural, linguistic and religious differences, when researching ethnic groups. This applies equally to policy makers and care providers seeking to provide care that meets the care ideals of society at a particular moment in time. The diversity within and between ethnic groups is not always recognized. For example, white ethnic groups, who appear to assimilate successfully, due in part to a common language as well as the ability not to stand out through physical appearance, may be overlooked when developing 'culturally sensitive or appropriate' services. Ethnic groups to whom this could apply in the UK are the Jewish population, and those who migrated from other European countries such as those whose ancestors were from Poland or the Ukraine.

How to ensure that cultural beliefs are respected for 'hidden' minorities can pose challenges for care providers, for example how to ensure that dietary preferences are met, cultural festivities upheld and religious requirements observed. These challenges are exacerbated when minority groups do not have the same common language as the majority culture, and who are visibly different in appearance, which contributes to the well-documented challenges of providing other services, such as housing and information about health care.

Looking specifically at ethnicity and old age, it has been suggested that barriers such as language need to be overcome and that service providers need to employ workers with the community languages of those they seek to serve (Blakemore and Boneham, 1994; Askham, 1995). Barriers such as these also need to be addressed when dementia is added to the equation. In a report on dementia care for minority ethnic older people in the UK, Denmark and France (Patel et al., 1998), it is highlighted that communication poses a key problem in establishing understanding about what the problem is and giving a diagnosis, that tests for diagnosing dementia are not culturally sensitive, and that professionals find it difficult to explain what the problem is. This can be a particular problem even when the professional speaks the language of the family and the person with dementia when there is no word for dementia in the minority language. Social and health care workers were also found to have gaps in their knowledge about the cultural context of the minority ethnic older person with dementia and had experienced problems working with the families of people with dementia.

Thus, to deliver person-centred care, first when it is difficult to communicate a diagnosis, second when there is a lack of cultural awareness of the individual client, and third when working with minority group family members is perceived to be difficult, contributes to a situation where the ideals of person-centred care are going to be put to the test. With service delivery geared towards mainstream populations, those from minority ethnic groups are often problematized as they are perceived not to suit or fit the services available (Beattie et al., 2005). Work in the US, for example, where outreach workers have been employed to go into local communities (Hart et al., 1996), highlights that it is possible to give a diagnosis, work with families and be very aware and sensitive to the cultural context of individuals with dementia; however, such work is often short-term funded and reliant on the recruitment of highly skilled workers who may be in short supply.

Geographical diversity

Many services are based in urban centres where health and social care services are located, for example in hospitals and other community care facilities. Living beyond an easy journey to such urban facilities poses challenges to those tasked with providing care services to those living in rural areas.

Dementia care is often focused on urban settings, and urban models that are inappropriate for rural and remote settings (Hamel-Bissell, 1992), a situation reflected in rural mental health generally (Gregoire and Thornicroft, 1998). These tend to be care models which do not account for the time, distance and transport required to access services based in centralized areas rather than, for example, outreach services which take the service to the remote or rural location of the user. There are recent exceptions to this urban bias, such as the study of carers in Canada by Morgan et al. (2002) and the study in Northern Ireland by Gilmour et al. (2003). These studies recognize that there are specific aspects of rurality that are barriers to using formal services, particularly access and transport. In Scottish research (Innes et al., 2005; Blackstock et al., 2006; Innes at al., 2006b), we found that individuals within communities provided support to people with dementia, rather than formal organizations and thus our findings questioned the findings in the general rural health literature about the importance of community *organizations* as sources of support (Voss, 1996; Jacob et al., 1997).

For care packages to respond to care needs, it is important that transport is available to enable users to access the service. This may involve developing new modes of delivery, in particular greater outreach services. Commissioners of services need to allow for flexibility and innovation to be built into the commissioning process to ensure that services are not rejected out of hand by potential users as inappropriate and inaccessible. Services need to develop that are welcomed by service users and which reflect their perceptions of their care needs. Our Scottish research findings extend the concept of person-centred care by stressing the importance of placing person-centred care within the individual's spatial and social context (see Morgan et al., 2003). Rural living can also, in some cases, provide *opportunities* for improved quality of living with dementia, including support from service providers (Blackstock et al., 2006). Thus, not meeting the 'norm' of urban-centred care delivery can create alternative ways of delivering care that actually meets the objectives of person-centred care. Indeed, the most negative account of services in the Scottish research came from a participant living in a market town, where it might have been expected that more people would have equated with more services, and this was not the case.

The diversity of care and service use experiences across remote and rural areas must also be acknowledged, as not all remote and rural areas are the same; they will have different community norms, different ranges of services available, and different resources allocated to them. So, rural/urban divides in themselves are not helpful, rather the aim here is to highlight differences in experiences where geographical location influences such experiences. Urban dwellers are also heterogeneous in their experiences and thus the use of any particular care model will have its deficiencies should they not allow for the individual needs of the client group such models seek to serve.

The challenge of providing dementia care in a way that meets the ideals of policy makers and the many other varied groups who write about dementia and dementia care cannot be underestimated. The challenge is not limited to those who live in geographically remote areas, or for people who come from ethnic groups whom mainstream service providers may find it difficult to identify and reach. These are but two examples of diversity and difference among people with dementia. To make person-centred care a reality for all with dementia is, and will perhaps continue to remain, a utopian ideal for two primary reasons:

1 Individuals within society experience inequitable treatment, discrimination and prejudice on a range of issues (e.g. gender, age, sexual orientation, disability, socioeconomic status). Dementia is likely to compound such experiences.
2 Those who provide care are a diverse group who have their own personal experiences of inequitable treatment, discrimination and prejudice. How all individuals can provide care that meets high ideals based on a moral basis that is not reflected in their day-to-day realities is paradoxical and, arguably, unrealistic.

This does not mean that the ideals of dementia care should be downgraded; having such goals offers society, not just care workers, or care organizations, the opportunity to strive to achieve such goals and ideals. It should be remembered, however, that ideals are not necessarily the social reality for those with dementia and their caregivers/workers, and if such ideals are not met it is not necessarily a personal failure of individuals, rather a reflection of the social framework surrounding perceptions of care, dementia and dementia care work.

Conclusions

This chapter has explored the expectations that surround care, it has demonstrated that the ideals set out by policy makers do not necessarily reflect the reality of the care situations paid and unpaid carers find themselves in. That women are expected to care, and that this is an extension of their 'natural' abilities, demonstrates the gendered notions of care and contributes to explaining the low value such work has within Western societies where women have yet to attain equality with men. Expectations about care and care ideals have implications for family and paid care workers who provide care, who work in situations where they receive very little support or training in an area allocated with finite resources. Achieving the ideals set out by policy makers is difficult in 'ideal' circumstances where resources are available and where services do meet the needs of an individual. When the heterogeneity of those with dementia is considered, and here we used ethnicity and rurality as examples, how to ensure that person-centred care, for want of a better term, for every individual, remains a huge challenge.

Difference can, however, promote opportunities to provide creative and innovative care that meets individual needs. Drawing on examples from the literature it is possible to see that outreach work to minority communities requires addressing the particular needs of community groups by a skilled and sensitive workforce. Thus, promoting quality care is possible should the needs of specific communities be taken into consideration. However, such schemes may be time and finance limited and occur as a result of local interest and enthusiasm rather than global policy making directives.

The decisions to take services to those in remote and rural areas rather than expecting physically and/or mentally frail older people to travel some distance to the location of services that may not quite meet their needs anyway is an example of services meeting the needs of commissioners and practitioners rather than service users. As such, care decisions do not always reflect principles of person-centred care and the care ideals of promoting individually tailored care packages suitable for individual circumstances.

Using these two examples – of minority groups and those living in rural areas – it can be seen that the ideals of care policies and theories about dementia care are not necessarily easy to transfer into day-to-day care practices for all people with dementia. Thus, ideals help to shape practice, they set the stage for what society has decided (articulated through policy and legal frameworks) should be in place for those in need of support and care.In addition, just as those with dementia are heterogeneous and diverse, so are those who care for people with dementia. This issue may become more apparent should migrant workers be employed in hard-to-fill care posts in the future. However, such issues remain largely empirical questions.

Care ideals may remain viewed as a utopian vision if, at the ground level, such ideals are not translated into tangible and concrete examples of how to provide the type of care that those writing about care practices, such as policy makers and academics, advocate. Those working at the coalface of service delivery are often not given adequate resources, support and training to enable them to put into place the ideals set from those who are at least one step removed from the reality of providing care. Thus, ideals may not even be known by those delivering care, with training opportunities limited to staff higher up the care-delivery hierarchy and information-sharing mechanisms which offer recommendations about care delivery confined to written reports that are not widely read by care practitioners.

Family caregivers provide care in a manner that may go beyond the relationship boundaries that existed prior to the onset of dementia and which stretch individuals' ability to juggle multiple roles and tasks, not to mention the emotional demands of caregiving. Supporting people with dementia within their families/relationships is important for the ideals of quality care and quality of life for people with dementia to be realized. However, if carers, family or paid, remain in a role where there is very little support offered to enable them successfully to continue a role that is often new and challenging in relational and practical terms, then it is unlikely that the ideals of care will be a reality for carers or people with dementia.

The crux of the matter can perhaps be seen as the basic undervaluing of care work and the stigma that surrounds dementia care in particular. Until care is valued, and in Western terms this has a monetary value, the work and world of care will remain marginalized. If the label dementia remains a medical category rather than a label that has particular social consequences for those who are given the label and those who provide care to those with the label, then the development of dementia care in the future will likely remain limited to examples of innovative practice. If expectations of care do not take into account the reality of those who are employed to deliver care services for people with dementia and their families, and if the social reality of those with dementia is not explored, then ideals are likely to remain just that, ideals.

An excellent, thought-provoking, book-sized account of the challenges of providing care to those with dementia is offered by Post (2000a). Innes et al. (2006b) provide a report-sized account of the issues surrounding the promotion and reality of person-centred care. The Beattie et al. (2005) research paper provides an overview of the challenges of finding services that meet individuals' needs.

4

DEMENTIA STUDIES WITHIN
CULTURAL CONTEXTS

■ ■ Chapter summary ■

- This chapter explores the study of dementia in two cultural contexts. First, across different cultural groupings, that is, people living in different countries and people from different ethnic groups living within a particular country. Second, it considers culture in relation to cultures of care promoted in care settings.
- By looking at culture in relation to social groupings based on constructions relating to national, social and ethnic identity, it is apparent that there are similarities in the needs and concerns of people with dementia and their carers across cultural groupings. This is not to detract from the specific needs individuals or ethnically grouped people may have, rather to highlight that dementia raises similar issues reflecting the marginal place older people and people with mental health difficulties occupy within and across societies.
- Focusing on the culture of care promoted in institutions provides an opportunity to reflect on: the variations between philosophies or theories about dementia and dementia care; policy and practice frameworks; and the reality of care provision in long-stay settings for people with dementia.

Cultural understandings about dementia

This chapter considers culture in two ways:

- Common societal values and beliefs influencing the actions of individuals and organizations which are influenced by policy structures.
- The daily work practices, norms and beliefs in care settings.

The impact of dementia does not stay with the individual diagnosed, nor the immediate family and circle of paid carers. This chapter will first review and explore societies' views and apprehensions about dementia and old age and misconceptions that dementia is a condition of the old.

How dementia is understood within different cultural groups within and across countries is then examined, highlighting the similarities and difficulties carers may experience when a relative develops dementia. Service providers' lack of understanding about ethnicity and cultural beliefs of individuals, and cultural groupings of carers and people with dementia, can compound the difficulties of living with dementia, either for the person diagnosed or the person(s) providing care.

From this consideration of broader cultural contexts the chapter goes on to examine the specifics of cultures of care settings. The approaches adopted by those promoting care at home and any support services used, compared to cultures of care within long-term care facilities, are of particular interest and provide the focus of the second part of this chapter.

Notions about dementia relating to stigma

Before considering cultural groupings and cultures of care settings, we will first consider the stigma surrounding the term 'dementia'. Stigma, that is, where a person is reduced from 'normal' to someone who is a person with whom something is wrong (Goffman, 1963), is evident in the field of dementia care and forms part of the cultural backdrop of the world people with dementia inhabit. This is in part due to the low social status awarded to older people and people with a mental health disorder (Benbow and Reynolds, 2000), leading to discrimination and stigma which may be directed towards the individual, their family and those who provide paid care (World Health Organization and World Psychiatric Association, 2002). Stigma relating to mental illness has been found to indiscriminately over-emphasize social losses, leading to social isolation and distress for those with mental illness (Crisp et al., 2000). Stigma may be subtle, in that the needs of older people in health care sectors may be ignored, and, indeed, in some areas of the world there may be a complete absence of health care programmes for older people (Mendonça Lima, 2003).

Although the research on stigma and dementia has been noted to be scarce (Poveda, 2003), a recent study has demonstrated that the stigma attached to dementia is well known amongst the mainstream Scottish population (Devlin et al., 2007). Such stigma was related to the negative public images of dementia as a disease bringing with it loss of ability of the person with dementia and associated emotional stress and physical burden for those providing care. The stigma attached to dementia varies within and across countries and appears to impact on diagnosis in some countries.

This may be due to a desire to avoid the term 'dementia' as it precludes entry to nursing homes (for example, in Portugal), but, conversely, making a diagnosis may be avoided due to fear of being removed from home into a nursing home, while the active Alzheimer Societies in, for example, the UK, France and the Netherlands, may have helped to reduce the sense of shame in having a family member diagnosed with dementia (Iliffe et al., 2005). It is interesting to note that stigma was found to be an important influence in the delay in recognition and diagnosis of dementia across eight European countries, regardless of the financial resources available to practitioners (Vernooij-Dassen et al., 2005) as there appears to be a belief that there is little to offer to a person with dementia due to the progressive nature of the disease. Thus, a biomedical understanding of dementia can be seen to have a direct impact on the early decision making and lack of action taken to provide either information or care interventions to the person with dementia and their family.

Stigma relating to dementia was evident in a study of South Asian and East European carers (Mackenzie, 2006) living in an English city. Carers reported stigma from within their cultural grouping, stemming from religious and cultural beliefs about mental health within South Asian communities; and the desire to hide traumatic experiences based on early life experiences reported by carers from Eastern European communities. Dementia was equated with loss and shame and led to a reluctance to seek help, diagnosis and services (Mackenzie, 2006: 245). The stigma experienced by the carers of the people with dementia can be conceptualized as 'courtesy stigma' (Goffman, 1963), whereby, through their association with a person with dementia, those who provide care also experience some form of shame and negative perceptions (MacRae, 1999). In her study of the experience of courtesy stigma and Alzheimer's disease, MacRae (1999) demonstrates that although at risk of experiencing stigma by their association with dementia, not all family members feel stigmatized. The reaction and support of family, neighbours and others in the community appears to be a key issue in whether family members felt stigmatized by their family member's condition. However, what promotes support or the withdrawal of support remains an area unexplored by research. The important point to note is that dementia tends to give rise to stigma but that it can be avoided should there be a supportive network. This applies equally to carers and people with dementia. Thus, negative perceptions based on misunderstanding and stigma can lead to negative experiences, but a network of understanding, empathic people can ease the experience of dementia.

In the limited research looking at dementia in Chinese communities, it is suggested that dementia may be hidden within the family (Elliott et al., 1996), as a diagnosis may trigger a negative response within the community to dementia due to the shame and stigma attached to mental illness (Lee, 1982; Phillips, 1993; Hinton et al., 2000). Such feelings of shame and stigma may prevent families seeking the help of professionals and using services that are available. The lack of a formal diagnosis will make accessing services and help more difficult, thus a 'double whammy' effect exists where stigma prevents seeking a diagnosis, the lack of which prevents access to services. Thus, cultural beliefs about dementia can contribute to avoidance of services. This raises particular challenges for service providers offering care services to people with dementia and support for their family carers. The challenges of providing care services to minority groups is compounded by the focus of existing services whose aim is ostensibly to meet the needs of the white majority population, but in reality the services available may be based on what it is possible to offer with the financial and staff resources available, rather than on the care needs of those with dementia.

Culture and the experience of dementia

The impact culture may have on the experience of dementia is an issue that has grown in popularity over the last two decades. In particular, sociocultural aspects of the experience of dementia have been subjected to scrutiny (Downs, 2000). It has been suggested that there are three ways in which culture may be conceptualized: according to geographical area (e.g., urban and rural, or country by country); family relationships (which reflect the expectations about spouses' and children's roles in caring for an unwell relative); and ethnicity (Kosloski et al., 2002). Such factors can be used to examine the impact of different values, beliefs and practices relating to geography, ethnicity and family structures on the experience of dementia. Similarly, Dilworth-Anderson and Gibson (2002: 56), considering the evidence about cultural influence on understanding about dementia in minority ethnic groups, conclude that cultural norms, values and beliefs help shape a collective knowledge within the group about a disease. This means that particular cultural groupings may respond to dementia in different ways, either by seeking information and support (as may occur within the white mainstream population) or by hiding dementia due to feelings of shame about the condition coupled with cultural values of a sense of duty towards elders.

Ethnicity

Often, the first grouping considered when thinking about culture is according to ethnicity, and minority ethnic groups in a given country may then be the focus of enquiry. Including people with dementia from different racial and ethnic groupings is an enterprise spanning international boundaries and contexts (Aranda, 2001: 116). How to recruit participants from specific ethnic groups has been discussed with three particular issues raised that are relevant not just to ethnic groups but to the majority population: that dementia is seen as part of normal ageing and not something that warrants the involvement in research; that the research will add to the worry that those with dementia are already experiencing; and that the label of 'dementia' may carry stigma and thus preclude an openness to research scrutiny (Hinton et al., 2000).

However, the experiences of minority ethnic groups and dementia generally have not been well documented in specific countries and difficulties recruiting participants may contribute to the dearth of knowledge in this area. For example, in the UK, although it is thought that the prevalence of dementia amongst such communities is set to increase as minority communities age (Ahmad and Walker, 1997), little dementia-specific knowledge has been generated. This perhaps reflects a general lack of interest in the impact of culture on the experience of dementia in favour of a focus on more biomedical areas of enquiry (discussed in Chapter 1). Yet, as Iliffe and Manthorpe caution 'as much as there is inter-group variation there may be important intra-group variations in behaviour and belief around needs and health related experiences' (2004: 288). This means that practitioners, policy makers and researchers need to remain alert to stereotypes based on group belonging and open to recognizing diversity, not just between groups, but within groups. However, the symptoms of dementia that give concern to caregivers from different ethnic groups may be remarkably similar to the concerns of caregivers from the majority population (Levkoff et al., 1999). Nevertheless, intra-ethnic differences in understanding dementia have also been reported (Hinton et al., 2000).

Thus, people from different racial and ethnic groups will have differences and similarities in their beliefs, attitudes and expectations. Such differences and similarities reflect the cultural norms for a given group. Further, similar values may not be interpreted in the same way, and how to include cultural issues within the development of dementia services and in service delivery research can be difficult for a variety of reasons. For example, difficulties can arise due to the invisible nature of culture, with the intangible nature of cultural beliefs, as well as the adaptive nature of culture, contributing to difficulties in detecting cultural factors that may be important in determining experiences of dementia and the use of care services (Henderson et al., 1994).

Difficulties in screening for cognitive impairment in minority ethnic older people may be due in part to the lack of culturally appropriate tests that depend not only on a common language but common understandings of the items included in tests. In addition, such screening tests rely on a certain level of educational attainment, for example to spell a word backwards. In their short review of screening tests, Parker and Philp (2004) suggest that developing culture-free tests that do not rely on common beliefs, common language or expected levels of educational ability may be the way forward in helping to identify dementia within minority communities. However, screening and diagnosis difficulties are not unique to minority communities but also to majority communities and rely to a large extent on the willingness and/or ability of the first primary care point of contact making a diagnosis and providing information about dementia and services available to support both the person and their carer. In addition, symptoms of dementia may be seen as part of normal ageing; this may then influence the pattern of caregiving adopted within a particular cultural grouping due to cultural beliefs about filial piety. For example, it is reported that Chinese Americans (Yeo et al., 1996) accept intergenerational dependence and accept that they will need to provide care.

Adamson and Donovan (2005) demonstrate that accounts of caring by UK carers from minority ethnic groupings were located within a cultural context where caring was valued, normal and expected. The underlying rationale varied for the two ethnic groups included in their study: for African/Caribbeans, this was linked to expectations about kin relationships through health and sickness; and in South Asian participants, this was linked to their religious and cultural beliefs that they should provide care to family members. Such findings do not preclude a need for services to help carers cope with a condition that can lead to considerable disruption to established relationships and lifestyles, and as the authors note, 'carers expressing their caring role in terms of their ethnicity has been misinterpreted as "looking after their own" and goes some way to explain the perpetuation of this stereotype as caring being culturally specific' (Adamson and Donovan, 2005: 47).

Such beliefs about 'other' cultures lead to marginalization of certain groups in relation to service delivery, particularly the stereotype that caregiving is normal and unproblematic for certain minority groups (Boneham et al., 1997). Looking at younger people with dementia as well as people from minority ethnic groups, Beattie et al. (2005) found that service providers felt that people with dementia from these categorizations did not fit the services offered. Three suggestions for providing services to marginalized groups are offered by Beattie et al. (2005). First, that services for marginalized groups be offered in their own homes; second, that specialist services are used (which could mean extensive travel to areas where such services exists); and, third, for service providers to be flexible in their organization of services to meet local needs. Of these three options, the third is the one that would require most systematic change, as this would also be the option that needs to address how to provide services to meet the care needs of all people in a locality. Such care needs may actually be more similar than different, as providers' expectations of difference are often based on little knowledge, and thus their perceptions of need may not reflect the reality of the needs of those with dementia and their carers, whom they serve.

In a study of four ethnic groups living in the Boston area, African-American, Chinese-American, Puerto Rican and Irish-American, it was found that there was heterogeneity within every ethnic group and that the desire to provide culturally competent services should not be based solely on ethnic groupings (Levkoff et al., 1999). Rather, 'the individual family migration patterns and other aspects of family history, financial concerns and degree of acculturation may have greater explanatory power than "culture" alone in understanding decision making for dementia' (Levkoff et al., 1999: 353).

In a review of the differences reported in caregiving experiences according to membership of a cultural grouping, Connell and Gibson (1997) highlight that non-white carers: were less likely to be a spouse than white carers, rather they were an adult child or other family member; who reported less stress and more use of spirituality and religion as a coping mechanism; and who held stronger views about filial duty. The importance of spiritual and religious beliefs was also found in caregivers and care recipients in African- Americans living in the Arkansas Delta (Gerdner et al., 2007), while Levkoff et al. (1999), found that the church itself did not necessarily provide support to caregivers from any group (African-American, Chinese-American, Irish-American or Puerto Rican), rather personal faith was perceived to help individual caregivers continue with their supporting role. Thus, the beliefs of individual caregivers are perhaps more likely to support their caregiving role than practical assistance from religious organizations.

However, such different experiences of caregiving do not provide an adequate explanation about how such situations arise: for example, what understandings about dementia underpin the experience of dementia across different cultural groups for both the person with dementia and their carer? Leibing (2002) charts the changes in perceptions and responses to dementia over time in Brazil. In doing so, she highlights the importance of popular cultural beliefs, changes in political circumstances and changes in patterns of ageing, and places such developments within the country's historical development. By doing so, she presents an account of understandings of dementia clearly located within Brazilian culture.

Without addressing questions about where understandings about dementia come from, it is difficult to see what advances can readily be made to improve the experience of living with dementia for those concerned. In a later review of culture and dementia caregiving studies, Janevic and Connell (2001) conclude that more research is required that explores cultural differences in caregiving that directly compares experiences of those from different cultural groups that goes beyond surface cultural differences, to begin to develop comprehensive understandings of the range of factors, cultural or otherwise, that shape the caregiving experience.

Gerdner et al. (2007) provide such an example of research that seeks to understand a wide range of factors that influence the caregiving experience. They highlight the historical position of slavery of the

African-American communities in the Arkansas Delta and the unchanging physical rural landscape; they contextualize dementia within the accounts of difficult emotional lives where domestic abuse and poverty were experienced as part of 'life's hardships'; the continued importance of the church; and the out-migration of younger people leaving only a small pool of potential caregivers. Thus, social, political, economic and historical factors are highlighted to contextualize the current position of caregivers and people with dementia. Within such a context, spirituality was important in helping caregivers to cope with their roles and also reported religious activities and faith as a continuing support factor in the lives of those with dementia, and therefore echoes previous findings about the importance of religion in African-American caregiving experiences (Connell and Gibson, 1997). However, Gerdner et al.'s (2007) research moves beyond such findings to provide a rich account of how dementia and caregiving are experienced within African-American communities in a particular area, and in doing so furthers knowledge about how and why dementia is understood and managed for this population.

Understanding the variability in conceptions of dementia in multiethnic populations has been suggested as necessary to improve care and guide future research (Hinton et al., 2005), yet the stigma and misunderstandings about dementia have been reported in studies of mainstream and minority populations (Hinton et al., 2000; Mackenzie, 2006). Indeed, Mahoney et al. (2005) found that African-Americans, Chinese and Latino caregivers all reported a lack of knowledge about Alzheimer's disease and had experienced an absence of referrals from local community physicians to obtain a firm diagnosis. This is a common report of caregivers, regardless of ethnic or cultural grouping. Hence, similarities in the experience of dementia relating to negative perceptions of dementia are as important to recognize as cultural differences, particularly if the aim is to challenge and improve the care and services offered to all people with dementia.

In their review of caregiving in black and Asian populations, Milne and Chryssanthopoulou (2005) take forward the idea of difference to explore what underpins understandings of dementia and the resultant experiences of caregiving. They identify four themes:

1 Illness meanings of dementia: stigma and shame are evident.
2 Caregiving patterns and relationships: the limited research that has explored this issue has found that women tend to provide the care, and that this is influenced by gender-role stereotypes as well as filial responsibility.

3 Impact of caregiving: there are mixed findings in relation to stress and burden experienced and this is sometimes explained by the positive cultural connotations of caregiving.
4 Social support and coping: in the US, it appears that minority groups have wide social networks to call on to help with caregiving, although this will not necessarily be the same in other countries, for example newly formed or emerging ethnic communities migrating to other countries.

Critiquing the literature and advancing an alternative research agenda, Milne and Chryssanthopoulou (2005) suggest that more needs to be done, as has been the case in the US, to look at the multi-dimensional impact of ethnicity, culture and life course experiences in relation to dementia caregiving. They also argue that more attention needs to be given to the views of communities, families or individual family carers to enable an exploration of caregiving through a 'lens of culture' (2005: 331). They argue that a move from service develop-ment is required to promote knowledge and theory generation. Thus, what is required is a moving on from examples of good practice and innovative services to explore what having dementia means for cul-tural groupings and how this reflects diverse identities and experiences, and not just belonging to an ethnic or racial group categorization. This is an important reminder, as many innovative services are short-lived due to limited financial support, so understandings of cultural group-ings' experiences need to be more inclusive than evaluations of esoteric initiatives.

Talk about developing 'culturally appropriate services' may not necessarily reflect the prerequisite need to identify hidden minor-ity ethnic groups, and to recruit staff who can speak the commu-nity language to deliver dementia services (Innes, 2003c). Indeed, Elliott and Di Minno (2006) found that misdiagnosis and inappro-priate recommendations were made for Chinese people attending a Californian clinic staffed by mainstream American clinicians who had little knowledge about Chinese culture. However, when cultural background was taken into account within the assessment, the clinical team was much better placed to make appropriate care recommendations.

As Forbat (2003) argues, the availability of leaflets giving informa-tion about a condition or service is not necessarily underpinned by a service where workers understand the community languages, and thus experiences of dementia services will relate to language and exacerbate the communication difficulties that commonly accompany dementia.

Although Mahoney et al. (2005) found similarities in the experiences of caregivers from African-American, Chinese and Latino groups, they also found that caregivers perceived health professionals to respond in ways that reflected the health professionals' views of cultural groupings. For example, African-Americans felt their views were dismissed by physicians, while Latinos feared that a diagnosis would end the provision of home care and the removal of the person with dementia to an institution without their consent. Such beliefs reflect experiences of dismissal by professionals and removal of control in other contexts as a result of their ethnic categorization. Levkoff et al. (1999) found that finding a service provider from a similar cultural background was important for some caregivers. For example, care homes linked to the Catholic faith (for Irish-Americans) or nursing homes for Chinese elders where food preferences are observed (Chinese-Americans).

Understanding the ethnocultural values of communities was a starting point for developing carers' support groups for African-American and Hispanic communities (Henderson et al., 1994). The process of developing these support groups involved recruiting volunteers from the community to promote the support groups, being aware of views about possible venues to hold support groups, all of which demonstrates the importance of considering cultural beliefs and attitudes when developing innovative services (Henderson et al., 1994). Developing strategies to reach minority ethnic communities demonstrates the need for innovation and commitment to the objectives set. For example, outreach work supported by service and community leaders which receives adequate funding, and by employing outreach staff themselves from minority communities who can act as cultural liaisons with the target client population, is one example of working innovatively (Hart et al., 1996). The benefits of overcoming difficulties in accessing cultural groupings produce useful insights into risk factors associated with dementia. For example, the common diet in a Cree community may partially explain low incidence of dementia, as might the high value older people have in Cree society (Hendrie, 2006), thus avoiding negative stereotyping and expectations accompanying old age in other societies. However, the danger of slipping into category fallacy, where ethnicity is misunderstood by professionals and when ethnicity is used as part of professionals' cultural (mis)understandings about groupings of individuals, can lead to the absence of services that meet individual needs (Iliffe and Manthorpe, 2004: 289).

The important questions about service experiences of people with dementia from minority groups appear to relate to the language they prefer to communicate in, the food they prefer to eat and any religious observances they wish to continue. As such, ethnicity is not necessarily the key question to consider, rather how to communicate and observe the preferences of all people with dementia, regardless of their ethnicity or cultural grouping. The impact ethnicity may have on the experience of dementia is the additional stigma and discrimination that those with dementia already experience, which is further compounded by discrimination based on cultural misunderstandings. The combination of 'folk' and 'biomedical' models which carers from a range of ethnic groups use to try and understand the condition labelled as 'dementia' (Hinton et al., 2005), reflects the dominance of the biomedical models of dementia, where deficits, decline and disease are the focus of enquiry, supplemented by the stigma and discrimination which loss of memory and cognitive functioning has across societies. Thus, the experiences of carers and those with dementia will reflect the common, dominant and popular discourse surrounding dementia used by professionals and represented to the public via various media.

Dementia in different countries

Looking at dementia in different countries with different cultural contexts highlights similarities in concerns about dementia across cultural groups. For example, concerns about memory problems and the decline in ability to perform activities of daily living may be common but the response to these issues may be to problematize such factors and seek an explanation, or alternatively to accept and adapt as necessary when an older person is no longer able to do specific tasks. Henderson notes that 'a myriad of interpretive constructs' can be found when looking at dementia in different cultures, and that 'everyone notices that the person has changed, but the change if viewed as a part of the elastic fabric culture that is incorporated within the bounds of reasonable experience' (2002: 195).

Lack of awareness of dementia within the community was evident in Kerala, India (McCabe, 2006), while across Europe there is variation in awareness and desire to diagnose (Iliffe et al., 2005). In McCabe's research, tension was apparent in attitudes towards dementia and dementia care: there was evidence of carers operating

83

within traditional cultural value systems where older people are valued and cared for within the family; there was also evidence of modern worries about dementia and the need for care services, and information and advice for carers on how to look after their relative with dementia.

Cultural traditions of family care are apparent in the developed and developing world and this will have an impact on beliefs about dementia and dementia care and the willingness to use services. Tensions in family members' desire to look after a person with dementia at home and their ability to do so is evident across the literature concerned with the majority population as well as those concerned with minority groups in a country or those interested in different countries. This suggests that there is a commonality of concerns that transcends cultural differences; a desire to protect the person with dementia from the gaze of others, a gaze which can be judgmental and negative (Sweeting and Gilhooly, 1997); a concern with protecting or promoting the well-being of the person with dementia; a lack of information and knowledge about dementia; a wariness about service provision, at least initially; and an uncertain reception from professionals. Thus, Aranda argues, 'Similarities across racial and ethnic groups are as important as differences, and should be highlighted as avenues for exploring intervention strategies that can be used with multiple populations' (2001: 121).

Cultural groupings and approaching dementia and dementia care

Different approaches to dementia and the impact this has for the person experiencing the condition in different countries with different cultural backgrounds have been discussed. For example, Ikels (2002) found that those with severe cognitive impairment in the Guangzhou region of China, were valued for their longevity and that this took priority over any physical or mental frailty. Thus, those who would be considered to be severely impaired by Northern American standards were welcomed, and, indeed, sought-after guests at public and family events such as weddings. Ikels (2002) considers the contrasting approaches of those she encountered in her Chinese research to those in North America and concludes that different cultural values shape the experience of those with dementia. A further interesting example of cultural differences in conceptualizing dementia is provided by Henderson and Henderson (2002) who use a case study from an American Indian tribe to demonstrate how symptoms of dementia are understood and explained in relation to wider cultural beliefs. Thus, for example, the person talking to people who family members cannot see is perceived as being part of having special powers and not given a disease-related label. Behaviours and symptoms that could be attributed to dementia in other cultures is understood within the folk culture and understandings of a particular family and the community where they live.

In China, filial piety continues to have a strong influence on caregiving, in part due to the stability of local communities where there is little geographical movement over time, allowing families and neighbourhoods to support those with dementia in ways that an individual living alone with dementia would not encounter, (a similar cultural context has been reported in rural Northern India (Chandra et al., 1998)). However, as geographical mobility increases and values change, the emphasis on duty and filial piety may alter over time. It is important to remember that just because families have always cared in the past that they may not continue to do so in the future.

A country that further exemplifies this point is Korea (Chee and Levkoff, 2001), where it has been found that beliefs about filial piety where traditionally the son provides the financial resources and the daughter-in-law provides the practical care underlie care arrangements of older people with dementia. Chee and Levkoff report a practice of '"face-saving" ... where family problems are deliberately hidden from the community at large. Adult children are fulfilling their filial responsibilities by caregiving in the home, while escaping public criticism' (2001: 118). However, the long-term viability of family caregiving in Korea is challenged as family structures change as a result of modernization and industrialization, where growing numbers of older people coupled with more women working may lead to a shortage of family caregivers and an increasing need for care services (Chee and Levkoff, 2001). Thus, a similar pattern of less carers and more older people can be identified across countries which is likely to lead to a demand for appropriate support services for people with dementia and their carers in the future.

It can be seen then, that the experience of those with dementia is not just related to the cognitive impacts of the disease but also to the response of family members and communities. However, it is important to remember that cultural groupings, within or between countries, are only one way to create subgroups of people with dementia or their family caregivers. As Aranda (2001: 121) reminds us, 'country of origin, regional and generational differences, degree of assimilation, religious preferences, family constellations, socioeconomic status, sexual orientation ...' may all be used to categorize and to try to explain experiences of dementia and dementia care.

A comparison of caregiving in Guatemala and Rhode Island in the US demonstrates that Guatamalans reported support networks that US participants did not, but also less formal service options they could use (Salguero et al., 1998). Thus, family and social networks exist and are used in Guatemala, perhaps pre-empting the demand for formal service provision; whereas in the US greater geographical mobility has led to dispersed family networks, resulting in the primary family caregiver not having a family network to hand and thus relying on services to provide support and respite from caregiving. Different countries will thus respond to dementia in different ways in part due to the dominant family structure at a particular moment in time.

The importance of Hulko's (2004) message about multiple oppressions or multiple privileges influencing the experience of dementia cannot be underestimated, as individuals with dementia and their carers will have multiple identities that may impact differently at different moments in time. The development of outreach services targeted at people with dementia from minority ethnic groups who are socially isolated and living in poverty (Edwards et al., 1999) is one example of a way to respond to the multiple oppressions people may experience. But such initiatives are not necessarily a panacea to providing care to people whom traditional services find it hard to reach. What such innovative work illustrates is that the structure of health and social care services responds to a set of expectations about who their users will be and a conventional approach to the delivery of services that is likely to exclude people who are marginalized in some way, be it through dementia, old age, ethnicity or other disability. The quadruple jeopardy that some people with dementia may experience (Bowes and Wilkinson, 2002) presents a serious challenge to service providers and wider society to question their approach to understanding experiences of dementia and care needs.

As McCabe reminds us, people with dementia are not fixed in time (2006: 117), but located within societies which are in a state of flux, with demographics, politics and culture interacting to influence the development of ideas about dementia and associated development of services. Thus, quick fixes in terms of time-limited service delivery are not going to address the underlying factors shaping individuals' experiences of dementia and dementia care (the giving or receiving). An example of usage of support services and unmet needs can be seen in the views of Asian-Americans on support services and unmet needs (Li, 2004). Li (2004) demonstrates that more than half of those using services report that these services did not meet their needs, the particular services mentioned were day care, meal services and personal care. Added to using services that do not meet their needs, around half the sample also reported not using services that were available due to feelings of obligation to care and that the services that were available would not match the care they needed.

In a series of case studies taken from research with Chinese-Americans, Hicks and Lam (1999) provide numerous examples of the different processes involved in making decisions about the care of a relative with dementia. They demonstrate the complex interplay between ethnicity, culture and decision making. Such an interplay provides a stark reminder that care decisions are not simply related to cultural beliefs, but, for example, to socioeconomic status (what care can be afforded) and family dynamics (who wields the power). Hicks and Lam make a powerful argument that without understanding the social context of decision making about dementia, it is impossible to understand the experiences of dementia for both the family carers and the person with dementia. Although Hicks and Lam use Chinese-Americans to illustrate their discussion about the complexity of decision-making processes around care for a person with dementia, they could equally use carers from different cultural groupings, as geographical mobility, family history, economic (dis)advantage will interact with the common societal expectations about dementia care, the services offered and the influence health professionals will exert over the decisions about what services a person with dementia will or will not receive. Indeed, Salguero et al. (1998) demonstrate that current family networks in Guatemala may preclude the need for formal services, they also highlight that dementia was identified earlier than for their American sample and that family caregivers reported poorer health.

Thus, a complex interplay between availability of formal service provision and the traditional family structures can be seen to influence the care that people with dementia receive. Going back to the earlier example of dementia care in Korea (Chee and Levkoff, 2001), it can be seen that policy making has not evolved to respond to the growing numbers of older people and the decline in availability of the traditional family caregiver due to more women entering the workforce. Thus, societal beliefs and expectations about filial obligation and duty have contributed to an absence of policy making and service development for dementia care.

Culture and ethnicity: examples of caregiving implications

Cultural perspectives impact not only on thinking about dementia but also on beliefs and approaches to caregiving. Defining experiences of dementia and dementia care according to categorizations of ethnic group may perpetuate myths that 'they look after their own' (Adamson, 1999; Adamson and Donovan, 2005). Thus, it is important to be aware of wider social processes at play when exploring categorizations of people according to ethnic, racial or cultural groups, where expectations can contribute to discrimination in the provision of services. Taking, for example, African-American caregivers, it has been found that less stress and burden are reported due to providing care to a person with dementia than that reported by white caregivers (Haley et al., 1996), and that African-American caregivers report less difficulty with care provision than white carers, despite often carrying heavy care responsibilities (Navaie-Waliser et al., 2001). However, this must be located within the broader cultural context of how care is perceived and valued (Dilworth-Anderson et al., 2002).

Tensions between respecting older people with dementia and protecting them from disease or other negative labels, and the disrespect encountered from care providers in relation to the views and concerns they held about their relative, provides a good example of when lack of cultural sensitivity creates further problems for the caregiver (Cloutterbuck and Mahoney, 2003), and in turn for the person with dementia reliant on the caregiver for support. Just because certain ethnic and racial groups share a common family values system that is linked to their 'culture' does not mean that support is not required, rather that the success of any intervention is dependent on it being culturally relevant and sensitive to a group (Dilworth-Anderson and Gibson, 1999).

An interesting example of approaches to caregiving by those from different cultures is reported by Knight et al. (2002), where the assumption that the greater the attachment individuals had to family loyalty and duty, the greater the acceptance of the caregiving role. This was not always found to be the case, particularly when those from 'different' cultural backgrounds had assimilated within mainstream American culture. The variance in burden and distress experienced by individuals from particular cultural groupings illustrates the complexity of culture as a way to explain difference in experience. Thus, cultural background is but one way to explain family caregiver experiences. The similarities in experiences of dementia across cultural groupings has also been remarked on in research in other countries where different minority groups' experiences have been explored, for example Bowes and Wilkinson (2003) looking at South Asians in Scotland. Stress and strain are experienced by caregivers across cultural groupings – ethnicity and culture may compound difficulties that dementia already brings to family carers.

Kontos (2006) provides moving examples of how individuals with dementia, who have lost the ability to remember how to do things, can, when provided with culturally specific rituals, speak coherently and remember and participate in religious ceremonies. Through the use of such examples, Kontos suggests that memory is not just displayed via cognitive means but by the body's ability to remember and respond to cultural prompts. This demonstrates that the self is 'embodied' within sociocultural socialization that is remembered by the body, even when the person cannot recall abilities or function in ways which rely on cognitive means. She demonstrates that the self is not just an abstract cognitive ability and that Sabat's concepts of Selves 1, 2 and 3 (2001) (see p. 14) remain with cultural support and prompts enabling this process to occur. Therefore, care situations require cultural cues to be offered to people with dementia to enable their well-being and sense of self to continue beyond the label of dementia.

Caregiving experiences and decisions have been found to reflect 'folk' understandings and beliefs about dementia as much as by information about the disease from health professionals (Jones et al., 2006). In a study including American caregivers originating from Japanese, Chinese and Korean backgrounds, it was found that caregivers had a range of knowledge about dementia (some accurate, some not), that drew upon popular cultural understandings about old age as well as what they had read about the disease produced by health professionals. The complexity of relating 'folk' beliefs about dementia to the predominantly biomedical accounts produced in written media impacts on when help is sought, as well as what services may be accepted or rejected. If a family member equates loss of memory to stigmatizing notions of mental illness then they may choose to try and hide the condition and refrain from seeking help until a crisis point is reached. The services then available to the person with dementia may not be ideal at the most basic level of the service provider not having a worker who can speak in the language of the person with dementia, which also takes account of the cultural connotations of discussions about loss of memory and cognitive function (Jones at al., 2006: 23).

In a review of service needs, service provision and models of good practice for people with dementia from minority ethnic groups, it was found that belonging to an ethnic group was not the crucial factor in determining service needs and access to services, rather the ability of care providers to be able to communicate with the person with dementia and their family members in their own language influenced access and use of services (Daker-White et al., 2002). While Kosloski et al. (2002: 85) argue that when trying to develop services to take into account cultural differences it is more important to look at what can be changed rather than factors where there is no control. They suggest that services should respect family values and elders, and facilitate access to services for groups who are less likely to admit a need for help due to expectations placed on their caregiving roles. However, as dementia services are constructed on a Western medical conceptualization, unless people with dementia and their families can describe their experiences in such terms, they are unlikely to be able to secure the help they need (Forbat, 2003).

If dementia care is to develop, it is argued that we must take account of the diverse backgrounds of those diagnosed with the condition, and that the experiences of minority groups require investigation (Lampley-Dallas, 2002). Perhaps in so doing the development of treatments and services may be more effective at meeting the needs of all people with dementia. For services to develop that meet the needs of service users and their families, including those from minority cultural groups, it has been acknowledged that their views and preferences must be included (Rait and Burns, 1997). However, it is not enough to hear the views and preferences of certain groupings, but to begin to understand the underlying subtext of such views: for example, the refusal to use some services and dissatisfaction with those that are used may reflect unfulfilled expectations based on what is culturally acceptable (and this applies to mainstream and minority groupings).

Thus, services need to develop to meet the needs and expectations of user communities rather than professionals' ideas about what should be happening in the care of people with dementia. This involves challenging ideas about the care that the mainstream culture of service providers think is 'best practice', to challenge and question what professionals do and where their knowledge underpinning their practice is based (see Harding and Palfrey, 1997, for a discussion of this topic). To do this demands a change in the thinking of service providers and the culture of care that they promote. It is to this issue of cultures of service provision that we now turn.

Service provision cultures

As Marshall reminds us, 'It is very difficult to specify a flexible, individually responsive service in our contract culture' (1999: 87). It is against this contract culture, where resources are finite and services are bound by conventions and bureaucracy, that those at the frontline, care workers and family carers, work to promote the ideals of dementia care (discussed in Chapter 3). Such ideals give rise to expectations of high quality support and care that address individuals' specific needs in ways that support and enhance the ideals of 'person-centred' or 'patient-centred' care, where the selves or personhood of individuals with dementia are valued and supported.

As well as broader sociocultural groupings within societies and between societies, there exist cultural norms, beliefs, values and expectations within the situation where care takes place. Thus, institutional care, that is nursing homes, care homes, residential homes and hospital wards, exists within a vacuum in society. By this I mean that people with dementia are removed from the community to live in a physical location that is often remote from their previous lifestyle, that is characterized by group living, that is easily demarcated from the small nucleus of family, couple or individual living. Those who work in such settings enter a private domain of where recipients of care live, but the public domain of their day-to-day work. Combining a physical place of paid work with the place where people live leads to a distinct social environment. Any particular care setting will have daily practices relating to the local cultural context (Parker, 2001: 340). Such daily practices will reflect the characteristics of care staff, care recipients, the physical environment and the wider communities staff and residents are drawn from.

Thus, a complex array of factors will influence the daily practices in a particular setting and the reality of what living with dementia and caring for a person with dementia might entail. The micro culture of an individual care setting is of course located within a society where there is knowledge about dementia and dementia care, and policy and practice frameworks guiding what is deemed to be acceptable or good standards of care provision, as discussed in Chapter 3. Although ideologies of person-centred care, most notably advanced by Kitwood (1997), may be embraced and recognized as a way to achieve a change in care cultures, how to achieve such changes is also recognized as problematic (Woodrow, 1998).

The difficulty in changing cultures of dementia care arises in part due to the stigma the label dementia attracts. In addition, the lowly status older people occupy provides a hotbed for the exertion of power by a small group of paid workers over residents who hold little value in wider society. That the paid care workers may be drawn from groups with low status in wider society compounds the difficulty of providing person-centred care that is relationship-based and seeks to promote the ideals of citizenship and social inclusion at the heart of many care ideals articulated through policy frameworks in the twenty-first century. As Beck et al. argue, there are a number of barriers that prevent direct care staff from providing high quality care, including lack of adequate staffing levels, little reward given when high quality care is provided, problems with recruitment and retention of staff, lack of dementia-specific training given to care staff and lack of knowledge about the best way to motivate and sustain staff and prevent burnout (1999: 199). Although discussing certified nursing assistants working in US nursing homes, these problems of staffing care settings are transferrable to different care settings: hospitals, care homes, day care and to different countries. How to ensure quality care provision when there is a lack of recognition of the value of low-status workers and the skill dementia care requires, should the desire be to enhance quality of life, is problematic.

The position and views of the manager of a care setting will impact on the way care is provided and organized. As McLean and Perkinson's (1995) research exemplifies, the head nurse's understanding of dementia, shaped through her training and work experiences, led her to focus on dementia as a disease and thus promoted a model of care based on bio-medicine. This particular head nurse also had a tendency to see the residents as individuals, leading to contradictions in her approach to care: at times the residents were to be protected, at other times to have their rights and preferences observed. Those whose dementia was seen as more advanced were perceived to need only basic custodial and medical care, and families keen to promote quality of life were seen to have unrealistic expectations. Thus, a medical focus shaped the care that she felt individuals could reasonably expect. Such a tension described by McLean and Perkinson (1995) between understanding and supporting approaches to care promoting psychosocial care needs, and the dominance of medical understandings of dementia, can perhaps partly explain the difficulty in providing care that meets the ideals of policy makers and theorists.

The practical constraints of many individuals with many care needs, with smaller numbers of care workers, alongside an ideology of the need to provide high-quality physical care, relegates psychosocial care to a lower place on the direct care agenda within care settings. In my own research, examining the culture of dementia care in three different care settings within the same organization, the position of each care home manager was key in determining the way staff worked (Innes, 2000). The support which staff received to spend time talking and interacting with residents varied according to the priorities set by the care home manager. Yet, those who reach managerial positions may have received their training at a time before person-centred care reached its popularity and when work experiences have helped to endorse medical doctrines of loss of abilities. Thus, working towards changing and improving care requires educating all staff, although it may often be assumed that it is those at the lower end of the care hierarchy who require training, it is likely that all staff require support to bring about the care that is referred to in policy documents and organizational mandates.

Despite their description of the organization of care provision in a particular setting that could be viewed as critical, particularly of the head nurse, and of the way care was provided, McLean and Perkinson go on to note that their account does not detract from the fact that working with people with dementia is 'extremely difficult and demanding. It requires resourcefulness, energy and intelligence, and it is undervalued' (McLean and Perkinson 1995: 147). This is perhaps the crux of the problem in trying to improve the quality of care offered to people with dementia: as long as dementia is misunderstood and those with dementia stigmatized and marginalized, those who work with them will similarly be marginalized and devalued.

An additional problem is supporting recently or in-training staff when they first work with people with dementia. Robinson and Cubit (2007) provide the example of student nurses' experiences while on placement in residential settings for people with dementia. In their study, student nurses were unsure how to respond to and work with people with dementia, even when they had theoretical knowledge about how to approach the care of people with cognitive impairments. In addition, staff working in the care facilities found it difficult to offer support and advice to student nurses and did not always identify that students were having difficulties working in the dementia field. Nurse mentors would assume that student nurses would be able to cope with residents' behaviours, including biting and hitting the nurse, as this was part of the workload they were used to (Robinson and Cubit, 2007: 258–9). Nursing students reported a lack of communication from their mentors about what they should expect with particular individuals with dementia and what the appropriate response might be. The authors conclude that current nurse training for dementia care is not adequate and that further information about dementia is required, as well as management strategies on how to work with people with dementia in care settings (Robinson and Cubit, 2007: 262).

If McLean and Perkinson's (1995) findings of the head nurse's out-dated education is coupled with Robinson and Cubit's (2007) findings of student nurses receiving little support from nurse mentors, then there is a dire picture for future dementia care provision. If those leading dementia care units have subsumed a biomedical approach to dementia care with a focus on disease and lack of abilities, and those new to the field are given very little information and support from those who are experienced practitioners, changing the culture of care provision from task-orientated care to psychosocial care will be a constant battle.

Those working in the field need to receive regular updates on approaches to care provision and to receive 'on the job' instruction to complement classroom learning and lead to learning being imple-mented in practice. I have discussed the difficulties of implementing learning and training into practice elsewhere (Innes, 2000) and con-cluded that an action learning approach is required should changes advocated in training sessions be implemented into day-to-day practice.

Such an approach requires a considerable investment from all those working in the care facility and good intentions can easily be subsumed by shortages and changes in the staff team through sickness or staff turnover alone. If the aim is to change the care offered, then an integrated approach is required, 'while management may promote a stimulating environment, nurses and caring personnel might cling to the strategies they have always used and which are passed on to new staff' (Declercq, 1998: 318). If this is the case, any ideology or approach embraced by management needs to be translated into care strategies that those at the frontline of care delivery can adapt and work with in their existing work cultures.

Further, the job satisfaction of those who perform direct care to people with dementia in nursing homes, in the US known as nursing assistants, has been reported as very low, contributing to the high turnover of this staff group (Friedman et al., 1999). One way to overcome low job satisfaction in the US is a model of care known as PACE (Program of All-inclusive Care for the Elderly). In a comparison of nursing assistants working with the PACE or nursing home environments, those working in the PACE environment were found to have higher levels of job satisfaction. This was explained by staff working within a setting where the philosophy was for team decision making; and where nursing assistants had some control over their daily workload; and the opportunity to use their personal judgements in caregiving situations (Friedman et al., 1999: 438). The implications for the lives of those receiving care were not examined, although the authors suggest that higher quality care is likely to be provided by workers who have higher levels of job satisfaction. This remains an empirical question open to study: what factors contribute to a culture of care where the quality of life experienced by people with dementia is high?

Subcultures within the caring work place have been described with rituals of resistance identified as part of the strategy adopted by care workers to get the job done (Lee-Treweek, 1997b). In light of this, it is not then surprising that the theories about dementia and dementia care, as well as policy and practice frameworks outlining care ideals, are not necessarily the reality. If care is framed as a form of work, then workers may seek to manage this work role to their advantage rather than to choose to engage emotionally with those in receipt of care, or to promote relationships with the person with dementia, an aspect required of the person-centred philosophy of dementia care (Kitwood, 1997).

95

Leibing (2006: 242) suggests that there is a division in the way individuals may view a situation and then interpret it. For example, very simply, different social actors will see different things: a doctor may 'see' one thing, the onset of dementia symptoms, whereas a social scientist will 'see' another, a person who is having difficulty with a particular aspect of their life. Thus, the erosion of personhood can occur when what the doctor sees is loss, whereas the social scientist, or lay family member may see instances where personhood remains. Leibing's application of Foucault's concepts of the Gaze to dementia as a divided gaze, may account for the difference in practice and ideals. The ideals may take account of diverse theoretical approaches to understanding dementia; the practice sees the deficits rather than abilities of an individual, the care tasks that they need to offer to keep the person, warm, fed and clean, rather than the care interactions that will reinforce and sustain the individual with dementia who may at first glance not be easy to find or recognize.

Those with dementia may not always be perceived by care staff to be the most difficult to work with: as Henderson notes, those with dementia were 'passive recipients of care. Their communication limits were so great that Certified Nurse Assistants (CNAs) could control virtually all of their circumstances' (1995: 46). Thus, if it is easier to get the tasks done when a person with dementia cannot communicate verbally, what is the incentive for care workers to seek the non-verbal cues and perform tasks in the manner that an individual may prefer? Again, the culture of care that has been labelled 'bed and body' care (Gubrium, 1975), where task-orientated care is the culture of work promoted, is likely to reduce the incentive to move towards a culture of care where the individual needs and preferences of all those with dementia are promoted, even if such care is part and parcel of the mission statement of individual homes, large organizations and governments.

There are numerous examples where initiatives have been taken to improve the experience of dementia, a process that involves changing the prevalent cultural understandings of dementia. The UK-published *Journal of Dementia Care* provides a good example of practitioners discussing their care practices where they seek to improve the lives of people with dementia – accounts which are too numerous to go into detail here – however, such accounts are relatively piecemeal, anecdotal and remain localized initiatives rather than national or international standards.

In the international literature, there are also accounts of good practice. For example, Fukushima et al. (2005) describe work in a Japanese day centre where care professionals worked with families and the person with dementia to encourage them to accept dementia and to see that those with the condition were 'living with dementia' and thus challenged the popular perception of a 'social death' (Sweeting and Gilhooly, 1997) that often accompanies the diagnosis of dementia. Such examples of good practice may not be easy to sustain over time. Even when a particular ideology is embraced, the normal way of working may create tensions in making care decisions that either embrace and promote personhood or maintain a controlling task-orientated approach that prevents person-centred working becoming a reality.

Interesting dilemmas commonly faced by those providing care are highlighted by Powers (2001). For example, where staff are able to understand and follow through on some individuals' preferences about what to wear and what to eat, but in contrast may not provide adequate standards of care if the person with dementia refuses 'care' and does not want to be, for instance, dressed or fed. Powers describes this as 'learning the limits of intervention' (2001: 336) within a culture of care which generally does not promote autonomy and decision making rights for people with dementia. A further example of the dilemma of promoting person-centred care within nursing homes is through a culture of surveillance and restraint in care homes, where the movements of individuals with dementia are, by a variety of measures, checked constantly. This could be through alarm devices on external doors, drugs to sedate and identification bracelets to monitor movements.

Such examples illustrate the tendency of institutions to seek to control the lives of people with dementia in ways that are difficult to reconcile to the person- or patient-centred approach to dementia care that determines the ideals of care provision set out in policy documents (as discussed in Chapter 3). As Powers suggests, the culture of care in institutions is often driven by a desire and/or duty to protect and care for people with dementia. However, this may not sit easily with the person-centred philosophy of care, where the individual rights and preferences of each person with dementia should be upheld. Thus, moving beyond surface niceties in care settings where individuals are given some choice over their food, the time they get up and where they may sit, is countered by a culture of control that is inherent in institutions with a remit to 'care', where restraints will be employed to avoid risk-taking behaviour that will have consequences, not just for an individual with dementia, but for staff and other service users.

To briefly consider those who are perceived as 'difficult' in some way, highlights the challenge in implementing ideals of person-centred care to all individuals with dementia. For example, the literature exploring treatment of older people (not specifically those with dementia) clearly provides examples of labelling individuals as 'difficult', resulting in the perpetuation of negative stereotypes about older people and those with dementia generally. Slocum (1989) provides the examples of 'crocks' and 'goners' used to describe older people who are perceived as being beyond hope and help. Such categorizations can be used by staff to justify care (or lack of care) offered to certain individuals who are labelled in particular ways. A study looking at how surgeons respond to and make decisions about treatment of older people (Fisher and Peterson, 1993) highlights the wider ageism that those with dementia experience and the depersonalization of individuals that can occur when making treatment decisions. Further, labelling an individual as 'difficult' is one way of ensuring that control of the care situation remains with health professionals (English and Morse, 1988) and an effective strategy for avoiding looking at why individuals behave in certain ways and adjusting care provision to meet individuals' needs.

The three selected examples from the literature used here are relatively 'old' and thus effectively demonstrate that patterns of care towards older people have remained. We still hear people with dementia being referred to in derogatory terms; staff can still choose to see dementia as a difficult part of their job and not move forward towards examining the ways in which people with dementia communicate through their observable behaviours. Thus, despite advances in theories about dementia and dementia care, as well as policy directives seeking to improve the care that is offered to those with dementia, there remains a pervasive culture of care that has not been able to accommodate in practice the ideals of person-centred dementia care.

Despite calls for improvements in the care offered to people with dementia, the culture prevalent in the majority of long-stay care settings is unlikely to deliver person-centred care. There are a range of reasons for this, as Henderson notes in his research in a home:

the emphasis was on tangible, mechanically delivered tasks amenable to check-list review. The actual subtleties and skills related to providing psychosocial care were reduced to congenial behaviour with no formal evaluation. There was no perceived need to truly upgrade staff psychosocial care skills. There was no reward for it. (1995: 46)

This lack of reward or recognition for care work includes lack of training, lack of support, dominance of physical care provision over social care and are issues that appear time and again in the literature reporting on the quality of care provision for people with dementia.

Changes in terminology may do little to change the culture of care settings. For example, the change in language from talking about those living in long-stay settings as inmates, to calling them patients, then residents, may mark a move to humanize and 'see' the individuals living in such settings, but may do little to change the reality of living in such settings, where individuals continue to experience 'dependency, stigma, lack of privacy' (Vesperi and Henderson, 1995: 3). Thus, theories, approaches and perspectives on the study of dementia may guide the way knowledge and understanding about dementia and dementia care develop over time however, the day-to-day reality of those living with dementia may remain constrained and restrained by a culture of caregiving shaped by biomedical discourse, where basic, physical care remains the priority.

The extent of the change required has been aptly discussed:

To follow Kitwood's instructions through completely would bring about a major revolution, not only because it would mean a large investment in time and staff during a period of ever tightening health budgets, but also because redefining 'memory as interactive' would only be possible after a major shift from what is deeply rooted in our thinking and practice: that memory is the carrier of individual identity and personhood. (Leibing, 2006: 255–6)

The challenge of improving the quality of care offered to those with dementia, to improve the quality of life experienced in the manner advocated by academics, policy makers and other practitioners, remains a challenge for all those concerned with improving dementia care.

Conclusions

This chapter has demonstrated that cultural groupings where common beliefs, values, norms and expectations are shared, contribute to shaping the experience of dementia and the way in which caregivers, family and care workers will respond to an individual with dementia. It can be seen that dementia brings with it negative emotions related to ideas of stigma and shame. This will have a direct bearing on how family members will relate to the person with dementia, their approach to family caregiving and their acceptance of formal service provision. Conversely, it has also been highlighted that in some cultures, those with dementia are valued and continue to be integrated into community events where elders are respected and perceived as central to community life. Mainstream interpretations of minority cultures will shape the service response to providing care to all cultural groupings within a society. Such interpretations of culture may exacerbate commonly held beliefs about the care that people with dementia *should* need, rather than the care and support services that individuals with dementia, regardless of their cultural grouping, *actually* need.

The second part of this chapter considered the culture of service provision using the example of long-stay care. Exploring the difficulties in interpreting calls for 'person-centred' or 'patient-centred' care within a social context where people with dementia are marginalized, as are those who perform care roles, demonstrates the gap between ideals and reality. Thus, this chapter provides further examples of why the ideals of care provision outlined in Chapter 3 are difficult to achieve in practice. This is, in part, due to the uniqueness of individuals and the lack of understanding and knowledge about individuals' uniqueness that service providers possess (of course, cultural groupings are only one facet of an individual's experiences and uniqueness). As Cohen-Mansfield (2000) has suggested, care models which embrace the heterogeneity of dementia have both strengths and weaknesses. Recognizing individuality is one way to promote an ideal of person-centred care, but how to translate this into care practices or 'treatments' remains problematic. This is not to say that the ideal is flawed. Indeed, if person-centred care was a reality, then the quality of life for those with dementia would improve: an aim that is laudable. Yet, over a decade on from Kitwood (1997), it is all too easy to find examples of care settings where individuals with dementia are subjected to a 'warehousing' model of care.

A further difficulty in working towards the ideals of care espoused by care policy is the prevailing cultures of care provision where tasks are key and responding to individuals' interactions are time-consuming and difficult. This is not to deny that good practice does occur and that enthusiastic, committed and skilled practitioners seek to improve and achieve patient-centred or person-centred care, rather that it is unrealistic perhaps to expect that a care ideology can transpose into care reality for those with dementia across the globe, while resources, training and physical environments are counter-productive to attracting and retaining the highly skilled, qualified and motivated staff who can work together to achieve the goals of person-centred care put forward by academics, practitioners and policy makers.

■ ■ Further reading ■

For a detailed review of race and ethnicity concerns in dementia research see Aranda (2001); although based on the US, the issues are relevant beyond the US and extend beyond issues of race and ethnicity. Dilworth-Anderson et al.'s (2002) review of race, ethnicity and culture in caregiving provides an overview of the key issues researched to date in this area of dementia studies and suggests future directions for research. Gerdner et al. (2007) provide an excellent account of contextualizing dementia care in one area within historical, economic, social and political developments. Downs (2000) provides a useful starting point to consider why culture is an important factor to consider in the study of dementia. Although not exclusively about dementia, Henderson and Vesperi's edited collection, *The Culture of Long-Term Care: Nursing Home Ethnography* (1995), is a good starting point for considering the culture of care settings.

5

RESEARCHING DEMENTIA AND DEMENTIA CARE: IMPLICATIONS OF THE GENERATION OF RESEARCH KNOWLEDGE FOR POLICY, PRACTICE AND APPROACHES TO RESEARCH

◼ ◼ Chapter summary ◼

- Dementia studies has emerged as a field of study cross-cutting academic and professional disciplines and boundaries. This is evident in the range of 'topics' dementia studies encompasses as well as the various approaches to the study of dementia. In trying to observe trends in the topics of social research on dementia it can be seen that the early concerns of researchers were with the experiences of family caregivers. In addition, but to a more limited extent, the role of professional carers was also explored, with unqualified direct care staff receiving little research attention. Research looking at people with dementia at first tended to obtain accounts of their lives and experiences through proxy means, in particular through accounts from family and paid carers. Later, observation was used to examine the lives of people with dementia and most recently through direct engagement with people with dementia as research participants. Also apparent is the move to be more inclusive and include the experiences of, for example, minority ethnic groups.
- Trends in approaches to dementia research are also apparent and parallel the topics that were the focus of empirical enquiry. For example, first a concern to hear the experiences of carers (paid and unpaid) through interviews and survey questionnaires, then to find out more about the lives of people with dementia from the point of view of proxy informants, and later a concern with how to hear the voices of people with dementia themselves.
- This chapter charts these developments in the focus of research enquiry and research approach and discusses the related challenges of how to obtain consent, choice of research methods, the impact of the researcher on the research process, and, finally, the impact of research dissemination for theory, policy and practice.

It is possible to chart the development of dementia as a subject of social study over time, from the early concern to know more about caregivers' experiences – in particular, carer burden and carer stress – to a concern to know more about the paid work of caring for people with dementia, to a more recent interest in knowing about the experiences of people with dementia as reported by people with dementia. Parallel to the change in focus of whose experiences were to be researched was a concern to include the experiences of diverse groupings of people, for example ethnic and racial groups and comparisons across different countries.

It is also possible to identify trends in the research approach adopted for the study of dementia and dementia care, for example from a concern with developing typologies of challenges in family care giving (Gilleard, 1984) to a concern in hearing the accounts of people with dementia themselves (Wilkinson, 2002). These research developments reflect the context of dementia studies where political, economic and social concerns can be used to bring attention to dementia-related issues, and the resulting parallel developments in policy and practice frameworks that have received attraction and attention from governments and voluntary organizations. For example, as discussed in Chapter 2, economic concerns have emerged from the changing demography of society, and humanistic concerns have emerged from policy ideals espousing social inclusion, social justice and human rights.

There are two trends evident within the conduct of social research on dementia: first, a concern to hear the voices of people with dementia; and, second, a concern to be more inclusive in the selection of research topics and research participants, with the aim of transcending taboo topics and seeking to include the views and experiences of individuals and social groupings traditionally marginalized. These trends emerged in the last decade of the twentieth century and are still in evidence at the time of writing. We will first examine the paradox of the changing focus of social research on dementia, where many issues appear to have come full circle due to a lack of evidence and information to inform our knowledge of dementia and dementia care, and thus formulate policy and practice that will provide the quality of life and care that the policy ideals of care for people with dementia are demanding (as discussed in Chapter 3).

The focus of social research on dementia

Social research on dementia reflects, to a degree, changes in the theorizing surrounding what dementia is (discussed in Chapter 1), and particular moments in time which shape public concerns about the numbers of people with dementia, the costs of dementia and who should and who can provide care (as discussed in Chapter 2). In this chapter, we will first look at those whose experiences of dementia have been explored, starting with family caregivers and professional caregivers, before moving on to discuss the trend for including people with dementia as participants in research studies.

Research with unpaid family caregivers

The focus of dementia research in the 1980s was very much about the experiences of carers of people with dementia. For example, the stress and burden experienced, gender differences and coping in caregiving, and access to information and services (Keady, 1996). However, despite the long-standing focus of research attention on family carers and interventions for family carers, is the lack of concensus about what works for family carers. It has been suggested that family care remains an area of enquiry were there still exists a huge gap in our knowledge (Zarit et al., 1999). Although a plethora of services for carers have emerged, there is still a lack of understanding about what works for carers, with uptake of services not necessarily reflecting the availability that research suggests carers may find useful. Nolan et al. (2002: 196–7) identify four questions that research into service delivery for dementia caregivers, has attempted to answer with differing degrees of success:

1 When is it appropriate to offer support to family carers?
2 Who is the primary target of care interventions?
3 What is the primary aim of the intervention? E.g., to promote knowledge or to promote well-being?
4 How is the intervention to be delivered?

Thus, despite the popularity of research looking into family caregiving, there is still remarkably little consensus about what works and does not work for family caregivers. Much research on family carergivers focused on stress and strain experienced in dementia caregiving. However, it has been argued that more research is required that explores the positive aspects of caregiving as well as the quality of care delivered by family caregivers (Schulz and Williamson, 1997). It has been well established over time that caregivers can experience stress, strain and burden (Lutzky and Knight, 1994; Coen et al., 2002; Cheung and Hocking, 2004), with studies demonstrating that high proportions of participants can be classified as highly burdened. For example, 68 per cent of carers out of a sample of 172 in Cyprus were found to be experiencing high levels of strain and burden as a result of caring for a person with dementia (Papastavrou et al., 2007).

The reasons for the stress and strain that has been labelled as 'caregiver burden' have been well documented. These include, for example, lack of support for the caregiver, lack of financial resources, further stress on already strained relationships and poor physical health on the part of the caregiver. These have been summarized as resources available to caregivers, care-related stressors and contextual variables (Zarit et al., 1999). While it is clear that the positive aspects of caregiving are beginning to receive more attention and have been identified as an area worthy of study (Maslow and Whitehouse, 1997: 195), the issue of the quality of care that family caregivers provide has been largely unexplored. This is perhaps due to the expectations surrounding caregiving that we discussed in Chapter 3, where it is expected that families will provide care and that the care they provide will be tailored to their individual relative, and thus be of a high quality. However, the quality of family care as experienced by the person with dementia is an issue that has received limited research attention, and as has been noted previously, the interests of people with dementia and their family caregivers do not necessarily coincide (Askham, 1991). Thus, it is important to find out from both the person with dementia and their family caregiver about their experiences of family caregiving and receipt. Generally, however, the views of caregivers have been sought rather than the views of those in receipt of care.

An exception to this is a Canadian study exploring the views of women who were receiving care from their adult daughters (Ward-Griffin et al., 2006). This study found that mothers reported feelings of 'grateful guilt' (Ward-Griffin et al., 2006: 132). This was due to two ideologies, familism and individualism, where mothers expect to provide the care for their daughters rather than the other way round, and wish to remain an independent individual despite being in need of support and help. Such perceptions of relationships and caregiving led to some of the mothers in the study suppressing their wishes and needs as they did not wish to add to the burden of their daughters' already busy lives. However, many women would accept care as they adhered to an ideology where daughters are expected to provide care and assistance to family members should the need arise.

Paid care workers

An area that is still generally overlooked within social research on dementia is that of the views and experiences of paid carers who tend to lack formal qualifications and the associated link with a professional body, who hold low status within the workplace and who may experience marginalization outwith the workplace due to their gender, ethnicity and class. The power and control that accompanies caring for another person creates a paradox of low levels of power and control within society due to low socioeconomic status, accompanied with opportunities to control the lives of those in receipt of care (Lee-Treweek, 1997a). The low status of those excluded from society through institutionalization still has resonance with the past, where the poor and sick ended up in institutions of the last resort, such as asylums and workhouses (Townsend, 1962).

For those who remain in the community, lack of opportunities to engage in social contact beyond their home or the day care provision offered, also presents a disengagement from society, although not at the extreme of incarceration within an institution. The primary focus of research including frontline dementia care workers' experiences and views is often the quality of care received by people with dementia and/or the impact such care has on the quality of life of people with dementia receiving care (Innes et al., 2006). Broadening the focus to look at care workers often brings attention to the lack of formal qualifications, lack of on-the-job training and the resulting difficulties in offering care that is deemed to be of high quality, although it should be remembered that defining quality care appears to be inherently problematic, given the lack of consensus about what this may mean for a given individual (as highlighted in Chapter 3).

The use of terms such as person-centred or patient-centred care, and the existence of standards of care does not necessarily reflect the complexity of such care ideals at the point of delivery or offering of care (McCormack, 2003, 2004). The importance of differentiating between approaches to care is important. For example, whether care is designated as a range of tasks to complete, or if care is seen to require an emotional engagement with the person with dementia (Ungerson, 2005). The general move in approaches to care has to be to develop care beyond regimes of feeding and cleaning towards interacting with individuals and establishing some kind of relationship.

The importance of research that addresses how to provide quality care is a complex endeavour that requires multiple factors to be explored, such as characteristics of staff, how staff are supported and managed, and how good care is recognized, valued and rewarded (Innes et al., 2006).

Research focusing on aspects of the experience of the person with dementia

The focus on the family caregiver's experiences of dementia care was not paralleled with research about the experience of the person with dementia of living with dementia. The earlier work of Kitwood (1993) and Sabat and Harré (1992) (discussed in Chapter 1 of this book), marked a shift in attention to the individual with dementia. With Goldsmith's (1996) seminal text 'Hearing the Voice of People with Dementia' making a clear case that it is both desirable and possible to communicate with people with dementia at all points in their illness trajectory. Thus, the development of research in the dementia field to seek to hear what people with dementia had to say about living with dementia and service use marked a major shift in dementia research.

Goldsmith's (1996) call for researchers, policy makers and practitioners to hear the voices of people with dementia, when he suggested that it was not just desirable to hear what people with dementia had to say but that it was also possible to communicate with people with dementia in meaningful ways, has been one that has since been responded to by many researchers. In an early example of this tradition Barnett, conducting her research in the mid 1990s (2000), demonstrated that is was possible to include the perspectives of people with dementia in research, through observation and conversation, and that they had opinions about the care they received. This concern to hear the voices of people with dementia themselves reflects a research tradition concerned with seeking service users' views (Heyman, 1995; Wilson, 1995).

This approach to research runs along a continuum of token representation of users' views to those who seek to empower service users throughout the research enterprise. Thus, user view research may seek to hear what service users have to say about a particular service they use, or it may involve service users' involvement throughout the research process, that is: from the design of a research study to the collection of data, to data analysis, to dissemination of findings. If the desire is to include the views and experiences of people with dementia, then the researcher must be willing to reassess their communication skills and techniques and adapt them accordingly to the communicative abilities of the person with dementia (Innes and Capstick, 2001; Haak, 2002).

Such an inclusive approach to social research allows for the voice of those at the margins to be heard as part of a research enterprise which favours the lived experiences of research participants who may be traditionally cast at the margins of society and research enquiry (Dressel et al., 1997). In her review of the emerging attention paid to the individual in dementia research, Downs (1997) outlines three issues of concern to researchers that emerged in the 1990s; the concern to recognize that the self or personhood of a person with dementia remained in some form even as the dementia progressed; a concern to recognize the rights of people with dementia to choose to participate in research as well as their right to a diagnosis of dementia; and the value of obtaining the perspectives of people with dementia to provide insights into what the experience of dementia felt like from the point of view of the person themselves and their views on services. A decade on and these issues are still evident in dementia research and have perhaps become more pronounced as a general policy agenda of social justice and inclusion has emerged.

In relation to dementia studies, the trend of 'social inclusion' can be seen to stem from a concern to promote personhood and recognition of the selves of individuals with dementia. Widening the focus of research to include younger people with dementia (Cox and Keady, 1999; Beattie et al., 2002), people from minority ethnic groups

(Dilworth-Anderson et al., 2002), people living in remote and rural areas (Innes et al., 2006) and people with multiple and complex health needs (Rosengard et al., 2007) represents a concern to broaden the focus of enquiry beyond the initial thrust of interest into family carers' experiences of dementia. Such an inclusive focus looked at people with dementia living in care homes (Innes and Surr, 2001), using services in the community, for example day care (Parker, 2005), and using services provided within their own homes (Cobban, 2004). It also included looking at people with so-called 'early' and 'late' stage dementia, and trying to include people with whom it was difficult to communicate by conventional conversation (Perrin, 1997).

O'Connor et al. (2007) identify three domains of research inquiry that relate to person-centred approaches to dementia care: subjective experience of dementia; interactional environment; and sociocultural context. Thus, social research on dementia may be concerned with understanding personhood or supporting personhood. This is an interesting and useful model in that it helps to conceptualize research which seeks to promote the self or personhood of individuals with dementia at the micro level (subjective experience), mid level (environment) and the macro level (social context). In so doing, this model may enable insights into why care ideals do not result in widespread practice – for example, due to the recruitment of unqualified staff into poorly paid, low status positions – and remain as ideals. This may be in part due to the focus of some research on the evaluation of interventions intended to preserve personhood in some way, and such research can tell us that certain interventions appear to have a positive impact on personhood at a particular moment in time, but it does not provide us with information about how to move isolated good practice in one setting to a broader social context.

A focus on the subjective experience of dementia is a fairly new trend and reflects genuine interest and concern not to marginalize the viewpoints of those with dementia in favour of accounts from family and professionals. Such subjective accounts also need to be located within a broader framework, the immediate environment as well as the social context, for such experiences to be understood, and perhaps factors influencing such experiences to be explored and challenged, and changed if necessary. Such developments in the conceptualization of dementia research are required to enable the development of understandings about dementia and dementia care that move beyond disciplinary and professional, theoretical boundaries in a way that begins to move the study of dementia into a distinct field of academic enquiry in its own right, rather than a specialist subject area located within a particular discipline.

The idea of providing as early a diagnosis as possible to people with dementia has been in vogue now for the last decade. Interestingly, this focus of research emerged more from a policy concern relating to user-centred principles (Marshall, 1999), that people should be given a diagnosis when they can still understand and make decisions about their lives (Fearnley et al., 1998). This time lag in research evidence following policy decisions is an interesting paradox in the quest for evidence-based practice when decisions about policy and practice initiatives are actually made in advance of the evidence! As Downs and Zarit (1999) noted, the idea of evidence-based practice may be laudable but is 'clearly premature'.

Almost a decade on, the evidence base surrounding decisions about care practice is still questionable, given the relative absence continued of the views of people with dementia themselves (Nygard, 2006). This is in part due to the lack of transparency between the theory about dementia and dementia care that drives and motivates the subject to be studied, and the approach to data collection. Dementia studies is still a relatively new area of social enquiry and arguably has thus to date not developed a critical agenda taking account of the interplay between theory and understandings of dementia and the impact this has, not only on care practice and policy but also on the research process.

Dementia research: including marginalized groups

Including individuals from different sociocultural groupings has received growing research attention, in part due to policies driving the funding of research, as exemplified in the US (Aranda, 2001), and in part due to government concerns about social inclusion and social justice (Scottish Executive, 2007).

Barriers to the inclusion of minority ethnic groups in dementia research have been highlighted in the literature. For example, race riots at the time of recruitment of participants in an English study had a knock-on effect on the number of people willing to be included in a study of dementia carers from minority ethnic groups

(Mackenzie, 2006), an unpredictable difficulty that compounded the predicted difficulty of access to communities where dementia tended not to be discussed openly. Allowing time for development of contact and making personal contact with key figures within the targeted communities, and allowing for the blurring of roles of project staff, are key lessons learned from the development of support groups for carers from African-American and Hispanic communities (Henderson et al., 1994). These lessons are transferrable to the research situation where making personal contact and allowing time to recruit participants is crucial when targeting 'hard to reach' groups. This includes people from minority ethnic groups but is not exclusive as it may also be difficult to include people, for example from certain socioeconomic groups.

Aranda discusses five types of barrier to the inclusion of ethnic and racial minorities in dementia research. Examples of each type of barrier presented below are selected from her detailed list of examples (2001: 118).

- *Individual*
  Individual reasons may relate to low levels of self awareness of the condition, negative biases about who can benefit from research, embarrassment about sharing information and fear of stigmatization.
- *Sociocultural*
  Linguistic difficulties and the absence of translators, fear of negative interactions due to historical experiences of discrimination and racism, fear of institutionalization or other undesired outcome.
- *Economic*
  Costs incurred due to participation, travel, care of person with dementia, loss of earnings, fear of cessation of benefits.
- *Scientific*
  Failure to understand retention and recruitment issues, exclusion of specific groups in the research design/questions.
- *Administrative*
  Too labour intensive to include minority groups, absence of culturally competent research staff, concerns that research may promote expectations about services.

Such barriers to including racial or ethnic minority groups in dementia research can be applied to other minority or marginal voices in the dementia field. For example, it may be considered to be too labour intensive to talk to people with dementia themselves due to the need to allow time to communicate. It may be considered too costly to include people with dementia or their carers living in more remote areas due to travel and time costs for either the researcher or participants. Yet, it is clear that there is a concern that dementia research does not explore the experiences of people with dementia and their caregivers from minority ethnic groups, with gaps in knowledge in this area highlighted as: what are the barriers to service use; what are the unmet needs; and how can education be used to support professionals to address minority needs (Lampley-Dallas, 2002)?

However, these concerns are not unique to minority ethnic groups, and arguably not enough is known about any of these issues for the 'generic' population of those with dementia, however this may be defined. The difficulty for dementia studies is to work out what applies to those with dementia generally and the cultural differences in dementia caregiving. Connell and Gibson (1997) highlight the lack of consideration given to the wider context of caregiving and the need to look at differences and similarities within and between sub-groups of people with dementia. Thus, ethnicity or racial group alone cannot be used to explore and explain experiences of dementia and dementia caregiving. This was reiterated and expanded upon in a later review (Dilworth-Anderson et al., 2002), where it is was found that caregiving was a varied experience across racial and ethnic groups, but that such findings were limited due to the lack of atten-tion to cultural beliefs, values and norms. Thus, race and ethnicity cannot be used on their own to understand experiences of family caregiving. This would also apply to experiences of living with dementia.

Yet, there is a concern to look at the esoteric experiences of dif-ferent groups of people with dementia, and although necessary, look-ing at such groups in isolation from the experiences of other groups makes it difficult to truly gain knowledge about what it means to live with dementia.

Take, for example, younger people with dementia. Interestingly, even younger people with dementia are traditionally excluded from research which seeks to explore the experiences of younger people with dementia, with family members and health professionals the favoured voices in research (Harris, 2004), reflecting perhaps a belief that dementia prevents individuals from recounting their experi-ences and thus the powerless position that those with dementia are placed in by families and professionals, whatever their age. Yet, very little is really known about the experiences of younger people with dementia (Beattie et al., 2002), with no consensus about whether specialist services are required for younger people with dementia, or whether the goal of individualized services to meet individual needs should be sufficient for all age groups of people with dementia (Reed et al., 2002). Harris (2004: 33) advocates that special space be given to allow younger people with dementia to discuss the impact of dementia for themselves and their families. However, this could equally be valuable for older people.

Not all older people with dementia are the same and the heterogeneity of those with dementia poses particular challenges, as to how to include the range of backgrounds and perspectives of those with this condition is not an easy task. In their review of studies seeking to find out from the point of view of the person with dementia what their experiences of living with dementia are, Steeman et al. conclude that, 'the influence of other factors such as gender, age, personality, type of dementia, type of relationship with family caregivers and educational level remain unclear' (2006: 735), although it was apparent that awareness of the condition and support of family members were two key aspects of coming to terms with accepting that there was a change leading to seeking help and then coping with the diagnosis.

O'Connor and her colleagues call for a research agenda that looks at the subjective experience of dementia within a broader sociocultural context,

> in particular, research is required that will transcend the borders between the personal, international and sociocultural domains, to recognize the connections between personal experience and how it is socially constructed, both within one's immediate environment and within a broader societal context. (O'Connor et al., 2007: 134)

However, dementia research is constrained by funding opportunities, and the differential in the research funding made available for Alzheimer's disease compared to cancer and heart disease in relation to the cost of providing care for the respective conditions has been noted, with the suggestion that state and publicly funded research councils should consider their research priorities (Lowin et al., 2001).

By looking at the focus of social research on dementia it can be seen that there has been a shift in who is included as research participants over time, from families, to professional caregivers to people with dementia. It can also be seen that in earlier dementia research, the needs and experiences of family caregivers, for example, remain pervasive concerns. Cooke et al. (2001) suggest that this is because the outcomes of family intervention studies are not always clear and when they are along the outcome measures used, no improvements were recorded for two-thirds of the studies they reviewed. This highlights the fact that despite an increase in interest in dementia studies, there have yet to be answers to the common concerns that appear to drive research in this field, how to improve quality of life and quality of care for those giving and receiving care.

Conduct of social research on dementia

We now go on to consider the conduct of social research on dementia which attempts to:

- Include the varied perspectives of the multitude of people who care for people with dementia who may commonly be excluded.
- Seek the views of people with dementia themselves about their experiences.

To do so requires an engagement with research processes, and as such social research on dementia reflects perennial concerns within social science research, including: how to obtain informed consent; how to ensure participants are representative of the broader population; and how to interpret the words and actions of research participants. The challenge facing researchers concerned with the social study of dementia is how to go about researching a complex social phenomenon that has been medicalized, then subjected to critiques and deconstruction. Also, research itself is influenced by, and part of, many wider social processes reflecting the discrimination and stigma attached to older people and people who are experiencing cognitive difficulties.

How to address such issues is challenging methodologically and epistemologically, (that is, how to establish what is known and what knowledge is), and ontologically, (that is, the approach taken to research that represents the assumption the research makes about the social world:

for example, that the social world is observable with different interpretations possible, or that there are 'facts' that can be documented).

Including people with dementia in dementia research

It has been suggested that one of the reasons that the views of people with dementia are now included in research is due to the higher levels of awareness of dementia brought about through diagnosis of dementia and services available to those who receive a diagnosis (Droes, 2007: 116). However, misconceptions about the ability of those with dementia to consent to taking part in research, and the value of the data collected, that is those who would pose the question – how reliable can an account from someone who forgets be? –create challenges for the researcher who wishes to include people with dementia in their research. One of the first challenges that a researcher may face is gaining ethical approval to include people with dementia in research, with the issue of gaining consent from individuals who have difficulty remembering. Thus, how to deal with the issues of consent is one of the first challenges facing researchers.

Consent

The difficulty in recruiting and retaining people with dementia in research has been discussed (Wilkinson, 2002), and has also been described as a concern of ethics bodies (Dewing and Pritchard, 2004) and may be seen as a barrier to the inclusion of people with dementia in the research process. Other difficulties in including people with dementia in research as participants in their own right relates to concerns to protect people defined as vulnerable by legislation, and the need for a proxy decision to be made as to whether a person can be included in research or not.

Different stakeholders may have different views on when it is appropriate to include people with dementia in research, but their views on this may be from a relatively uninformed position about what research involves and also from a position where they seek to protect the person with dementia from any risk or harm (Bravo et al., 2003). In a Canadian study, informal carers and older adults were found to be more likely to exclude those with cognitive impairment from research than would ageing researchers and members of review boards, reflecting perhaps a difference in perception of research, dementia and potential risk of harm (Bravo et al., 2003). However, researchers who have included people with dementia in research argue that ethical issues should not pose a barrier to engaging people with dementia in research. Indeed, they state that 'it would be unethical to exclude them' (Preston et al., 2007: 141). Thus, there is arguably a 'turn' occurring in dementia research where the aim now is to place the person with dementia at the centre of the research enterprise.

However, the desire to include people with dementia and the final result of their eventual participation in dementia research is a complex undertaking. Taking two examples of approaches to including people with dementia in research illustrates the complexity of the process, and also how the different starting points for understanding dementia influence the suggested ways of involving people with dementia in research.

It has been suggested that there are five conditions that should be met for ethical considerations to be upheld should research be non-therapeutic (Berghmans and Ter Meulen, 1995). By non-therapeutic the authors mean research that has no obvious immediate benefit to the research participants but also that they will be exposed to no obvious harm. The suggested conditions are:

1 That the research could not be conducted with those who do not have dementia, or as progressive a dementia.
2 That the research must be 'scientific'.
3 The research must have low burden and risk to participants.
4 Proxy consent must be obtained.
5 Research should stop if non verbal signs indicate that participants are unhappy with the process. (Berghmans and Ter Meulen, 1995: 650–1)

These suggested conditions appear to perceive dementia as a disease and thus people with dementia are 'subjects' in research where they are researched on rather than included as people who can share their subjective experiences. As such, a traditional approach to research, referred to as the scientific paradigm or positivist paradigm, is apparent. The researcher will make the decisions as s/he is the 'expert'. Indeed, Berghmans and Ter Meulen state that a 'responsible scientist ... will know how to implement these conditions in practice' (1995: 651). However, such a premise is based on a largely biomedical understanding of dementia and thus overlooks the active role people with dementia can have in decision making. Yet, Berghmans and Ter Meulen's paper is important in that it argues for including people with dementia in research, and thus marks a move forward from a concern with hearing the views of families and professionals about dementia rather than the views of the person with dementia.

A contrasting position is presented by Dewing (2007), in her discussion of participatory research, where she proposes a method to gain the consent of people with dementia. This method of gaining consent involves a reflective process on behalf of the researcher who must:

- Do background preparation to gain access.
- Establish the basis for consent: for example, when and how to ask and on what basis capacity to consent is decided.
- Gain initial consent, through giving verbal, written or visual information.
- Monitor ongoing consent; this is a way to ensure that visual or verbal signs from participants expressing unease or distress with being involved in the research are taken into account and that initial consent does not mean that a person will be willing to participate at all times.
- Provide feedback and support if required to carers about the well-being of the person and make any notes about the research process for personal reflection at a later date.

Dewing's position in relation to obtaining consent to participate in research reflects a belief that people with dementia retain a sense of self and can express their views about participating in research if the researcher takes care to engage subjectively with potential research informants.

Thus, deciding whether or not to include people with dementia in research, and then whether to obtain consent through the decision of a proxy, be it caregiver or professional, or whether to directly engage with individuals with dementia to seek their individual consent, is a process that is complex and challenging. But how to achieve the goal of including people with dementia relates to theoretical understandings of what having dementia means. In very simple terms, resonant with Kitwood's (1997) position on dementia care, in research terms, does the disease come before the person, or does the person come before the disease? A further complication is highlighted by Beck and Shue (2003) where the trend for surrogate decision making, a form of proxy consent, may lead to such control being exerted over the research process that it could lead to the exclusion of the very group of people who have only started to be consulted about what it is like to live with dementia, and their support requirements. Proxy informants have been found to be able to report on aspects of quality of life such as observable symptoms and quality of services. However, they have been found to be less in agreement with those in receipt of care when it comes to their subjective views and experiences of illness and services (McPherson and Addington-Hall, 2003).

Thus, as the growing body of work about awareness in dementia (Clare, 2004) has demonstrated, people with dementia can report on their subjective experiences and views and add to our knowledge about dementia, and also influence care providers' and professionals' debates about care services required. However, it very much depends on the theoretical understandings surrounding dementia being applied and understood, as to whether asking people with dementia what they think is considered a reliable and valid way of collecting data about dementia and dementia care (Cotrell and Shultz, 1993).

The role of the researcher in facilitating the research process

There are also discussions in the literature about how to do person-centred research with people with dementia. McCormack (2003), for example, calls for research to meet five conditions: informed flexibility; sympathetic presence; negotiation; mutuality; and transparency. If researchers adopt such an approach, then they will be demonstrating person-centred care sentiments through their research, in much the same way that educators can demonstrate person-centred care in their approach to facilitating learning about person-centred care with care staff (Innes, 2001).

Immediate implications of when and where interviews and observations of people with dementia take place are apparent, leading Nygard to conclude that 'the context is indeed a key issue for support for informants with dementia when eliciting their perspective' (2006: 105). She provides the example of asking people with dementia about a device for a stove; if questions were asked about the device in the kitchen where the stove was visible, this helped participants answer the question, whereas asking questions in a different room made it more difficult for the person with dementia to understand what was being asked.

The importance of taking into account the context of the research extends beyond the room in which an interview is conducted. For example, if a family member is present during an interview, this may lead to the collection of data where there are competing perspectives (Sands et al., 2004). The question may then arise about whose perspective is most 'accurate', as one of the concerns which is often used as a rationale to prevent people with dementia being included in research is a concern with the accuracy of their accounts of their experiences of aspects of their lives. The importance of allowing sufficient time to conduct research with people with dementia has been stressed, whether this is to gain consent, build rapport, or time required to cover interview topics (Nygard, 2006; Dewing, 2002, 2007).

Yet, the call to include people with dementia in research began in the early 1990s, with Cotrell and Schultz (1993) arguing that it was desirable to hear what people with dementia themselves had to say and that research methods should and could be adapted to enable individuals with dementia to participate as fully as possible in research. Indeed, it has been argued that researching dementia is no different from researching any other complex social phenomenon (Bond and Corner, 2001), in that researchers need to locate their work within theoretical debate and be clear about the beliefs and understanding of dementia they are using and bringing to their research, while selecting appropriate methods for their selected research questions. With this comes the need to remember that any account that is presented, where perspectives and experiences are shared, is not a quest for a 'correct' answer, rather an attempt to hear what research participants have to say about aspects of their lives. As such, dementia research where, for example, an ethnographic approach is adopted, can help to provide insights into a crucial domain, what people with dementia themselves have to say about living with dementia, which has, it has been argued, still been relatively unexplored (Nygard, 2006: 110).

However, the real crux of the problem in doing social research on dementia relates to the paucity of reflective accounts of the research process, which would help to inform others seeking to embark on researching an area of social life that has been categorized in a way that makes the starting point for doing research difficult. To hear the views of people with dementia involves complex entry processes where there is a concern to protect, and in the process exclude, the person from research, and to rely rather on proxy information or the information of those with dementia who are deemed to be 'early' in their dementia and thus capable of giving accounts that are seen as reliable by those who do not have dementia.

An example of a reflective account of the research process where power in the research relationship is explored can be found in Proctor's (2001) small study where four women with dementia attending a day hospital were interviewed about their views of the service. Proctor describes difficulties in obtaining consent from a woman who felt she had nothing to say that could be valuable. She also describes difficulties in understanding what it is that the women were trying to say, and concludes that it would be useful to spend more time with each woman prior to doing the interviews. She also highlights the importance of looking at her role as researcher in the interview and the power relationship between herself as a health care worker and researcher and the research participants who were older women, labelled with dementia, who were health care recipients.

A second example of a reflective account of conducting observations and interviews with people with dementia living in long-stay hospital wards is provided by Kelly (2007). She describes the difficulties she encountered in the care setting, her lack of control and power over situations she observed and her feelings of relief at being able to leave such an environment. Such accounts are valuable in that they alert us to the difficulty of conducting social science research where the participants are often assumed to be unable to participate, although this is now widely repudiated, and also how people with dementia as research participants may be in marginalized positions which require a sensitive approach to data collection. Further, the impact of conducting such research for the researcher who empathizes with the participants is only beginning to occupy a central place on the wider social science agenda (Lee-Treweek and Linkogle, 2000) but is of particular significance for those studying dementia and dementia care.

The moral or ethical concerns that the social science orientated researcher seeking to conduct research about dementia or dementia care encounters, can be further complicated by a range of practical issues that are not unique to dementia research but which raise questions about the value and esteem that is accorded to dementia studies, in comparison say, to funding decisions about research for other health conditions or for other groupings in society. The multiple jeopardy surrounding dementia discussed in further detail in Chapter 6, relating to mental health and old age in particular, has an impact on the practical constraints surrounding the conduct of dementia research where cost and time constraints have given an added dimension to the collection of data, where it is widely accepted that people with dementia need time to communicate and cannot be rushed (Killick and Allen, 2001).

Costs incurred of including any carer may be prohibitive to their participation: travelling to a research venue does not only involve travel costs, but could also include loss of earnings to be able to attend, or loss of a day's break from work or caring responsibilities, and could also incur costs of having an alternative person cover the caring responsibilities. A similar dilemma exists for including the person with dementia. For a person with dementia to come along to a research venue will incur travel costs and perhaps the costs for a carer to accompany them. It may involve additional research time costs for travel to where they live and the time required to establish rapport, and find ways to communicate effectively with the individual with dementia, which may require repeated interviews (Bond and Corner, 2001).

The fear of decisions being made about the care situation, whether economic, through the loss of benefits, or social, through the institutionalization of the person with dementia, or at an individual level through embarrassment in sharing experiences, may all influence the decision to participate. Of course, information sheets can be provided offering reassurance about such issues, but previous experiences may shape the decision.

Funding decisions about how much financing is required and if the research offers 'value for money' through the added benefit of hearing the views and experiences of marginal groups. Similarly, ethics bodies may be concerned with protecting the person with dementia based on beliefs about limited capacity and the limited value of what a person with dementia may share due to concerns about accuracy of accounts and ability to recall events.

How to include the views of people with dementia: a question of research methods

A range of research methods are at the disposal of those concerned with studying social aspects of dementia, from questionnaires, to interviews, to observation methods. The purpose of this chapter is not to discuss the merits of such approaches, as many research texts adequately address these issues. Rather, the intention here is to discuss one particular method, the research interview, to demonstrate the potential of this method to obtain the views of research participants who have dementia.

Interview is an increasingly popular research method to obtain the views of people with dementia about aspects of their lives, as Steeman et al.'s (2006) review of 28 qualitative studies exploring living with early stage dementia, published between 1990 and 2004, readily demonstrates. The use of interviews enables participants to speak about their lives, and for researchers to begin to understand what living with dementia is like for those with the condition. There is a growing body of literature adopting such an approach which does much to add to knowledge about what living with dementia is like, not just for family and paid carers, but also for the person with dementia. The use of interviews is argued to be a way to facilitate communication with the person with dementia (Moore and Hollett, 2003). For example, the use of open-ended questions and the researcher's skill in rewording questions that interviewees appear to find difficult to understand, enables the person with dementia and the interviewer to have a conversation that is meaningful to the person with dementia, and which also elucidates the person's views and experiences of living with dementia.

The complexity of talking about a diagnosis of dementia is demonstrated by Langdon et al. (2007) where participants reported being happy to share their diagnosis with close family and friends but reluctant to talk about it beyond a small circle of trusted people. This reflects an awareness of the stigma that dementia attracts and a desire to avoid drawing attention to a condition that receives potentially negative consequences when it is shared with others. However, participants in this study were happy to share their experiences with a researcher. This demonstrates that people with dementia are able and willing to talk about their experiences of dementia and that they can adjust their discussion according to whom they are interacting with, and they are clearly articulating their experiences within the context of their social world – a context we explored in Chapters 2 and 3, where we established that those with dementia are marginalized and stigmatized on account of being 'old' and on account of their 'dementia'.

Clearly then, interviews do allow a way for people with dementia to share their views, although it should be noted that this approach has only had reported success for those whose dementia is deemed to be 'mild' or 'early stage'. To illustrate this approach, I have selected three examples of small-scale qualitative research which included people who were considered to be at an early stage in their dementia. These studies were conducted in Sweden (Holst and Hallberg, 2003), in the UK (Preston et al., 2007) and Belgium (Steeman et al., 2007).

Using a biographical approach to interview, where throughout the interview 11 participants were asked to talk about important events in their lives, Holst and Hallberg (2003) established that the experience of dementia for their participants was an emotionally overwhelming life event. For some participants, taking up new activities, for example, golf, helped them to experience living with dementia positively. For others, the gradual erosion of abilities and the ability to participate in activities, such as a sewing circle, that also served a socializing function, was a real difficulty to cope with in their day-to-day lives and in their efforts to maintain a sense of identity and sense of purpose in their lives.

In a similar vein, Preston et al. (2007) conducted 12 qualitative interviews with people with dementia. Their aim was to investigate how participants coped with their dementia in their day-to-day lives. Three themes are discussed by Preston et al. (2007: 139–41) of managing identity in relation to dementia, making sense of dementia, and coping strategies and techniques. The discussion of these three themes presents a clear case that the person with dementia actively works to preserve their identity and to cope with the difficulties that accompany their cognitive decline.

In Belgium, Steeman et al. (2007) interviewed 20 older people with a probable mild dementia. They found that people wanted to be valued as individuals in their own right and that this was more important than their cognitive abilities. However, they also found that cognitive abilities, or the lack of them, contributed to feeling worthless and having little value, thus a struggle between maintaining a sense of value alongside recognizing their cognitive decline was evident. Steeman et al. suggest that narratives need to be understood as attempts to negotiate their dementia.

The common issues that are highlighted by these three studies is that they demonstrate that through the use of sensitive interviewing techniques it is possible to hear what people with dementia think about their dementia and what their perceptions are about the condition's impact on their lives. A common theme emerges from studies seeking to hear people's experiences of their illness – that living with dementia is a balancing act of maintaining identity and associated sense of worth and value alongside their own and others' reactions to their decline in cognitive abilities.

Attempts to hear the views of those with more advanced dementia through the use of interview are also evident. For example, Aggarwal et al. (2003) interviewed people with dementia at all stages of dementia and found that all could report their views about either the day care or residential care services they used. They were also able to report the losses they had experienced through their dementia and how they felt about their loss of abilities. Thus, including those with a more advanced dementia using interviews in research has been found to be possible with similar findings to studies exploring the views and experiences of those with a less advanced dementia.

Multi-method studies using interview as one research tool are also popular, and reflects a trend in critical gerontology to use different methods to help 'get the story right' (Holstein and Minkler, 2007: 22). For example, Beard's US study (2004), using individual interviews and focus group interviews supplemented with observation, has also demonstrated that it is possible to find out how people with dementia view their diagnosis and the impact it has on their sense of self and personal identity. Participants in Beard's study demonstrated their awareness of others' negative assumptions about their abilities, and in interview and through observations Beard found examples of individuals striving to preserve a sense of self worth. Similarly, Phinney (1998) used observation and interviews to form her analysis of the experiences of five people living with dementia.

She found that they tried to be 'normal' and continue with their lives to counteract the negative impacts of living with their dementia. Thus, multi-method studies not only hear what the person's views are but can observe what their interactions are like to further illustrate participant experiences.

As such, research that seeks to hear the views of people with dementia begins to circumnavigate concerns of researchers interested in issues of outcomes for people with dementia. However, research that fails to look at outcomes may fail to have an immediate and direct impact on the lives of those with dementia in terms of developing services and improving quality of life.

This is not to diminish the contribution of researchers including the views of people with dementia, who have undoubtedly challenged preconceptions about what it means to have dementia, and the importance of moving beyond proxy accounts of what this condition involves to accounts from those who directly experience it. Thus, the contributions of research including the views of people with dementia are perhaps at a theoretical level, and by this I mean that accounts of what it means to have dementia, how individuals seek to cope and adjust to cognitive decline, provides information to add to theoretical understandings about what dementia is and what it means for those who are given this label/medical diagnosis.

In addition, research presenting accounts of the experiences of people with dementia adds to the research process literature by providing examples of how to include groups traditionally viewed as 'difficult' in the research process. Contributions to policy and practice may be less direct and as such not an obvious outcome of the research, but by changing conceptualizations about what it means to have dementia may have a slow lead-in to future discussions about the shape and direction of care policies.

Outcomes and the challenge of measurement

A further issue that has perplexed researchers is how to measure outcomes of quality of care or quality of life for people with dementia. This is in part due to the difficulty in defining what quality of life means (Lawton, 1997). It has been noted that current debates about the goals of interventions for people with dementia 'provide food for thought' not only for researchers but for policy makers and practitioners as well (Nolan et al., 2002: 202). Thus, process, structure and outcome are important dimensions to evaluate when exploring aspects of dementia care (Bond et al., 1989: 355).

There are many methods available to audit and evaluate the quality of life and/or quality of care for older people in general and people with dementia in particular. Measures encompass a wide range of domains, including health status characteristics, cultural factors, personal autonomy factors, personality factors and subjective satisfaction (Bond, 1999: 567). The measures often reflect a world view stemming from the biomedical model, which is of limited use when exploring the impact of quality of care for persons with dementia, as subjective satisfaction is often overlooked.

While such measures may provide a piece of the jigsaw (Bond, 2000) and, indeed, researchers often piece together methods in the hope that an incremental picture will emerge, Bond argues that a multi-factorial process is required to understand and change, if necessary, cultures of care. A review of assessments of quality of life for people with dementia (Selai and Trimble, 1999) highlights the methodological difficulties inherent in measuring a subjective state of being. Lawton (1997: 93) discusses the range of measures that can be used to try and assess quality of life, including the desire of some to avoid subjective outcomes that would involve hearing what the person with dementia thought, to objective measures that avoid direct consultation with the person with dementia but allow proxy responses to be included.

Nonetheless, there have been a number of innovative attempts to measure the quality of life of people with dementia, and/or the quality of care that contribute to our understanding about the extent to which care settings meet the psychosocial care needs of people with dementia, an area that has received increasing attention as the focus of empirical enquiry. For example, Smith et al. (2005) demonstrate that it is possible for people with dementia to describe health-related quality of life domains, and that their accounts differed from the response by their proxy caregiver. This raises two important issues: that people with dementia can discuss their quality of life along health-related domains; and that their views are not necessarily accurately represented by their family members.

Who decides on measures of success is an important research consideration. Post (2001), for example, argues that from an ethical standpoint, it should be family caregivers and people with dementia who decide which measures should be used to gauge the success of a service, intervention or piece of research. However, the outcomes selected to evaluate the success or otherwise of an intervention research study may not be designed with success for the family carer or person with dementia clearly in mind (Schulz, 2001). Rather, success may be measured in terms of professional, care provider or practitioner (or researcher) rather than from the viewpoint of those who were the focus of the research enquiry. Looking at outcomes of community care from the perspective of people with dementia and their carers, Bamford and Bruce (2000) conclude that quality of life and service-process outcomes should be used to ascertain the outcome for those using the service, rather than only using measures relating to the aims of the service. They point out that one outcome for service users was preservation of their autonomy and that this was not perceived as an outcome for the service providers. Thus, service providers and service users will have different perceptions of outcomes and research needs to be aware of these different perceptions of outcomes.

A Japanese study (Fukushima et al., 2005) demonstrates that the measures of quality of life important to those with dementia were not necessarily those that professionals felt comfortable with, given their desire to deliver care. When people with dementia were given the opportunity to talk about what was important to their quality of life, it was clear that they were able to do so, and that by listening to their views, care practice could be reorientated accordingly to meet the understanding of dementia that those with the condition had developed.

Accepting dementia and the changes and challenges that can arise appeared to be key to quality of life as reported by people with dementia themselves (Fukushima et al., 2005). The difference in needs, and thus successful outcomes, was found to vary from the perspective of service users, carers and staff (Hancock et al., 2003), with service users reporting less need for social support than their family member or staff of services. This is echoed when health-related quality of life was examined (Smith et al., 2005), and people with dementia were found to rate their quality of life higher than their family members did, demonstrating the danger of relying solely on family members' proxy reports.

It has been suggested that there are two reasons for differences in reports of quality of life as reported by people with dementia and by their carers. The first is that carers report lower quality of life than the person with dementia when the carer is experiencing high levels of burden. The second is when carers report higher quality of life than the person with dementia – this occurs when the person with dementia is in a depressed mood (Sands et al., 2004). This highlights the importance of hearing what people with dementia have to say, as their viewpoints may not converge with the accepted professional wisdom or, indeed, the views of the people, family members, who think they know the person with dementia best. This does not mean that the views of paid and unpaid carers are not important, only that the views of the person with dementia are equally important should the aim of dementia studies be to develop and grow our understanding and knowledge of what having dementia means for the range of people affected by this condition.

Disseminating research: impacts on theory, policy and practice

Common outlets for research findings are short papers appearing in journals targeted at academics and practitioners. Following on from developments observed in gerontology (Holstein and Minkler, 2007: 19), those working in the dementia field need to be aware of potential difficulties in getting their social research on dementia published if it is not perceived as 'scientific'. However, there are a growing number of outlets for the publication of dementia work in specialized dementia journals as well as related fields, such as gerontology, where the mushrooming of journals dedicated to old age has already been highlighted (Warnes and Phillips, 2007: 146). Book chapters, conference papers and workshops are also common research 'outputs' that researchers use to share their findings. However, what impact do such writings and verbal presentations have on the theory upon which the study of dementia is grounded? On the policy developments that shape the care expectations of, for example, families and people with dementia? On the care practices of individual care workers who are employed to 'care' for those with dementia living in either their own homes or in institutions?

Research has a potentially important role to play in the development of dementia studies and the recommendations that can be made for policy makers and practice development. Indeed, Beck et al. (1999: 208) call for researchers to frame their research questions in a way that can provide data for policy makers, that can inform changes in policy. For example, Ward-Griffin et al. (2006: 139) argue that their findings of women receiving care from their daughters who report feelings of 'grateful guilt', present a clear challenge to home care services policy makers to be aware of gendered ideologies of care and to develop alternative care services that do not rely on the expectations within families that daughters will provide care. However, the gendered expectations of caregiving are pervasive within society and to challenge such expectations would require a radical overhaul of policy making, and this is beyond the remit of researchers who can only seek to advise and inform policy makers in their decision making, and as such, recommendations from researchers are an important part of the research enterprise.

A further issue relating to the impact of research is how it was funded in the first place. Researchers conducting small studies attracting small amounts of funding from, for example, care organizations or voluntary sector funds, may have very little funding devoted to disseminating their findings. Attracting funding from large research councils, where awards are competitive across disciplines and topic of enquiry, may be difficult to win. And even when funders make an active decision to make awards for dementia research, the impact of such research may not be particularly effective. As has been noted in an interesting short piece, where Adelman (1998: 157) suggests that, despite a large US funding organization – the National Institute of Aging – devoting a disproportionately large amount of its funds to Alzheimer's research, there is a lack of effective political action as a result of the research.

Newcomer et al. (2001) suggest that there are opportunities for researchers to make an impact on policy and future dementia practice if they engage effectively with contemporary policy concerns relating to budgets and outcomes, that is, the cost-effectiveness of services and interventions for people with dementia and their carers. However, they also note that politics rather than research will make the decisions about the future (2001: S135); research can only seek to inform the direction politics may take.

That said, researchers can help to shape new directions in policy making by highlighting new areas. Whitehouse (1999) and Post (2001) concur in their respective suggestions that more research is required about end-of-life care for people with dementia. That we still do not know enough about how dementia impacts on the person with dementia is apparent from the brief overview of selected small studies where the views of those with dementia were sought. Post (2001) also talks of the need to look to the future impacts of medications and other treatments on the lives of people with dementia, and in a similar vein Whitehouse warns of the dangers of 'medicalization or economization of quality of life' (1999: 109). Thus, given the current trend of looking for a cure, the advent of the so-called 'anti-dementia' drugs are not an end in themselves. Rather, the impact of these for carers (paid and unpaid) and those with dementia remain areas open to enquiry. Although including people with dementia in research is an undoubted move forward in helping to increase knowledge about what it means to have dementia, there is a need to ensure that people with dementia can help set the research agenda of the future (Post, 2001: S17), although there is now a flourishing literature in this area.

When the relatively small time frames of socially orientated dementia research are considered (mainly from the 1980s onwards), dementia studies research has had a remarkable journey in a short timescale. There have been positive moves to be more inclusive in terms of whose views and experiences are included, and there have been innovative attempts to use research methods in appropriate ways to ensure that the experiences of the key stakeholders in the dementia experience have been included. However, the extent of the impact of greater understandings about what it means to have dementia, and what could be assumed to be examples of good care practices on the lives of people with dementia, are not fully known. Longitudinal studies in the dementia field would be one way to explore the impact of dementia over time on the individual, that could take account of changing policy contexts and care expectations. This could enable a comparison of the lives of individuals with dementia as the effect of changes in common understandings about dementia and policy decisions filter down to the actual lived experiences of dementia.

Those studying dementia have many avenues open to them to further knowledge and inform future policy and practice developments.

An agenda favouring social inclusion offers many new topics to explore, while building on the ever-growing literature in this area.

Conclusion

This chapter has charted the change in focus of dementia studies research over time, highlighting the initial exclusion of those with dementia from the research process in favour of a focus on the experiences of family carers and care professionals. It has demonstrated that this change in focus has also led to changes in research approaches. Perennial research concerns of how to obtain consent, how to hear the voices of individuals that have previously been unheard, how to adapt existing research methods to enable the researcher to engage effectively and interact with the targeted research group, have been approached by researchers in this field with reported success. Reflective accounts of the research process are helpful in alerting those studying dementia, and beyond, of how to approach topics that may be perceived to be sensitive, with groups perceived to be vulnerable and lacking in capacity in some way.

There is thus much to be commended about dementia research to date. That is not to say that those researching in this field can be complacent. The impact of research on the lives of people with dementia remains relatively unknown: identifying good practice through a research study has not necessarily led to a broad adoption of practices. Care situations remain unique in many ways and as such, universal improvements are guaranteed, which is why research continues to highlight issues that would be considered poor practice by policy makers, care professionals and family caregivers (Kelly, 2007 provides a recent example).

The challenge of ensuring that people with dementia are not just seen as passive research participants, but that they are enabled to become active in deciding the direction dementia research can take, has been embraced by Alzheimer movements where people with dementia sit on research-funding decision-making panels. Thus, there continue to be developments in the process of research. Those studying dementia therefore have a wide literature to draw upon, both of empirical studies, as sketched out above, and of theoretical developments (as discussed in Chapter 1). We shall now move on to the final chapter of this book, which seeks to map out a social science based model for the study of dementia.

Wilkinson's (2002) edited collection of papers is excellent, considering various aspects of including the person with dementia in research. O'Connor et al.'s (2007) paper presents suggestions for creating a research agenda that builds on the popularity of Kitwood's (1997) notion of personhood underpinning person-centred care perspectives.

6

A MODEL OF DEMENTIA STUDIES:
KNOWLEDGE GENERATION AND DEVELOPMENT

■ ■ Chapter summary ■

- This final chapter proposes a reflective model for the study of dementia that takes account of key issues that underlie thinking about dementia and dementia care practice. This chapter discusses such a model through the engagement of theory, social context, policy frameworks and research. The book began by first considering the theorizing about dementia and dementia care from three broad theoretical perspectives or approaches: biomedical, social-psychological and social-gerontological. The knowledge – upon which policy and practice frameworks about the care and place of people with dementia in society are based – can be interrogated, if we question the starting point for thinking about, conceptualizing and understanding dementia and dementia care.
- A further contextualization for the study of dementia involved looking at the political, economic and social concerns that surround the discourse about dementia and dementia care. We then moved on to explore policy frameworks as ideologies about care with care ideals central to their articulation.
- It is again possible to question how knowledge about dementia can lead to ideas about best practice. Taking the examples of cultural groupings and cultures of care settings demonstrated the potential of a separateness of daily living from theoretical conceptualizations and policy ideals. Looking at the research process – from the selection of topic to be studied, to the methods of data collection adopted, and the approach to interpretation of data and resultant dissemination messages – demonstrates the influence that theory, care ideals and care practice can have on the research process. This, in turn, may or may not confirm conventional or current wisdom about dementia and dementia care.
- This concluding chapter builds on these preceding discussions to argue that dementia studies is part of a knowledge questioning, generation and production process: a process that requires acknowledgement of the rights of people with dementia and a quest for an agenda that embraces values of social inclusion and citizenship.

Introduction

Studying dementia and dementia care from a social science perspective requires taking on-board the ideas and assumptions from a range of disciplines, namely bio-medicine, psychology and social-gerontology. Specific sociological concepts and ideas can also be used to illuminate the study of dementia. In this chapter, I draw on a body of sociological work, the sociology of knowledge, borrowing some ideas about how knowledge is generated and applying these to dementia studies. I also use the ideas of social inclusion and citizenship to demonstrate alternative ways of viewing people with dementia. I do this in an applied way, as the intention of this book is to demonstrate that the study of dementia requires an openness to different perspectives, an awareness of the contributions different approaches have to our understandings about dementia, and the resulting policy frameworks which guide care practices. An awareness of the limitations of different approaches is also required to further our knowledge of this field of study and to develop the potential to learn more about dementia and how to find care practices that work for both those who receive and deliver care.

To reach the point of proposing a model for the study of dementia, I first considered the theorizing about dementia that has been evident throughout Western countries since early in the last century (Chapter 1). The developments since the medicalization of dementia, where the critics of such an approach presented alternative perspectives drawing on social-psychology and social-gerontology, provide a rich literature for those studying dementia. That dementia is a social construct is readily apparent, although it is also clear that those with the label do experience a set of symptoms and that their lives are shaped by this experience. Thus, the contributions of different approaches need to be recognized, as well as the limitations of a particular approach highlighted. To study dementia from a social science perspective requires an understanding of the various theoretical starting points for the key disciplines and professions which are interested in dementia and dementia care. It requires a critical and questioning approach to the perspectives offered by different disciplines as has been argued in detail by Harding and Palfrey (1997). Questioning the assumptions underlying care policies and principles is a necessity before it is really possible to begin to understand care practices, and why and how such practices may be deemed to be inadequate and thus need to be challenged to promote change for people with dementia and their carers.

Before moving on to consider policy frameworks, we explored the political, economic and social contexts (Chapter 2) that create the climate for the study of dementia. As such, policy decisions cannot be seen in isolation from the political, economic and social concerns of a society, nor can they be easily separated from the dominant theoretical discourses surrounding the applied nature of the dementia world.

Chapter 3 considered how this theorizing about dementia is operationalized into ideas about dementia care and the subsequent framework of principles and policies upon which dementia care is then based. These utopian ideals reflect a step between abstract thinking and day-to-day practice and experiences of dementia. Care principles and policies can be seen not only to reflect the theoretical contributions from disciplines and professions, but also from within the social context dementia and dementia care is located. This helps to move knowledge forward from theoretical discourses and the policy and principles surrounding dementia care, to look specifically at the day-to-day challenges of providing dementia care, and meeting the somewhat utopian ideals offered by abstract theoretical thought and the somewhat disconnected social, political and economic context of dementia care provision.

Culture was used in two ways in Chapter 4 to demonstrate some of the gaps between theorizing, policy making and practices. Cultural groupings were first explored, either across countries or cultural groupings within countries, demonstrating the diversity in experiences and the gaps in knowledge about experiences of dementia and dementia care across different groupings of people. The chapter then moved on to consider the cultures that those who receive and provide care operate within. By looking at cultures of care settings it was possible to explore what is acceptable, what is expected, and what may be open to challenge and further debate within care settings and in turn by wider society. This chapter thus provided examples of how theory, policy and practice can diverge and the difficulties in applying these components of dementia studies systematically. The social, political and economic contexts that shape individuals' lives are also illustrated by the use of 'culture', as it demonstrates the complexity of living with dementia and how where one is cared for, which cultural grouping one is allocated or belongs to, shapes the experiences of dementia and dementia care.

Those who research dementia care are informed by theoretical discourse and are, or arguably should be, aware of care principles and policy frameworks shaping dementia care practices. Thus, research can provide a way to evaluate, reflect on, offer challenges to and further knowledge about theory, policy and practice. Chapter 5 considered the empirical study of dementia care. It highlighted tension in methods, topic of enquiry, personal interests and funders' control over the research agenda. Research (including evaluation) can offer a way to move knowledge, policy and practice forward, as well as to consolidate existing views. However, if the underpinning ideas shaping the conceptualizations of dementia are not articulated, it becomes difficult to challenge existing knowledge and move our knowledge of this field forward.

Research applications will often clearly state the starting points for the researcher's proposal, for example a concern to hear the views of people with dementia, or to ease the burden experienced by caregivers. However, published work resulting from research may not articulate this as clearly. The intention may be to promote the 'findings' of the research rather than raise questions about what this means for our knowledge about dementia and dementia care. This type of writing may be the task of a different paper. This means that the accounts of research available in published formats are partial and incomplete. The task of those studying, and indeed researching dementia, is to pull these different research outputs together to make sense of the area they are studying: a complex undertaking.

This final chapter builds on the preceding arguments by presenting a model for the study of dementia. This model stresses the importance of taking into account theorizing, policy principles and ideals, care practices and social science research. An awareness of all these areas is important for those interested in dementia to enable a social science of dementia to emerge in the future. A social science that will help to establish dementia studies as a discipline in its own right.

A model for the study of dementia from a social science perspective

It is clear that dementia affords opportunities for the medicalization of symptoms, and opportunities for psychosocial interventions to meet the care needs of people with dementia and the support needs of those providing care. Dementia also affords social gerontologists the opportunity to highlight the social, political and economic context of dementia care and the lived realities of those with dementia. Social science can add to such worthy concerns through opportunities to extend, challenge and stimulate debates about what dementia is, what this means for care principles and ideals, and through research, whether any of this is apparent at the coalface of dementia care practices.

'We have come to know that every individual lives, from one generation to the next, in some society; that he lives out a biography, and that he lives it out within some historical sequence' (Mills, 1959: 10), is a reminder from a seminal work that research, in this case dementia research, has to be contextualized within personal experiences that are grounded within a social context at a particular moment in time. Thus, the importance of contextualizing the study of dementia within past and current theorizing, policies and practice cannot be understated.

Of course, applying a social science perspective to the study of dementia is but one way to examine, explore and begin to understand how knowledge has been developed, applied and challenged to a distinct phenomenon commonly known as 'dementia'. It is, however, a place to position challenges to existing knowledge in this field. There are interesting parallels that can be drawn between movements in the dementia field and the disability movement.

Disability was initially located within a medical model, which is similar to initial understandings of dementia which were initially derived from a medical model of dementia where the disease is emphasized. The social theory of disability stressed the discrimination and barriers those with a disability faced within society; 'Disability is therefore an outcome of social attitudes and structures, and the interaction between the person and environmental factors' (Gannon and Nolan, 2007: 1426).

This shift has also been occurring for dementia; a social model of dementia has emerged (Lyman, 1989; Bond, 1992; Harding and Palfrey 1997; Downs, 2000) where wider social factors are taken into account. The social model of disability argued that the solution to disability was not a cure for impairments but for social and political solutions to challenge and address the discrimination faced by disabled people (Oliver, 1996). Although the search for future cures for those with dementia is a laudable enterprise if it will alleviate future

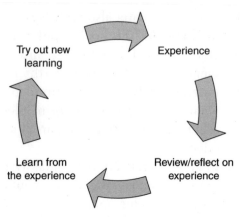

Figure 6.1   A learning cycle – adapted from Kolb, David, A., *Experimental Learning*
© 1984: 42. Adapted with the permission of Pearson Education Inc., Upper Saddle River, NJ.

suffering, the challenge is first to acknowledge the discrimination faced by people with dementia on multiple levels, for example on the basis of age, mental health and gender, and then to challenge and address such discrimination and the impact such discrimination has on the experience of living with dementia.

A useful starting point in considering how we may develop our thinking about dementia is found through Kolb's (1984) notion of a learning cycle (Figure 6.1). This begins with what Kolb described as a concrete experience (experience or problem); reflective observation (when the individual reflects on the experience or problem encountered); abstract conceptualization (when they then move on to think about what they have learnt from that experience); and, finally, active experimentation (where one tests this new learning out in practice).

Studying dementia could be understood as thinking about a problem (dementia), reflecting on that problem, thinking about other ways of looking at it and then testing this out in practice, which then goes on to influence theorizing or thinking about dementia. Of course, the starting point may be thinking about why dementia has been labelled, as a problem in the first place!

Thus, applying a cyclical learning process to the aspects of dementia studies that this book has argued are important, could mean a cyclical process where one starts by thinking about what dementia is, what policies exist to support this view of dementia, the care practices that follow on from policy, that may then be researched and the findings of which then influence thinking or theorizing about dementia (Figure 6.2).

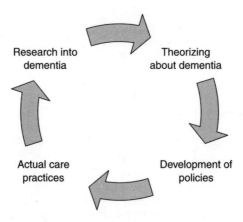

Figure 6.2   Applying the notion of a cyclical process for the study of dementia

However, the process of moving between theory, policy, practice and research is not a simple stage process where one moves from one stage to another and then continues to do so in a cyclical way. Rather, dementia studies may involve looking at policies, then moving back to considering the ideas that shaped these. Care practices may be considered from a research evidence base or from a policy framework angle, or, again, from ideas that shape understandings about dementia. Thus, the way in which studies of dementia progress will vary according to the primary focus of interest. However, for our knowledge of dementia to move forward, the interplay between all of these factors needs to be considered. Otherwise, our knowledge base will not substantially alter.

In Figure 6.3, I present a model for the study of dementia. This model requires that those studying dementia think about the theorizing that underpins their understandings about dementia and the assumptions they then have about the nature of dementia. For example, is dementia viewed as a disease with distinct stages that require different care interventions at different points in time? Or, alternatively, is dementia viewed as a socially constructed label applied in ways that result in stigma and marginalization of those who hold the label? Thinking about what dementia is, or indeed is not, provides one way of questioning existing beliefs about dementia that shape care ideals.

Ideas about care presented, for example, in care policy frameworks are not just a result of thinking about dementia; they also reflect the political, social and economic contexts at a particular

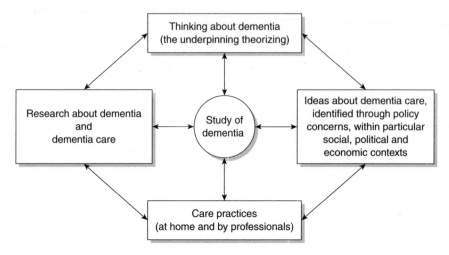

Figure 6.3   A model for studying dementia

moment in time. Political, economic and social concerns collide and help to shape the policy decisions that will shape the experiences of care. Research about dementia is an enterprise spanning disciplines and countries; this suggests a universal interest or concern about dementia. This may be partially explained by the demographic time bomb images used effectively by lobbying bodies to grab the attention of governments, or it may be due to a personal interest in the lives and experiences of older people, and those with dementia in particular. The concern may be about how to provide care interventions that impact positively on the well-being/quality of life of those with dementia.

Research questions reflect individuals' personal research interests, approaches to research represent different disciplinary backgrounds and different methods reflect different preferences in how to do research that answers the questions of interest to researchers. It has also been argued that 'socially shaped hierarchies of power inform questions of research method, and they are also inevitably present in the research process' (Oakley, 1999: 160). Research that is funded illustrates the particular concerns of funding bodies that reflect in turn the political, economic and social concerns at a particular time. Funded research is one example of power hierarchies at work, as the concerns of funders may not be the concerns of those researched.

The interplay between theory, policy, practice and research is where the study of dementia sits. As such, the study of dementia can be visualized as a web, where various strands of theory, policy making, practice ideas and research meet. Different individuals will spin different webs in their 'story' or accounts of dementia, reflecting their starting points for their story and the extent to which, for example, a concern with care practices is woven into the web.

Thinking about dementia, that is, theorizing about dementia, influences the ideas about appropriate dementia care. Thus, the underlying beliefs about dementia manifest themselves in ideas about cure and care. Wider social, political and economic issues influence the ideas put forward about dementia care that may or may not be supported by policy recommendations from states, special interest groups and care providers. Care practice, that is, the reality of care provided at home and in institutions shaping the experiences of those with dementia and those who observe dementia in others, is in turn influenced by the various theories about dementia and how these are operationalized on a day-to-day basis through care principles and ideals.

The social science research that is conducted into 'dementia' is influenced by theorizing about dementia (the researcher's own theorizing influenced by dominant thinkers/writers of the time), the policy and ideas framework surrounding dementia care, and the care practices that are reported by others and observed during research. Thus, research reports may impact on thinking about dementia at micro or macro levels (practice or theory levels, for example) and pose a challenge to ideas about dementia care that are in turn used to support or challenge common care practices that are then subject to research scrutiny and empirical enquiry. Bond (2001) has argued that sociology can be used in the study of dementia in two ways. First, as a sociology of dementia, where dementia is seen as a 'social state of affairs' (2001: 60), which can be demonstrated through recognition of the social context of dementia and the different perceptions health professionals, family carers and the person with dementia may hold about experiences of dementia. Putney et al. (2005) talk about social gerontology as public sociology in action. They suggest that it is 'social gerontology's commitment to help older people and solve the mysteries of old age and ageing that energizes and inspires, whether the domain is professional, critical, policy or public' (2005: 100). Dementia studies can be seen as part of this application of public sociology where the 'problems' that dementia brings to society in relation to the projected increase in the costs of dementia and the need for care services can be brought to the attention of the public, policy makers and the media (all of which have occurred in recent times). Thus, the sociological enterprise can be applied through dementia as the topic of enquiry.

The second way Bond suggests that sociology can be used in the study of dementia is through sociology in dementia care. This involves applying specific sociological concepts to dementia and dementia care. An example of applying sociological theory to the study of ageing generally comes from Powell and Biggs (2003) where they apply the ideas of Foucault to the study of ageing. Transferable to the study of dementia in their application of Foucault to understanding ageing is their point that 'Historical critique should be used to shatter taken for granted assumptions surrounding aging' (Powell and Biggs, 2003: 3). The study of dementia from a social science perspective involves looking at the broader context surrounding thinking about ideas about dementia, challenging them and presenting alternative ways of knowing and understanding what dementia means for those who experience this condition. As such, the 'shattering' of taken-for-granted assumptions can be seen as a key area of work for social scientists studying dementia.

The sociological concepts most applied to the study of dementia have come from the sociology of health and illness. In their discussion of common conceptualizations used in the sociology of health and illness, Kelly and Field (1998) demonstrate two common approaches, which come from structuralist or interpretivist positions. Discussing a structuralist approach, Kelly and Field (1998: 4) highlight the focus on the experience of an illness expanding from the biological pathology of chronic disease to the disruption of social relationships. Kitwood (1997) presents an example of this tradition, as he sought to bring attention to the Malignant Social Psychology experienced by people with dementia. Thus, the experience of dementia is more than the biological pathology, but the disruption of social relationships. Discussing interpretivist conceptualizations of the sociology of health and illness, Kelly and Field (1998: 7) describe the focus of interest on the self of the person with the illness and attempts to maintain identity when a particular label has been applied. For example, the strength of critical gerontology is that it sees that individuals are 'active agents who can change the nature of their social environments' (Putney et al., 2005: 92), which, if applied to the study of dementia, brings to the fore the person with dementia as not the object of care but a partner in the care process who can influence by his/her actions the experience of dementia.

This movement towards recognizing the agency of those with dementia can also be seen within the study of dementia with the work of Sabat (2001), who was concerned about the self of those with dementia (discussed in Chapter 1), and Clare (2004), who is concerned about the self awareness of those with dementia and their attempts to negotiate their identity while living with the label of dementia. Thus, it can be seen that studying dementia from a social science perspective takes account of conceptualizations of health and illness found within the sociology of health and illness. This is an example of using sociology in the study of dementia described by Bond (2001).

Applying ideas from the sociology of knowledge to the study of dementia

To further illustrate my ideas about the study of dementia I will borrow from another body of sociological work – the sociology of knowledge. This is a particular area of sociological enquiry which is concerned with the organization of knowledge, and by knowledge I mean ideas that are accepted by certain social groups or wider society. The sociology of knowledge can be broadly conceived of as the study of social origins of ideas, and the impact prevailing ideas have on societies/sections of society.

There are two sociological or philosophical terms used when thinking about knowledge production. The first is epistemology, which is essentially concerned with knowledge and knowing, so it sets out to address: 'What is knowledge?' and 'How is knowledge acquired?' Critical gerontology in particular has tried to address such questions in relation to understandings of the position of older people in society, and the implications this has for the knowledge produced (von Kondratowitz, 2003) with stress placed on the importance of acknowledging the standpoint adopted by the researcher (Holstein and Minkler 2007). Estes (2001a) has argued that the situated nature of different knowledge and the influence of dominant theoretical approaches must be acknowledged to help develop a more scientific epistemology in gerontology, the same sentiments could be applied to the study of dementia: the dominance of bio-medical perspectives must be recognized and alternative ways of knowing should not be discounted if we are to further develop understandings and knowledge about dementia. Biggs and Powell argue that '"knowledge" as a socially constituted category through which "power" is manifested and deployed' can be challenged so that the '"subject" becomes open to deconstructive scrutiny' (2001: 3).

Essentially, the study of dementia involves asking epistemological questions that seek to explore and challenge the assumptions that underlie what is 'known' about this condition. Doing this helps to identify the 'disciplinary techniques that constitute knowledge of subjects/objects' (Powell and Biggs, 2003: 11). Indeed, it has been argued that social gerontology (of which dementia studies can be seen to be closely related) 'continues to see epistemological debates surrounding different kinds of knowledge and the use of theory' and that different perspectives can provide 'complementary lenses that can broaden our understandings of the multiple facets of aging' (Putney et al., 2005: 96).

That dementia attracts the attention of a multitude of disciplines/professions with different perspectives is a way of pushing our knowledge forward. Thus, it is important not to discard 'knowledge' produced by any discipline, rather the task is to explore and critique such knowledge. As the study of ageing is a multi-disciplinary and applied enterprise, it is important to acknowledge the different ways of knowing that come from studying dementia from a biomedical, psychological or sociological perspective, for example. This is very similar to the study of ageing, where it has been stressed that an important feature of gerontology is its multidisciplinary and applied character, with the relationship between the theories underlying research and the policy developed as a result are closely linked (Biggs et al., 2003a). Thus, it is important to recognise and question the 'knowledge' that is presented to us about what dementia is and what this means for, and how it relates to, care policies and care practices.

It must be remembered that social researchers looking at dementia can do much the same as social gerontologists who 'approach problems and issues from various theoretical or epistemological perspectives ... . Indeed because the best social gerontological research is likely to consider the motives and interests of all groups ... researchers are not put in the position of "taking sides'" (Putney et al., 2005: 99), and thus avoid the pitfalls in trying to answer the question, 'Whose side are we on?' posed by Becker (1967) that was referred to in Chapter 1 of this book. Rather than 'taking sides', the study of dementia involves acknowledging, recognizing and interrogating the knowledge that is presented about dementia from a range of different perspectives stemming from different disciplinary starting points and using this information to further our understandings and knowledge about dementia and what this means for dementia care.

A second term that is often confused with epistemology is ontology – ontology refers to a particular way of looking at the nature of social reality. In practice, this can involve asking questions or revisiting questions in novel ways and has been argued to be one way to develop theory in gerontology (Biggs et al., 2003b), a related field that dementia studies can arguably learn much from. By challenging the knowledge we have about dementia, from a range of standpoints, it is possible to move beyond the traditional paradigm constraints which perceive dementia as a disease with an inevitable decline to explore what it means for different people who are living with or caring for people with dementia. Remembering ontological views is important to the study of dementia as much 'knowledge' of dementia is based on a biomedical way of looking at this condition.

Further, biomedicine still holds much of the power in decisions about the care and lives people with dementia live. Those with dementia are perhaps typical of the example Biggs and Powell give where, 'Those who are labelled "old" are in the grip of power, this power would include that operated by professionals through institutions and face to face interactions with their patients and clients' (2001: 97). Those labelled with dementia are immediately placed in a less powerful position, and, indeed, as was highlighted in Chapter 5, it is only relatively recently in the history of dementia research that the views of those with dementia are now being actively sought.

Epistemology and ontology have been debated widely within the social sciences, and it is not my intention here to review or enter such debates. Rather, my purpose is to highlight that the sociology of

145

knowledge provides us with some tools to study dementia. However, for those interested in further exploring theory and research practice links, an accessible account is provided by Layder (1998).

To return to the study of dementia, if the broad questions guiding the sociology of knowledge are about the origins of ideas and the impact ideas have for societies, then we can begin to consider what this might mean if applied to the study of dementia. Dementia studies requires one to look at the social origins of the ideas about dementia and the effects such ideas have on dementia care practices. So, to resume with the analogy of the web, the study of dementia can be seen as weaving a web. Different webs may be in evidence that begin with different theoretical assumptions or different ideas about care practices, but such ideas bring together a range of thoughts and approaches about what dementia is and what appropriate care practices should involve.

To give an example, a dementia studies 'web' founded on biomedical understandings of dementia may be presented in the following way (Figure 6.4): as a disease, which requires treatment. Thus, policy frameworks should support the need to administer treatment. Research may then be interested in the effectiveness of treatments, but ideas of effectiveness will be framed from the starting point of dementia is a disease which requires treatment.

It is useful when thinking about knowledge surrounding dementia to stop and think a little more about the different theoretical approaches that influence the discourse surrounding dementia care. Are the different

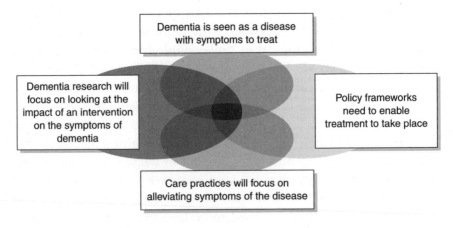

Figure 6.4   A web of understanding about dementia – from a medical viewpoint

theoretical assumptions of the approaches that influence the study of dementia which we considered in Chapter 1 so far apart? Do they all not seek to understand what dementia is, how to support/care for people with dementia and their carers? They may do so in different ways, but dementia studies alerts us to the usefulness of a variety of approaches in the quest to know more about dementia and to develop care practices and policies, accordingly. Just as the health care disabled people receive is influenced by theories about disability (Oliver, 1998), so too is the care offered to people with dementia based on theories about dementia.

Deciding on whose accounts of dementia to listen to and write about provides an example of the impact that our decisions, based on our implicit understandings of dementia, have on the knowledge we have about dementia and dementia care. Who we decide to include demonstrates how important those whose stories we listen to are perceived; policy, practice and theory influence whose stories we select to hear. The accounts we hear and report on will then impact again on future decision making about care practices. As one of the first to explore knowledge construction has said, 'A given social position so limits one's point of view as to obscure various facets of the situation under scrutiny' (Merton, 1937: 497). If we choose to hear what professionals have to say, we will have their views; if we ask caregivers, we have their views. If we do not include the voices of those who have dementia then we will miss aspects of their experiences that can help us shape knowledge about what dementia 'is' and means for those labelled.

Hammersley (2000: 5) suggests that there are two broad approaches to thinking about knowledge; that objective knowledge is possible if a rigorous enquiry process is followed, through epistemological privilege and through involvement in practice. The other approach would argue that objective knowledge is not possible, as research is simply a political device that can be used to serve particular goals, because such research should be pursued in a way to realize ethical human relations. Depending on the perspective one adopts, that it is possible to produce definitive knowledge, or that knowledge will be partial and incomplete, will have a bearing on the approach to studying dementia and dementia care. However, Oakley argues that the question should not be about particular approaches characterized through the use of particular methods, but to consider how best to match methods to research questions and to find ways of 'integrating methods to carry out socially useful inquiries' (1999: 66). The study of dementia then is open to the same concerns of researching any complex social phenomenon (Bond and Corner, 2001).

As individuals begin to pose questions about the expertise of the medical profession at the expense of forgetting about the expertise of those who live with a condition, the medical dominance evident within dementia studies may begin to erode: 'Without some element of trust exhibited by ordinary members of society towards experts, expertise would vanish' (Stehr, 2003: 648). In the case of dementia, medical expertise is unlikely to vanish, but it may diminish as lobbying groups and researchers suggest alternative ways of seeing what the experience of dementia involves. The dementia field lags behind developments in the disability field where research now actively seeks the involvement of disabled people at all stages of the research process and where medical assumptions are readily challenged (Oliver, 1998). Thus, challenges from other groups labelled as 'disabled' are leading to changes in thinking and conceptualizations about disability.

It can be seen that research about dementia is now including the views of people with dementia (discussed in Chapter 5) but that there has yet to be a major political movement similar to research on disability. The dementia field has reflected, albeit at a slower pace, developments in the gerontological field in the 1980s and 1990s, where critique of biomedical models prevailed alongside a traditional gerontological approach which was very individualistic and failed to call attention to social structures and economic contexts of the ageing experience (Biggs et al., 2003a). A critical gerontology has been called for that involves 'a critical approach to theory and policy ... that goes beyond everyday appearances and the unreflective acceptance of established positions. It examines the structural inequalities that shape the everyday experience of growing old' (Biggs et al., 2003a: 3). Those studying dementia should be mindful of this call, as, if the field of dementia is to move forward and develop, it is essential that established positions are critiqued.

Kitwood (1997) roundly critiqued what he called the standard paradigm or medical model of dementia care and introduced what is in essence an individualistic approach to looking at people with dementia. What is needed now in the dementia field is a move forward from this individualistic or micro level of analysis to one that examines the social structures that shape the position of those with dementia, as 'without an understanding of social structure ... an overly humanistic approach to ageing is isolated from context and history' (Biggs et al., 2003a: 147). This, of course, applies to a condition that older people may experience, dementia, the focus of this book, and as has been demonstrated, the field is slowly moving beyond the individual as the unit of analysis in taking dementia knowledge forward. Just as social gerontology has been described as being 'inherently multidisciplinary' and to involve the 'borrowing' of ideas from a range of disciplines to help develop insights into aspects of ageing and to 'engaging multiple publics and working toward improvements in well-being' (Putney et al., 2005: 101–2), so, too, does the study of dementia involve building on one's starting discipline and then 'borrowing' ideas from different disciplines to help gain insights and understanding about dementia.

The dementia literature contains a growing number of accounts which include the perspective of those with dementia (see Chapter 5). Could this be seen as a move towards self knowledge where 'expert' knowledge can now be questioned – and, indeed, in time may develop to expert knowledge being openly questioned by those with dementia? If those with dementia share their views and experiences and their attempts to preserve their identity become more widespread, this will impact on what is known about dementia and therefore the taken-for-granted 'knowledge' that forms part of our common discourse in this very applied field of research, policy and practice.

Merton, discussing the work of Mannheim, suggests that, 'The sociology of knowledge could itself arise only in such a society where, with the emergence of new and the destruction of old basic values, the very foundations on which an opponent's beliefs rest are challenged' (Merton, 1937: 499). Thus, the study of dementia requires new ideas and values to emerge. The work of Kitwood (1997) is an example of a challenge to conventional wisdom about dementia, suggesting that the person did remain despite loss of abilities and memory. This was in stark contrast to the popular view of the time of his earlier writings that dementia was a disease that left the shell of the person. Thus, Kitwood's (1997) talk of a paradigm shift represented a challenge to the foundations of the beliefs of the dominant ideology of biomedicine.

Writh, in his preface to Mannheim's work, discusses problems that can be tests of facts. These include:

- Studies of the social evaluation of types of knowledge and of the factors determining the proportion of social resources devoted to each of these types. (1936: x)

If we apply this to the study of dementia, we can consider the move towards researching care as well as cures for dementia as new types of knowledge that are emerging.

- Studies of the conditions under which new problems and disciplines arise and decline. (Ibid., p. x)

Applying this to the study of dementia, this book has demonstrated the demographic time bomb that dementia has been problematized within. It also demonstrates the growth of interest in this field, a topic of study is emerging as a discipline in its own right, influenced by the core disciplines of medicine, psychology and social gerontology, itself a throw-off from sociology.

- Determination of the shifts in the foci of intellectual interest which are associated with changes in the social structure (changes in differentiation, stratification). (Ibid., p. x)

The developments in theorizing about dementia over time demonstrate a range of intellectual interests, some concerned with the impact of social structures on the agency of individuals with dementia (shown in Kitwood's (1997) work on personhood and Sabat's (2001) work on the self). The interest in cultures of care in care institutions demonstrates an interest in the way people are marginalized and excluded on the basis of difference that has stigma attached to it (discussed in Chapter 4). Hulko's (2004) work exploring the privileges and oppressions that impact on the experience of dementia reflects a move towards looking at the social position individuals or groupings of individuals occupy that will impact on the experience of dementia. Thus, we may be at a crossroads where our knowledge base about dementia care can radically develop and move forward.

How we might achieve developments in our knowledge has been suggested as falling to research: 'The burden of further research is to turn from this welter of conflicting opinion to empirical investigations which may establish in adequate detail the uniformities pertaining to the appearance, acceptance and diffusion, or rejections and repression, development and consequences of knowledge and ideas' (Merton, 1937: 503). Thus, those researching dementia can use the conflicting ideas that are present in theoretical discourses about dementia to conduct empirical work that can question conventional and contemporary ideas and wisdom.

However, doing 'new' research that breaks with traditional approaches may present itself with some practical problems. An example is that those seeking to hear the views of people with dementia have to defer to the medical professions' dominance, work within their approach and language to enable ethics approval to be granted to undertake research with people with dementia. Thus, the language used demonstrates a status differential, so, although many may intuitively like the idea and use of the phrase of 'a person with dementia', there appears in the literature the phrase 'dementia sufferers' which may be used even when talking about person- or patient-centred care practices. Thus, it is likely that qualitative researchers in the dementia field will have to justify their approach to those who follow or understand the language of more positivistic perspectives using quantitative approaches, in a way that is typified within qualitative research generally (Becker, 2003).

Discussing the impact of a medical perspective of understanding dementia and the resulting burden on caregivers and costs to society, Antuono and Beyer (1999) demonstrate that a particular approach and the expert knowledge held by health professionals will lead to particular outcomes for people with dementia that pose profound ethical dilemmas. They conclude that 'Health-care professionals, caregivers and society may differ in the perceived worth of the patient with dementia, therefore issues of patient autonomy, physicians' benevolent paternalism, or truth in telling, become complex and challenging issues' (Antuono and Beyer, 1999: 11). Thus, expert knowledge and control over knowledge will impact on the information that a person with dementia receives, the treatment that they may or may not be offered and the resulting 'management' of their condition. This is a useful reminder of the use of expert power, language and control of health care professionals over the person with dementia, a position that is reflected in research trying to hear the views of people with dementia.

Becker (1996) argues that all social scientists have a point of view and place their interpretations on to the people we study. He suggests that the key question is not about the point of view we have but how accurately we report our findings. This means that our point of view has to be made clear. If we see dementia as a social construct, we need to present our research within this framework. If we see dementia as a disease requiring treatment, we need to state this clearly.

The danger, no matter what our opinion of dementia, is that we place our interpretations on people and that we may not get it right. By hearing proxy accounts we are even more likely to fail to hear what living with dementia is like. So, unless we hear from people with dementia themselves about their experiences of living with dementia, the danger is that we will not be getting it right, rather we will be putting our own views about what living with dementia is like. Even when we collect accounts from people with dementia we are still likely to place our own interpretations of events through our selection of quotes, and the themes we choose to structure our discussion of findings. Thus, whose views are heard and whose accounts presented, are intrinsically important to questioning the knowledge we have about dementia and dementia care, and future accounts are crucial if we wish to generate new ways of thinking about dementia and generate new knowledge bases.

Those interested in including people with dementia tend to have a focus on questions they think need to be answered. So, the procedure to get the answers to such questions is not necessarily their primary concern, hence the anecdotal reports of difficulties with ethics boards representing the medical profession who control the knowledge of dementia and the information that is passed to families and the person themselves, rather than a concern to further knowledge about dementia based on what those with dementia have to say. This demonstrates a problem that arises when those from different disciplines are interested in the same research topic, where those who are in control and dominate the field can insist that their language is used to describe the research process, and are often powerful enough for their insistence to be adhered to. These more dominant voices can also insist that their viewpoint is more valid than the researchers from a less dominant discipline who seek to find new knowledge that may profoundly challenge what is 'known' about dementia.

Talking specifically about sociology, Becker's question of the relevance of sociology applies to social science research in general:

> The relevance of sociology consists in solving, or contributing to the solution of, the problem as someone has defined it. Which means that we should be very attentive to the way this or that situation is singled out as the kind of problem to which our work should be relevant. (Becker, 2003: 1)

When the findings of research arising from smaller numbers of participants who are often included in qualitative research are questioned for their relevance or their wider applicability, we have a classic case of those working within the dominant research paradigm (where results arise from research with a larger sample size), where dementia is viewed in a particular way (disease with inevitable decline), questioning the starting point of those interested in hearing the views of people with dementia. This leads researchers to having to justify themselves within a 'double whammy' effect, as they are not only questioning conceptualizations of dementia held by the 'experts', but are also conducting their research in a way that is not fully understood by those seeking to have large numbers of 'subjects' and generating statistics to 'prove' a cause and effect relationship.

This should not deter us from looking at new ways to understand and explore dementia and dementia care: 'Look at everything that might be worth looking at even when others think you're wrong, and don't worry about whether anyone finds your results useful. It's the best way to produce knowledge that will really work, if anyone is willing to try it' (Becker, 2003: 6). Although this may be difficult to do in practice, the impact of findings could be profound if, for example, those with power are willing to change the way they have 'always done' things.

Therefore, just as the sociology of health and illness has offered useful concepts that can be applied to the study of dementia, the sociology of knowledge offers conceptualizations that can be usefully applied to the study of dementia and reminds us of debates within the literature about the research enterprise that are also applicable to dementia study and research.

Citizenship, social inclusion and dementia

How then can we continue to push the boundaries of knowledge about dementia? Applying existing social science ideas to the study of dementia is one way to continue the challenge to conceptualizations of dementia that have now been in circulation for three decades or so. There are two related social science concepts that can be usefully applied to dementia studies, providing insight into the current state of play in the dementia field, and the advances required to move the study of dementia beyond that of an illness category or disease label, to a socially experienced condition that because of its disease and illness connotations has an impact on the social realities of those affected by dementia, people with dementia and their carers. These are citizenship and social inclusion.

Citizenship is an ideal of Western societies where individuals have rights and responsibilities. In the wider social science literature there have been long-standing conceptual debates and developments about what citizenship actually is (Turner, 1990), and whether citizenship is now being eroded (Turner, 2001). Turner (2001) demonstrates that citizenship has been traditionally associated with the ability to work, reproduce and fight. As older people move out of the paid workforce and are no longer able to fight or reproduce, the consequences are that they are likely not to be seen as full and active citizens. Rather, older people are perceived as a passive group who live out their lives in the private domain and who are likely to be in need of support and help, a position that Turner highlights is a false stereotype (2001, 195). Passive citizenship is, however, one of the domains identified by Turner (1990: 209), and the right to the provision of welfare and support is one of the classic foundations of citizenship conceptualizations (ibid., p. 212). However, as Townsend (2006) has noted, not all older people will experience the provision of welfare in a way that promotes basic human values of dignity, choice and respect. For example, citizenship is not something that everyone will experience equally age, gender, class are but some of the factors that will influence how the rights and benefits citizens can expect (Estes, 2001b). The presence of dementia and the associated cognitive impairment is but another dimension in how the notion of rights will be applied to those citizens afflicted with the label of this condition.

Feminist critiques of citizenship pose the challenge that for individuals to exercise their rights and responsibilities may require the facilitation of participation (Lister, 1997). This is particularly pertinent for the study of dementia, when the struggle to maintain the personhood or self of an individual with dementia through compassionate and empathic care practices have been clearly articulated (Kitwood, 1997; Sabat, 2001).

If it has been a struggle to see the person or self that remains with the advance of dementia, to apply a citizenship model requires a consideration of how to facilitate such an ideal. A social science view of dementia can usefully apply these ideas, and, in so doing, it can be demonstrated that people with dementia are cast as 'other', where their rights are often systematically diminished and the idea of preserving responsibility is simultaneously eroded. Dementia studies can again draw on insights from disability research: Oliver and Barnes argue that disability or impairment are linked with 'social isolation, stigmatisation or second class citizenship' (1998: 66). Dangers of limited application of ideals of citizenship for older people have also been noted:

> Dominant economic interests and privilege are preserved by not examining as equally valid options the opposing thought structures of constructing and implementing other systems of governance that would promote a citizen right to the benefits of health and long term care and to an adequate quality of life with economic security. (Estes, 2001a: 234–5)

Thus, inequality and social exclusion can be perpetuated, even when the ideals of rights implied by citizenship are supposedly a cornerstone of social policy. As such, social inclusion is a concept that can be closely aligned to citizenship. The disability field again highlights the importance of seeing disability as an 'outcome of social attitudes and structures and the interaction between the person and environmental factors' (Gannon and Nolan, 2007: 1426). Thus, it is important to bear in mind the dynamics between disability and social inclusion when thinking about how to achieve citizenship. The concept of social inclusion and its association with social justice for all, regardless of social grouping, has been embraced by governments (Scottish Executive, 2007) who seek to find ways to promote equality across social divisions such as race, gender, age and disability. Thus, addressing social inequalities has a political life that can help to deal with

155

concerns about the exclusion of any particular group, as well as those with dementia.

We can easily apply the insights from disability research about citizenship and social inclusion to dementia. The stigma attached to dementia was discussed in Chapter 4, where it was seen that the stigma dementia attracts can lead to a process of social exclusion. The label 'dementia' thus promotes social isolation, rather than social inclusion where the person can participate within society through exercising rights and responsibilities, and the resulting 'care' people receive leads to a second-class citizenship, where the rights of an individual are systematically eroded as the disease progresses and health care professionals increasingly take over decision making.

The concept of citizenship has been applied within a European context to long-term care for older people. Leichsenring (2004: 42–3) suggests that conceptualizations of long-term care have moved along a continuum from 'poor law' to 'citizens rights' ideals. Thus, the goal of long-stay care to house society's poor has moved towards a model where society seeks to ensure all its members have rights, no matter where they reside. However, the combination of having a dementia coupled with institutionalised living is likely to detract from the promotion of the social inclusion citizenship requires. In addition, the lack of human rights, a basic tenet of citizenship can be eroded by the structured dependency that continues to be prevalent in the way the position of older people is understood (Townsend, 2007). Townsend presents a series of examples to demonstrate how the treatment of older people in care homes do not uphold a basic human rights of dignity, for example in not providing pain relief to a dying woman and expecting people to eat breakfast while sitting on a commode (2007: 36). Thus, the provision of welfare, a basic tenet of citizenship (Turner, 1990), is not always applied to older people in receipt of care.

Early indications of aspects of citizenship as important to dementia research can be seen in the concern with the rights of the person with dementia to a diagnosis and concerns to seek consent to be involved in research by the person with dementia themselves (Downs, 1997: 599). Citizenship and dementia may be first seen as an odd combination, however, although dementia may take independence and communication abilities away, it does not take away the human. By promoting relationships to preserve citizenship, the person with dementia can remain part of society, where inclusiveness is valued and the voices of all citizens are heard (Brannelly, 2007). Townsend argues that 'used best, human rights offer a framework of thought and planning that will enable society to take a fresh and hopeful direction' (2006: 177). Applying a human rights framework to the care of people with dementia would enable practitioners and families to think about how far the care environment meets such ideals or whether in fact the long-standing dependency of older people is being reinforced (Townsend, 2006), and in turn to what extent the voices of all citizens are heard.

An interesting paper by Bartlett and O'Connor (2007) argues that applying a citizenship lens to the study of dementia places emphasis on the socio-political nature of living with dementia that helps move the focus from a micro level–where the 'personhood' of an individual with dementia is the focus of study – to the macro level, which considers the broader social context of dementia and dementia care. In many ways, the increasing recognition of the need to look at both micro (individual) and macro (structural level) issues reflects developments in gerontology. However, there has been a time lag in mapping the theoretical developments in, for example, gerontology, from the individual as the unit of analysis, to the consideration of broader social forces (Estes, 2003), to the study of dementia. Of course, an inclusive study of dementia requires both micro and macro levels of analysis to occur. The concepts of personhood and citizenship allow such an approach to the study of dementia. Applying the concept of citizenship to the care for people with dementia, Brannelly (2004: 11) found that for those living in the community, care packages reaffirmed the personhood and agency of the care recipient. However, she also suggests that the micro level of care practice is open to contradictions, in that legal frameworks can take away the capacity of people with dementia to make decisions (Brannelly, 2004: 13), while simultaneously, good care practice demands the views of the person with dementia to be considered. Thus, it is through adhering to good practice ideals rather than citizenship models that enables citizenship to be upheld. The tension between care and policy ideals may not necessarily always promote or lead to citizenship or person-centred care for people with dementia receiving care.

Yet, notions of citizenship are evolving over time (Turner, 2001). As Townsend (2006) has noted, human rights provides one way of extending and developing ideas about challenging ideas of dependency, which could in turn promote the use of conceptualizations of citizenship as a way to approach the care and support of older people. Turner argues that new forms of citizenship emerge as global social issues arise which are characterized by 'new causal processes that are more closely connected with social movements, status contradictions and identity' (2001: 204). Application of the concept of citizenship to the study of dementia (Brannelly, 2004, 2007; Bartlett and O'Connor, 2007) may perhaps be a clear indication that dementia is now recognized as an international phenomenon. Alongside this is a growing awareness of the marginal position that people with dementia are or have been relegated to, based in part on erroneous assumptions about a loss of identity that has been perceived to accompany the diagnosis of dementia. The works of Sabat (2001, 2002, 2006) and Clare (2003, 2004), in particular, challenge assumptions about loss of identity, and there has been a growing attention given to the need for the social inclusion of people with dementia (Innes et al., 2004).

The concepts of citizenship and social inclusion offer those studying dementia opportunities to broaden the research, practice and policy agendas beyond individual examples of good quality care provision in one specific area at one moment in time, to research, policy and practice that encompasses individual and collective levels of analysis to understanding the social worlds of people with dementia. Locating the study of dementia within broader debates relating to older people where social gerontology is seen as an expression of public sociology in action (Putney et al., 2005), where the human rights of older people are seriously considered (Townsend 2006, 2007) and where social changes are being charted which have global significance, such as changes in what it means to be a 'citizen' (Turner, 2001). These are some ways where dementia studies can contextualize understandings of dementia while simultaneously learn from other related areas of academic enquiry. As Cantley and Bowes (2004: 265–6) have argued, social inclusion of people with dementia is more than focusing on specialist services or defining a 'group' as having special needs. Doing so may serve to exclude those who do not have the same special need. It does not reflect the multiple 'groups' that an individual may belong to, and, further, a focus on 'special' cases can serve to reinforce stereotyping and exclusion.

Tantalizingly, Parkes suggests that we must consider how the disease (dementia) and its characteristics are interpreted by the sufferer, carer, professionals and wider society as 'these understandings have a great bearing upon the approaches to intervention taken and in a wider sense the policies and care provided' (2001: 341). The question is how to do this? By adopting a model for studying dementia outlined above (Figure 6.3), it may be possible to consider, and most importantly to question, the knowledge that we have about dementia, how it is generated and perpetuated and the impact this has on the care ideals advanced by policy makers and organizational providers of care. Gerdner et al. (2007) offer one rare example of a research study exploring meanings and approaches to care for those with dementia living in one ethnic community and contextualizes this within local economic and social history. This approach has not been systematically applied, particularly for mainstream populations, with a further step in the analysis of linking such understandings and conceptualizations to policy making and care decisions a recurring omission.

Linking knowledge to policy frameworks to practice situations is not a new idea. Applying this idea systematically to the study of dementia is perhaps a rarer occurrence. This is not surprising, however, given the relatively passive position people with dementia are placed in, where attempts at resistance are too often interpreted as challenging behaviour, that may be renamed behaviours that challenge in an attempt to follow the person-centred philosophy of Kitwood (1997) and other like-minded contemporaries.

If the task of a social study of dementia is to bring to the centre a group traditionally cast at the margins of discourse (in the tradition described by bell hooks (1984)) then there are numerous challenges to be addressed. First, should the study of dementia be mainstreamed into existing academic disciplines and discourses, or should it emerge as an area of study in its own right in a similar way to the emergence of gender studies or race studies as academic fields of enquiry (Anderson and Collins, 1995)? Just as social gerontology can be seen to encompass a range of perspectives (Bond et al., 1993), can the study of dementia progress to include a multitude of perspectives that will enhance our understandings and develop knowledge about dementia and dementia care? Or is it that much thinking surrounding research, policy making and notions of good or best practice is restricted by a lack of clarity about what dementia is? From a social science viewpoint, it can be seen that dementia is a social construction used to help decide how people with a medical label should be cared for or a medical condition to be diagnosed and then treated. The way dementia is socially constructed over time has and is likely

159

to continue to change and reflects the changes in the way old age generally has been constructed and dichotomized over time (von Kondratowitz, 2003: 49).

The social study of dementia allows for the adoption of an eclectic position to researching this complex social phenomenon. It is not possible to develop understanding about dementia without considering biomedical models which point to the causes, treatments, diagnosis and care needs of people with dementia. It is also important to remember the contribution of social psychology to identify the individual level characteristics that influence the experience of dementia. Just as important is to remember the wider social structures within which the experiences of the individual with dementia are located.

Using a case study, Bond et al. (2002) demonstrate the power and control that is exerted over a person with dementia because of the spouse's and health and social care provider's understandings of what having dementia means for safety and risk taking. Lay understandings about dementia are demonstrated, through the withdrawal of friendship and offers by contemporaries of the person with dementia to join them in running, for example, again a consensus by others about the lack of ability, appropriateness and risk taking that running would involve, is reached by those who do not have dementia, which has a marked impact on the person with dementia who still feels he would be able to run. Thus, the common knowledge held by people that those with dementia need to be protected from taking risks, and the control over the lifestyle of the person with dementia, are clearly illustrated, which echoes Powell's (2001) arguments about the loss of power of older people and the control exerted by care professionals.

Nolan et al. (2002) argue that for a truly inclusive vision for the future of dementia care practice and research to emerge requires a move towards 'relationship-centred care', where the importance of interaction between people is key rather than the more individualistic model suggested by 'person-centred care', an issue we considered in Chapter 3. Although it should be noted that Kitwood (1997: 10–12), who promoted the idea of person-centred care, clearly stated the need to recognize that for personhood to occur, the relationships of people with dementia needed to be nurtured. Relationships or sense of belonging are part of being socially included, that is, relationships within communities, rather than isolation within an institution. Similarly, taking away rights because of the health professionals' fear of lack of capacity or understanding on the part of the person with dementia, implies that the person has lost key aspects of citizenship, that is, the right to be involved in care decisions and to make decisions that may incur risk, but in an increasingly risk-averse society, the curtailment of citizenship for people with dementia appears likely to be a continuing theme.

Sociology and social gerontology can do much to alert the dementia scholar to the interlocking oppressions (Dressel et al., 1997) or privileges a person with dementia may experience, according to race, class, gender and age (to name the most studied social divisions in society). Thinking about social divisions alongside the economic concerns that shape policy and practice decisions about treatments and care for the person with dementia and those who provide care and support, and the resultant politicization of dementia is in large part due to the growing concern with the number who will be affected by dementia in the future (due to prevalence and incidence of dementia), and is one way to broaden out from the recurrent focus on the individual with dementia that does not take account of structural frameworks.

This book has demonstrated that there are now serious efforts underway to hear the views of people with dementia who have been excluded from research, and often excluded from the communities they were part of until their dementia posed problems to their continuing membership of those communities (for either the individual or the community). The stigma attached to dementia is being questioned. Marginalized areas within dementia studies have made valuable contributions to highlighting commonalities and differences that different groups of people who have dementia experience (see Chapter 4). Thus, that which has been excluded is now open to inclusion, in particular, including the views and voices of those with dementia and those who are paid to care. It is important to remember to contextualize the voices that are heard (Gubrium, 1992) to enable the individual to be located within broader social forces of a particular point in time. By doing so, the individual is the unit of analysis, while taking into account the broader social context of the experiences voiced.

Thus, the direction of future work in the dementia field may continue to move forward along the lines of that of the disability field where inclusion and citizenship ideals are being embraced (Oliver and Barnes, 1998), and in critical social gerontology where micro, meso and macro levels of analysis are being employed to understand the position of older people in society (Biggs et al., 2003b; Baars et al., 2006). This process is already in evidence in recent writings in the dementia field (Innes et al., 2004; Bartlett and O'Connor, 2007).

Knowledge of dementia: a history of confusion made orderly?

Dementia studies is in essence exploring knowledge about dementia and dementia care. Potentially, dementia studies can offer ways to develop and contribute to furthering knowledge about dementia by questioning contemporary thinking and challenging taken-for-granted assumptions about the nature of dementia and the resulting models of care offered to people with dementia.

Our knowledge about dementia is partial and incomplete, and based on this, services have developed that reflect this partial knowledge and also the dominant knowledge that determines the diagnosis a person may receive, and any further information and advice that may be offered. Fox (2000) presented a history of Alzheimer's disease movements, while Gubrium (1986) presented the history of the popularization of dementia. Both accounts go some way to demonstrating that knowledge about dementia can be used to great effect by lobbying bodies to raise interest and aware-ness in their particular cause, in this case Alzheimer's disease. Such accounts demonstrate how incomplete and conflicting ideas can be presented as a set of ideas that appear to be consensual. Just as dementia is typified as confusion – while attempts are made to con-trol this confusion by giving anti-dementia drugs or other treat-ments or interventions – with those whose behaviour or abilities are deemed too difficult or lacking and are removed from communities to care institutions, so we can see that society attempts to make this confusion an orderly procedure. Although our knowledge about dementia may be confusing, we can present it as a cohesive position (Harding and Palfrey, 1997).

Talking about mental illness, Aneshensel (1999: 601) urges us to remember that:

> The unique aspects of each person's experience should not obscure the com-monality in experience that arises because people encounter similar social sys-tems, institutions and processes, or because they occupy the same social role, that of psychiatric patient. ... the study of mental health deals as much with society as it does the psyche.

The study of dementia has to date moved outwards from the 'disease', to focusing on the individual person with dementia. It has as yet to move beyond this to examine fully the social systems and processes at work which will continue to define the experiences of those who have dementia. Future studies of dementia need to look at the micro level of experiences, especially the reported experiences of those with dementia themselves and this is an important development in this field. However, if the theoretical underpinnings about dementia are not examined, if policy frameworks are not questioned, how can care practices be effectively challenged and changed? Dementia studies is not just about the individual with dementia and their relationships with those who provide care. Dementia studies must move beyond this individualistic way of conceptualizing dementia and dementia care, to reach a position where social structures and processes are interrogated to illuminate the impact such structures and processes have on the lives of those with dementia. Then we shall perhaps be able to move forward our knowledge about dementia.

Thus, students – and by this I mean all those studying dementia – along the continuum of those who are new to this field, to those who are established in the dementia field today, are presented with a wealth of information that is presented as dementia knowledge. The challenge is to look past this information, to begin to question how such knowledge was arrived at, and what assumptions knowledge was based upon. In so doing, we may begin to be able to question the appropriateness of services offered and to understand why wholesale change and improvement has not occurred, despite the popularity of ideas about promoting the well-being of individuals with dementia and enhancing the care offered in a range of care settings. Changes are apparent – previously marginalized areas within the dementia field are now being addressed (Innes et al., 2004), thus posing questions about the extent to which the 'knowledge' base of dementia is partial and incomplete.

However, looking at distinct questions can lead to claims of research being esoteric and not addressing wider issues. Nevertheless, the question should be, how can esoteric research and insights help to further debate and knowledge about a condition that remains challenging and difficult for those who live with dementia and those who provide care and support to them? How we move beyond a theoretical, policy and research position that has placed emphasis on the individual or on a particular care service, to developing knowledge that embraces the structural, cultural and individual factors, is key to the future of dementia studies.

■ ■ Further reading ■

Both Layder's (1998) and Hammersley's (2000) books provide useful discussion of the links and tensions in the theory, methods and practice of research. Harding and Palfrey's (1997) book is an excellent example of questioning and critiquing existing knowledge about dementia and considering what this means for dementia care practice. Oliver's (1996) book provides an accessible account of understanding disability that could be developed and applied to the study of dementia.

REFERENCES

Adams, T. (2005) 'From person-centred care to relationship-centred care', *Generations Review*, 15 (1): 4–7.

Adams, T. (2008) 'Nursing people with dementia and their family members – towards a whole systems approach', in T. Adams (ed.), *Dementia Care Nursing: Promoting Well-Being in People with Dementia and their Families*. Hampshire: Palgrave Macmillan. pp. 105–26.

Adams, T. and Gardiner, P. (2005) 'Communication and interaction within dementia care triads: developing a theory for relationship-centred care', *Dementia*, 4 (2): 185–205.

Adamson, J. (1999) 'Carers and dementia among African/Caribbean and South Asian families', *Generations Review*, 9 (3): 12–14.

Adamson, J. and Donavan, J. (2005) '"Normal disruption": South Asian and African/Caribbean relatives caring for an older family member in the UK', *Social Science and Medicine*, 60 (1): 37–48.

Adelman, R.C. (1998) 'The Alzheimerization of aging: a brief update', *Experimental Gerontology*, 33 (1/2): 155–7.

Aggarwal, N., Vass, A.A., Minardi, H.A., Waed, C., Garfield, C. and Cybyk, B. (2003) 'People with dementia and their relatives: personal experiences of Alzheimer's and of the provision of care', *Journal of Psychiatric and Mental Health Nursing*, 10 (2): 187–97.

Ahmad, W.I.U. and Walker, R. (1997) 'Asian older people: housing, health and access to services', *Ageing and Society*, 17 (2): 141–65.

Alzheimer Europe (2007) 'The population of people with dementia in Europe': <http://www.dementia-in-europe.eu> [accessed 14 August 2007].

Alzheimer's Society (2006) *Facts about Dementia*: <http://www.alzheimers.org.uk/Facts_about_dementia/What_is_dementia/index.htm> [accessed 12 December 2006].

Anderson, M.L. and Collins, P. (1995) *Race, Class and Gender: An Anthology*. 2nd edn. Belmont, CA: Wadsworth.

Aneshensel, C.S. (1999) 'Mental illness as a career: sociological perspectives', in C.S. Aneshensel and J.C. Phelan (eds), *Handbook of the Sociology of Mental Health*. New York: Plenum. pp. 585–603.

Antuono, P. and Beyer, J. (1999) 'The burden of dementia: a medical and research perspective', *Theoretical Medicine and Bioethics*, 20 (1): 3–13.

Aranda, M.P. (2001) 'Racial and ethnic factors in dementia care-giving research in the US', *Aging and Mental Health*, 5 (1): S116–23.

Askham, J. (1991) 'The problem of generalising about community care of dementia sufferers', *Journal of Aging Studies*, 5 (2): 137–46.

Askham, J. (1995) *Social and Health Authority for Elderly People from Black and Minority Ethnic Groups.* London: HMSO.

Askham, J., Briggs, K., Norman, I. and Redfern, S. (2007) 'Care at home for people with dementia: as in a total institution?', *Ageing and Society*, 27: 3–24.

Audit Commission (2000) *Forget Me Not: Mental Health Services for Older People.* London: Audit Commission.

Baars, J., Dannefer, D., Phillipson, C. and Walker, A. (2006) 'Introduction', in J. Baars, D. Dannefer, C. Phillipson and A. Walker (eds), *Aging, Globalization and Inequality: The New Critical Gerontology.* Amityville: Baywood Publishers. pp. 1–14.

Ballard, K., Elston, M.A. and Gabe, J. (2005) 'Beyond the mask: women's experiences of public and private ageing during midlife and their use of age-resisting activities', *Health*, 9 (2): 169–87.

Bamford, C. and Bruce, E. (2000) 'Defining the outcomes of community care: the perspectives of older people with dementia and their carers', *Ageing and Society*, 20 (5): 543–70.

Barnett, E. (2000) *Including the Person with Dementia in Designing and Delivering Care: 'I Need to Be Me!'* London: Jessica Kingsley.

Bartlett, R. and O'Connor, D. (2007) 'From personhood to citizenship: broadening the lens for dementia practice and research', *Journal of Ageing Studies*, 21 (2): 107–18.

Beard, R.L. (2004) 'In their voices: identity preservation and experiences of Alzheimer's disease', *Journal of Aging Studies*, 18 (4): 415–28.

Beattie, A.M., Daker-White, G., Gilliard, J. and Means, R. (2002) 'Younger people in dementia care: a review of service needs, service provision and models of good practice', *Aging and Mental Health*, 6 (3): 205–12.

Beattie, A.M., Daker-White, G., Gilliard, J. and Means, R. (2005) '"They don't quite fit the way we organize our services" – results from a UK field study of marginalized groups and dementia care', *Disability and Society*, 20 (1): 67–80.

Beck, C., Ortigara, A., Mercer, S. and Shue, V. (1999) 'Enabling and empowering certified nursing assistants for quality dementia care', *International Journal of Geriatric Psychiatry*, 14 (3): 197–212.

Beck, C. and Shue, V. (2003) 'Surrogate decision-making and related issues', *Alzheimer Disease and Associated Disorders*, 17 (1): S12–16.

Becker, H.S. (1967) 'Whose Side Are We On?', *Social Problems*, 14: 239–47.

Becker, H.S. (1996) 'The epistemology of qualitative research', in R. Jessor, A. Colby and R.A. Shweder (eds), *Ethnography and Human Development: Context and Meaning in Social Inquiry.* Chicago: University of Chicago Press. pp. 53–71.

Becker, H.S. (2003) 'Making sociology relevant to society', Paper given at the European Sociological Association in Murcia, Spain, 2003: <http://home.earthlink.net/~hsbecker/relevant.htm> [accessed 21 June 2006].

Bell, D. and Bowes, A. (2006) *Financial Care Models in Scotland and the UK.* York: Joseph Rowntree Foundation: <http://jrf.org.uk/bookshop/ebooks/1859354408.pdf> [accessed 12 December 2006].

Bell, V. and Troxel, D. (2003) *The Best Friends Approach to Alzheimer's Care.* Baltimore, MD: Health Professions Press.

Benbow, S.M. and Reynolds, D. (2000) 'Challenging the stigma of Alzheimer's Disease', *Hospital Medicine*, 61 (3): 174–7.

Berghmans, R.L. and Ter Meulen, R.H.J. (1995) 'Ethical issues in research with dementia patients', *International Journal of Geriatric Psychiatry*, 10 (8): 647–51.

Bettio, F., Simonazzi, A. and Villa, P. (2006) 'Change in care regimes and female migration: the "care drain" in the Mediterranean', *Journal of European Social Policy*, 16 (3): 271–85.

Biggs, S., Estes, C. and Phillipson, C. (2003a) *Social Theory, Social Policy and Ageing: A Critical Introduction*. Berkshire: Open University Press, McGraw Hill.

Biggs, S., Lowenstein, A. and Hendricks, J. (2003b) 'Where is theory headed?', in S. Biggs, A. Lowenstein and J. Hendricks (eds), *The need for Theory: Critical Approaches for Social Gerontology*. Amitville, NY: Baywood Publishing Company. pp. 245–8.

Biggs, S. and Powell, J. (2001) 'A Foucauldian analysis of old age and the power of social welfare', *Journal of Aging and Social Policy*, 12 (2): 93–112.

Black, W. and Almeida, O.P. (2004) 'A systematic review of the association between the behavioural and psychological symptoms of dementia and burden of care', *International Psychogeriatrics*, 16 (3): 295–315.

Blackstock, K., Innes, A., Cox, S., Mason, A. and Smith, A. (2006) 'Living with dementia in rural and remote Scotland', *Journal of Rural Studies*, 22 (2): 161–76.

Blakemore, K. and Boneham, M. (1994) *Age, Race and Ethnicity*. Buckingham: Open University Press.

Bloom, B.S., Pouvourville, N. and Straus, W.L. (2003) 'Cost of illness of Alzheimer's disease: how useful are current estimates?', *Gerontologist*, 43 (2): 158–64.

Boejie, H.R., Niewaard, A.C. and Casparie, A.F. (1997) 'Coping strategies of enrolled nurses in nursing homes: shifting between organizational imperatives and residents' needs', *International Journal of Nursing Studies*, 34 (5): 358–66.

Bond, J. (1992) 'The medicalization of dementia', *Journal of Aging Studies*, 6 (4): 397–403.

Bond, J. (1999) 'Quality of life for people with dementia: approaches to the challenge of measurement', *Ageing and Society*, 19 (5): 561–79.

Bond, J. (2000) 'The impact of staff factors on nursing-home residents', *Aging and Mental Health*, 4 (1): 5–8.

Bond, J. (2001) 'Sociological perspectives', in C. Cautley (ed.), *Handbook of Dementia Care*. Buckingham: The Open University Press. pp. 44–61.

Bond, J., Bond, S., Donaldson, C., Gregson, B. and Atkinson, A. (1989) 'Evaluation of an innovation in the continuing care of very frail elderly people', *Ageing and Society*, 9 (4): 347–81.

Bond, J., Coleman, P. and Peace, S. (eds) (1993) *Ageing in Society: An Introduction to Social Gerontology*. London: Sage.

Bond, J. and Corner, L. (2001) 'Researching dementia: are there unique methodological challenges for health services research?', *Ageing and Society*, 21 (1): 95–116.

Bond, J., Corner, L., Lilley, A. and Ellwood, C. (2002) 'Medicalization and insight and caregivers' response to risk in dementia', *Dementia*, 1 (3): 313–28.

Bond, J., Stave, C., Sganga, A., Vincenzino, O., O'Connell, B. and Stanley, R.L. (2005) 'Inequalities in dementia care across Europe: key findings of the Facing Dementia Survey', *International Journal of Clinical Practice*, 59 (S146): 8–14.

Boneham, M.A., Williams, K.E., Copeland, J.R.M., McKibbin, P., Wilson, K. and Scott, A. (1997) 'Elderly people from ethnic minorities in Liverpool: mental illness, unmet need and barriers to service use, *Health and Social Care in the Community*, 5 (3): 173–80.

Bowes, A. and Bell, D. (2007) 'Free personal care for older people in Scotland: issues and implications', *Social Policy and Society*, 6 (3): 435–45.

Bowes, A. and Wilkinson, H. (2002) 'South Asian people with dementia: research issues', in H. Wilkinson (ed.), *The Perspectives of People with Dementia: Research Methods and Motivations*. London: Jessica Kingsley. pp. 223–41.

Bowes, A. and Wilkinson, H. (2003) '"We didn't know it would get that bad": South Asian experiences of dementia and service response', *Health and Social Care in the Community*, 11 (5): 387–96.

Brannelly, T. (2004) *Citizenship and Care for People with Dementia: Summary Research Paper*. Birmingham: University of Birmingham: <www.socialresearch.bham.ac.uk/downloads/Citizenship_and_Care_for_People_with_Dementia.pdf> [accessed 12 December 2006].

Brannelly, T. (2006) 'Negotiating ethics in dementia care: an analysis of an ethic of care in practice', *Dementia*, 5 (2): 197–212.

Brannelly, T. (2007) 'Citizenship and care for people with dementia: values and approaches', in S. Balloch and M. Hill, *Care, Community and Citizenship: Research and Practice in a Changing Policy Context*. Bristol: Policy Press. pp. 89–101.

Brannelly, T. (2008) 'Developing an ethical basis for relationship-centred and inclusive approaches towards dementia care nursing', in T. Adams (ed.), *Dementia Care Nursing: Promoting Well-Being in People with Dementia and their Families*. Hampshire: Palgrave Macmillan. pp. 243–59.

Bravo, G., Paquet, M. and Dubois, M.F. (2003) 'Opinions regarding who should consent to research on behalf of an older adult suffering from dementia', *Dementia*, 2 (1): 49–65.

Brooker, D. (2004) 'What is person-centred care in dementia?', *Reviews in Clinical Gerontology*, 13: 215–22.

Brooker, D. and Surr, C. (2005) *Dementia Care Mapping: Principles and Practice*. Bradford: University of Bradford.

Callahan, C.M., Hendrie, H.C. and Tierney, W.M. (1995) 'Documentation and evaluation of cognitive impairment in elderly primary care patients', *Annals of Internal Medicine*, 122 (6): 422–9.

Callahan, D. (1991) 'Dementia and appropriate care: allocating scarce resources', in R.H. Binstock, S.G. Post and P.J. Whitehouse (eds), *Dementia and Aging: Ethics, Values and Policy Choices*. Baltimore, MD: Johns Hopkins University Press. pp. 141–52.

Cantley, C. (2001) 'Understanding the policy context', in C. Cantley (ed.), *A Handbook of Dementia Care*. Buckingham: Open University Press. pp. 201–39.

Cantley, C. and Bowes, A. (2004) 'Dementia and social inclusion: the way forward', in A. Innes, C. Archibald and C. Murphy (eds), *Dementia and Social*

Inclusion: Marginalised Groups and Marginalised Areas of Dementia Research, Care and Practice. London: Jessica Kingsley. pp. 255–71.

Capstick, A. (2003) 'The theoretical origins of Dementia Care Mapping', in A. Innes (ed.), Dementia Care Mapping: Applications Across Cultures. Baltimore: Health Professions Press.

Chandra, V. (1998) 'Dementia and the care giving family', Global Perspective: A Newsletter for Alzheimer's Disease International, 8 (2): 6–7.

Chandra, V., Ganguli, M., Pandav, R., Johnston, J., Nelle, S. and DeKosky, S.T. (1998) 'Prevalence of Alzheimer's disease and other dementias in rural India: the Indo-US study', Neurology, 51 (4): 1000–8.

Chee, Y.K. and Levkoff, S.E. (2001) 'Culture and dementia: accounts by family caregivers and health professionals for dementia-affected elders in South Korea', Journal of Cross-Cultural Gerontology, 16 (2): 111–25.

Cheung, J. and Hocking, P. (2004) 'Caring as worrying: the experience of spousal carers', Journal of Advanced Nursing, 47 (5): 475–82.

Clare, L. (2003) 'Managing threats to self: awareness in early-stage Alzheimer's Disease', Social Science and Medicine, 57 (6): 1017–29.

Clare, L. (2004) 'Awareness in early-stage Alzheimer's disease: a review of methods and evidence', British Journal of Clinical Psychology, 43 (2): 177–96.

Cloutterbuck, J. and Mahoney, D.F. (2003) 'African-American dementia caregivers: the duality of respect', Dementia, 2 (2): 221–43.

Cobban, N. (2004) 'Improving domiciliary care for people with dementia and their carers', in A. Innes, C. Archibald and C. Murphy (eds), Dementia and Social Inclusion: Marginalised Groups and Marginalised Areas of Dementia Research, Care and Practice. London: Jessica Kingsley. pp. 50–66.

Coen, R., O'Boyle, C., Coakley, D. and Lawlor, B.A. (2002) 'Individual quality of life factors distinguishing low-burden and high-burden caregivers of dementia patients', Dementia and Geriatric Cognitive Disorders, 13 (3): 164–70.

Cohen, D. and Eisdorfer, C. (1986) The Loss of Self: A Family Resource for the Care of Alzheimer's Disease and Related Disorders. New York: W.W. Norton.

Cohen, L. (1994) 'Old age: cultural and critical perspectives', Annual Review of Anthropology, 23: 137–58.

Cohen-Mansfield, J. (2000) 'Heterogeneity in dementia: challenges and opportunities', Alzheimer Disease and Associated Disorders, 14 (2): 60–3.

Comas-Herrera, A., Wittenberg, R., Pickard, L. and Knapp, M. (2007) 'Cognitive impairment in older people: future demand for long-term care services and the associated costs', International Journal of Geriatric Psychiatry, 22 (10): 1037–45.

Connell, C.M. and Gibson, G.D. (1997) 'Racial, ethnic and cultural differences in dementia caregiving: review and analysis', Gerontologist, 37 (3): 355–64.

Conrad, P. (1975) 'The discovery of hyperkinesis: notes on the medicalisation of deviant behaviour', Social Problems, 23: 12–21.

Cooke, D.D., McNally, L., Milligan, K.T., Harrison, M.J.G. and Newman, S.P. (2001) 'Psychosocial interventions for caregivers of people with dementia: a systematic review', Aging and Mental Health, 5 (2): 120–35.

Cotrell, V. and Schultz, R. (1993) 'The perspective of the patient with Alzheimer's Disease: a neglected dimension of dementia research', Gerontologist, 33 (2): 205–11.

Cox, S. and Keady, J. (eds) (1999) *Younger People with Dementia: Planning, Practice, and Development.* London: Jessica Kingsley.

Crisp, A.H., Gelder, M.G., Rix, S., Meltzer, H.I. and Rowlands, O.J. (2000) 'Stigmatisation of people with mental illnesses', *British Journal of Psychiatry*, 177 (1): 4–7.

Daker-White, G., Beattie, A.M., Gilliard, J. and Means, R. (2002) 'Minority ethnic groups in dementia care: a review of service needs, service provision and models of good practice', *Aging and Mental Health*, 6 (2): 101–8.

Dalley, G. (1988) *Ideologies of Caring.* London: Macmillan.

Davis, D.H.J. (2004) 'Dementia: sociological and philosophical constructions', *Social Science and Medicine*, 58 (2): 369–78.

Dawson, S. (1996) *Analysing Organisations.* London: Macmillan Business.

De Mendonça Lima, C.A., Levav, I., Jacobsson, L. and Rutz, W. (2003) 'Stigma and discrimination against older people with mental disorders in Europe', *International Journal of Geriatric Psychiatry*, 18 (8): 679–82.

Declercq, A. (1998) 'Organisational culture as an instrument in residential care for dementing elderly', in J. Graafmans, V. Taipale and N. Charness (eds), *Gerontechnology: A Sustainable Investment in the Future.* Amsterdam: IOS Press. pp. 317–19.

Department of Health (2001) National Service Framework for Older People: Standard Two – Person-Centred Care: <http://www.dh.gov.uk/PolicyAnd Guidance/HealthAnd SocialCareTopics/OlderPeoplesServices/Older PeopleArticle/fs/en?CONTENT_ID= 4002286 &chk= IBaLdY> [accessed 12 December 2006].

Devlin, E., MacAskill, S. and Stead, M. (2007) '"We're still the same people": developing a mass media campaign to raise awareness and challenge the stigma of dementia', *International Journal of Nonprofit and Voluntary Sector Marketing*, 12 (1): 47–58.

Dewing, J. (2002) 'From ritual to relationship: a person-centred approach to consent in qualitative research with older people who have a dementia', *Dementia*, 1 (2): 156–71.

Dewing, J. (2007) 'Participatory research: a method for process consent with persons who have dementia', *Dementia*, 6 (1): 11–25.

Dewing, J. and Pritchard, E. (2004) 'Including the older person with a dementia in practice development', in B. McCormack, K. Manley and R. Garbett (eds), *Practice Development in Nursing.* Oxford: Blackwell. pp. 177–96.

Dillman, R.J.M. (2000) 'Alzheimer Disease: epistemological lessons from history?', in P.J. Whitehouse, K. Maurer and J.F. Ballenger (eds), *Concepts of Alzheimer Disease: Biological, Clinical and Cultural Perspectives.* Baltimore, MD: Johns Hopkins University Press. pp. 128–57.

Dilworth-Anderson, P. and Gibson, B.E. (1999) 'Ethnic minority perspectives on dementia, family caregiving and interventions', *Generations*, 23 (3): 40–5.

Dilworth-Anderson, P. and Gibson, B.E. (2002) 'The cultural influence of values, norms, meanings and perceptions in understanding dementia in ethnic minorities', *Alzheimer Disease and Related Disorders*, 16 (2): S56–63.

Dilworth-Anderson, P., Williams, I.C. and Gibson, B.E. (2002) 'Issues of race, ethnicity and culture in care giving research: a twenty-year review (1980–2000)', *Gerontologist*, 42 (2): 237–72.

Douthit, K. (2006) 'Dementia in the iron cage: the biopsychiatric construction of Alzheimer's dementia', in J. Baars, D. Dannefer, C. Phillipson and A. Walker (eds), *Aging, Globalization and Inequality: The New Critical Gerontology*. Amityville, NY: Baywood Publishing Company. pp. 159–80.

Downs, M. (1997) 'The emergence of the person in dementia research', *Ageing and Society*, 17 (5): 597–607.

Downs, M. (2000) 'Dementia in a socio-cultural context: an idea whose time has come', *Ageing and Society*, 20 (3): 369–75.

Downs, M. and Zarit, S.H. (1999) 'Editorial: what works in dementia care? Research evidence for policy and practice: Part 1', *International Journal of Geriatric Psychiatry*, 14 (2): 83–5.

Dressel, P., Minkler, M. and Yen, I. (1997) 'Gender, race, class and aging: advances and opportunities', *International Journal of Health Services*, 27 (4): 579–600.

Droes, R.M. (2007) 'Insight in coping with dementia: listening to the voice of those who suffer from it', *Aging and Mental Health*, 11 (2): 115–18.

Edvardsson, D., Winblad, B. and Sandman, P.O. (2008) 'Person-centred care of people with severe Alzheimer's disease: current status and ways forward', *Lancet Neurology*, 7 (4): 362–7.

Edwards, D.F., Baum, C.M., Meisel, M., Depke, M., Williams, J., Braford, T., Morrow-Howell, N. and Morris, J.C. (1999) 'Home-based multidisciplinary diagnosis and treatment of inner-city elders with dementia', *Gerontologist*, 39 (4): 483–8.

Elliott, K.S. and Di Minno, M.D. (2006) 'Unruly grandmothers, ghosts and ancestors: Chinese elders and the importance of culture in dementia evaluations', *Journal of Cross-Cultural Gerontology*, 21 (3–4): 157–77.

Elliott, K.S., Minno, M.D., Lam, D. and Mei Tu, A. (1996) 'Working with Chinese families in the context of dementia', in G. Yeo and D. Gallagher-Thompson (eds), *Ethnicity and the Dementias*. London: Taylor & Francis. pp. 137–49.

English, J. and Morse, J.M. (1988) 'The "difficult" elderly patient: adjustment or maladjustment?', *International Journal of Nursing Studies*, 25 (1): 23–39.

Estes, C.L. (2001a) 'Concluding observations on social policy, social theory and research', in C.L. Estes (ed.) (2001) *Social Policy and Ageing: A Critical Perspective*. London: Sage. pp. 231–7.

Estes, C.L. (2001b) 'Political economy of aging: a theoretical framework', in C.L. Estes (ed.), *Social Policy and Ageing: A Critical Perspective*. London: Sage. pp. 1–22.

Estes, C.L. (2003) 'Theoretical perspectives on old age policy: a critique and a proposal', in S. Biggs, A. Lowenstein and J. Hendricks (eds), *The Need for Theory: Critical Approaches for Social Gerontology*. Amitville, NY: Baywood Publishing Company. pp. 219–43.

Estes, C. (2006) 'Critical feminist perspectives, aging and social policy', in J. Baars, D. Dannefer, C. Phillipson and A. Walker (eds), *Aging, Globalization and Inequality: The New Critical Gerontology*. Amityville, NY: Baywood Publishing Company. pp. 81–101.

Estes, C.L. and Binney, E.A. (1989) 'The biomedicalisation of aging: dangers and dilemmas', *Gerontologist*, 29 (5): 587–96.

Fearnley, K., McClennan, J. and Weaks, D. (1998) *The Right to Know? Sharing the Diagnosis of Dementia*. Edinburgh: Alzheimer Scotland – Action on Dementia.

Featherstone, M. and Hepworth, M. (1991) 'The mask of ageing and the post-modern life course', in M. Featherstone (ed.), *The Body: Social Process and Cultural Theory*. London: Sage. pp. 371–89.

Ferri, C.P., Prince, M., Brayne, C., Brodaty, H., Fratiglioui, L., Ganguli, M., Hall, K., Hasegawa, K., Hendrie, H., Huang, Y., Jorm, A., Mathers, C., Menezes, P.R., Rimmer, E. and Scazufca, M. (2005). 'Global prevalence of dementia: a Delphi consensus study', *Lancet*, 366 (9503): 2112–7.

Fisher, B.J. and Peterson, C. (1993) 'She won't be dancing much anyway: a study of surgeons, surgical nurses and elderly patients', *Qualitative Health Research*, 3 (2): 165–83.

Fontana, A. and Smith, R.W. (1989) 'Alzheimer's Disease victims: the unbecoming of self and the normalization of competence', *Sociological Perspectives*, 32: 35–46.

Forbat, L. (2003) 'Concepts and understandings of dementia by "gatekeepers" and minority ethnic "service users"', *Journal of Health Psychology*, 8 (5): 645–55.

Forbat, L. (2008) 'Social policy and relationship-centred dementia nursing', in T. Adams (ed.), *Dementia Care Nursing: Promoting Well-Being in People with Dementia and their Families*. Hampshire: Palgrave Macmillan. pp. 227–42.

Fortinsky, R.H. (2001) 'Health care triads and dementia care: integrative framework and future directions', *Aging and Mental Health*, 5, (Supplement 1): 35–48.

Fox, P.J. (1989) 'From senility to Alzheimer's disease: the rise of the Alzheimer's movement', *Milbank Quarterly*, 67 (1): 58–102.

Fox, P.J. (2000) 'The role of the concept of Alzheimer Disease in the development of the Alzheimer's Association in the United States', in P.J. Whitehouse, K. Maurer and J.F. Ballenger (eds), *Concepts of Alzheimer Disease: Biological, Clinical and Cultural Perspectives*. Baltimore, MD: Johns Hopkins University Press. pp. 209–33.

Friedman, S.M., Daub, C., Cresci, K. and Keyser, R. (1999) 'A comparison of job satisfaction among nursing assistants in nursing homes and the program of all-inclusive care for the elderly (PACE)', *Gerontologist*, 39 (4): 434–9.

Fukushima, T., Nagahata, K., Ishibashi, N., Takahashi, Y. and Moriyama, M. (2005) 'Quality of life from the viewpoint of patients with dementia in Japan, nurturing through an acceptance of dementia by patients, their families and care professionals', *Health and Social Care in the Community*, 13 (1): 30–7.

Gannon, B. and Nolan, B. (2007) 'The impact of disability transitions on social inclusion', *Social Science and Medicine*, 64 (7): 1425–37.

Geldmarcher, D.S. (2002) 'Cost-effective recognition and diagnosis of dementia', *Seminars in Neurology*, 22 (1): 63–70.

Gerdner, L.A., Tripp-Reimer, T. and Simpson, H.C. (2007) 'Hard lives, God's help, and struggling through: caregiving in Arkansas Delta', *Journal of Cross-Cultural Gerontology*, 22 (4): 355–74.

Gilleard, C.J. (1984) *Living with Dementia: Community Care of the Elderly and Mentally Infirm*. London: Crook Helm.

Gilmour, H., Gibson, F. and Campbell, J. (2003) 'People with dementia in a rural community: issues of prevalence and community care policy', *Dementia*, 2 (2): 245–63.

Gladman, J.R.F., Jones, R.G., Radford, K., Walker, E. and Rothera, I. (2007) 'Person-centred dementia services are feasible, but can they be sustained?', *Age and Ageing*, 36 (2): 171–6.

Goffman, E. (1961) *Asylums: Essays on the Social Situation of Mental Patients and Other Inmates*. New York: Doubleday Aschor.

Goffman, E. (1963) *Stigma: Notes on the Management of Spoiled Identity*. Englewood Cliffs, NY: Prentice Hall.

Goffman, E. (1991) *Asylums: Essays on the Situations of Mental Patients and other Inmates*. Harmondsworth: Penguin.

Golander, H. and Raz, A.E. (1996) 'The mask of dementia: images of "demented residents" in a nursing ward', *Ageing and Society*, 16: 269–85.

Goldsmith, M. (1996) *Hearing the Voice of People with Dementia*. London: Jessica Kingsley.

Goldstein, M., Abma, T., Oereburg, B., Verkerk, M., Verney, F. and Widdershoven, G. (2007) 'What it is to be a daughter? Identities under pressure in dementia care', *Bioethics*, 21 (1): 1–12.

Gordon, D., Carter, H. and Scott, S. (1997) 'Profiling the care needs of the population with dementia: a survey in Central Scotland', *International Journal of Geriatric Psychiatry*, 12 (7), 753–9.

Gove, D. (2002) 'Ethical and legal approaches to Alzheimer's disease in the EU', in M. Warner, S. Furnish, M. Longley and B. Lawlor (eds), *Alzheimer's Disease: Policy and Practice across Europe* . Abingdon: Radcliffe Medical Press. pp. 27–59.

Graham, H. (1981) 'Caring: a labour of love', in J. Finch. and D. Groves (eds), *A Labour of Love: Women's Work and Caring*. London: Routledge and Kegan Paul.

Graham, H. (1991) 'The concept of care in feminist research: the case of domestic service', *Sociology*, 25: 61–78.

Gregoire, A. and Thornicroft, G. (1998) 'Rural mental health', *Psychiatric Bulletin*, 22 (5): 273–7.

Gubrium, J.F. (1975) *Living and Dying at Murray Mauer*. New York: St. Martin's.

Gubrium, J.F. (1986) *Oldtimers and Alzheimer's: The Descriptive Organization of Senility*. Greenwich: JAI Press.

Gubrium, J.F. (1991) *The Mosaic of Care: Frail Elderly and their Families in the Real World*. New York: Springer.

Gubrium, J.F. (1992) 'Voice and context in a new gerontology', in T. Cole, A.W. Achenbaum, Jakobi, P. and Kastenbaum, R. (eds), *Voices and Visions of Aging: Toward a Critical Gerontology*. New York: Springer. pp. 46–63.

Haak, N.J. (2002) 'Understanding communication from the perspective of persons with dementia', *Alzheimer's Care Quarterly*, 3 (2): 116–31.

Haley, W.E., Roth, D.J., Coleton, M.I., Ford, G.R., West, C.A.C. and Collines, R.P. (1996) 'Appraisal, coping and social support as mediators of well-being in black and white family caregivers of patients with Alzheimer's Disease', *Journal of Consulting and Clinical Psychology*, 64 (1): 121–9.

Hall, R.H. (1997) *Organizations: Structures, Progresses and Outcomes*. London: Prentice Hall.

Hamel-Bissell, B.P. (1992*)* 'Mental health and illness nursing in rural Vermont: case illustration of a farm family', in P. Winstead-Fry, J.C. Tiffany and

R.V. Shippee-Rice (eds), *Rural Health Nursing: Stories of Creativity, Commitment, and Connectedness.* New York: National League for Nursing Press. pp. 55–78.

Hammersley, M. (2000) *Taking Sides in Social Research: Essays on Partisanship and Bias.* London: Routledge.

Hancock, G.A., Reynolds, T., Woods, B., Thornicroft, G. and Orrell, M. (2003) 'The needs of older people with mental health problems according to the user, the carer and the staff', *International Journal of Geriatric Psychiatry*, 18 (9): 803–11.

Handy, C. (1993) *Understanding Organizations.* Harmondsworth: Penguin.

Harding, N. and Palfrey, C. (1997) *The Social Construction of Dementia: Confused Professionals?* London: Jessica Kingsley.

Hardy, B., Young, R. and Wistow, G. (1999) 'Dimensions of choice in the assessment and care management process: the views of older people, carers and care managers', *Health and Social Care in the Community*, 7 (6): 483.

Harris, P.H. (2004) 'The perspectives of younger people with dementia: still an overlooked population', *Social Work in Mental Health*, 2 (4): 17–36.

Hart, V.R., Gallagher-Thompson, D., Davies, H., Deminno, M. and Lessin, P.J. (1996) 'Strategies for increasing participation of ethnic minorities in Alzheimer's Disease diagnostic centers: a multifaceted approach in California', *Gerontologist*, 36 (2): 259–62.

Hellstrom, I., Nolan, M. and Lundh, U. (2005) 'We do things together: a case study of couplehood in dementia', *Dementia*, 4 (1): 7–22.

Henderson, J. and Forbat, L. (2002) 'Relationship-based social policy: personal and policy constructions of "care"', *Critical Social Policy*, 22: 669–87.

Henderson, N.J. (1995) 'The culture of care in a nursing home: effects of a medicalized model of long-term care', in N.J. Henderson and M.D. Vesperi (eds), *The Culture of Long Term Care: Nursing Home Ethnography.* London: Bergin and Garvey. pp. 37–54.

Henderson, N.J. (2002) 'The experience and interpretation of dementia: cross-cultural perspectives', *Journal of Cross-Cultural Gerontology*, 17 (3): 195–6.

Henderson, N.J., Gutierrez-Mayka, M., Garcia, J. and Boyd, S. (1994) 'A model for Alzheimer's Disease support group development in African-American and Hispanic populations', *Gerontologist*, 33 (3): 409–14.

Henderson, N.J. and Henderson, L.C. (2002) 'Cultural construction of disease: a "supernormal" construct of dementia in an American Indian tribe', *Journal of Cross-Cultural Gerontology*, 17 (3): 197–212.

Henderson, N.J. and Vesperi, M.D. (eds) (1995) *The Culture of Long-Term Care: Nursing Home Ethnography.* London: Bergin and Garvey.

Hendrie, H.C. (2006) 'Lessons learned from international comparative crosscultural studies on dementia', *American Journal of Geriatric Psychiatry*, 14 (6): 480–8.

Herskovitz, E. (1995) 'Struggling over subjectivity: debates about the self and Alzheimer's Disease', *Medical Anthropology Quarterly*, 9 (2): 146–64.

Heyman, B. (ed.) (1995) *Researching User Perspectives on Community Health Care.* London: Chapman and Hall.

Hicks, M.H.R. and Lam, M.S.C. (1999) 'Decision-making within the social course of dementia: accounts by Chinese-American caregivers', *Culture, Medicine and Society*, 23 (4): 415–52.

Hinton, L., Franz, C.E., Yeo, G. and Levkoff, S.E. (2005) 'Conceptions of dementia in a and multiethnic sample of family caregivers', *Journal of the American Geriatrics Society*, 53 (8): 1405–10.

Hinton, L., Guo, Z., Hillygus, J. and Levkoff, S. (2000) 'Working with culture: a qualitative analysis of barriers to the recruitment of Chinese-American family caregivers for dementia research', *Journal of Cross-Cultural Gerontology*, 15 (2): 119–37.

Hockey, J. (1990) *Experiences of Death*. Edinburgh: Edinburgh University Press.

Holst, G. and Hallberg, I.R. (2003) 'Exploring the meaning of everyday life, for those suffering from dementia', *American Journal of Alzheimer's Disease and Other Dementias*, 18 (6): 359–65.

Holstein, M.B. (1997) 'Alzheimer's Disease and senile dementia, 1885–1920: an interpretive history of disease negotiation', *Journal of Aging Studies*, 11 (1): 1–13.

Holstein, M.B. (2000) 'Aging, culture and the framing of Alzheimer Disease', in P.J. Whitehouse, K. Maurer and J.F. Ballenger (eds), *Concepts of Alzheimer Disease: Biological, Clinical and Cultural Perspectives*. Baltimore, MD: Johns Hopkins University Press. pp. 158–80.

Holstein, M.B. and Minkler, M. (2007) 'Critical gerontology: reflections for the 21st century', in M. Bernard and T. Scharf (eds), *Critical Perspectives on Ageing Societies*. Bristol: Policy Press. pp. 13–26.

hooks, b. (1984) *Feminist Theory from Margin to Center*.Cambridge, MA: South End Press.

Hulko, W. (2004) 'Social science perspectives on dementia research: intersectionality', in A. Innes, C. Archibald and C. Murphy (eds), *Dementia and Social Inclusion: Marginalised Groups and Marginalised Areas of Dementia Research, Care and Practice*. London: Jessica Kingsley. pp. 237–54.

Husaini, B.A., Sherkat, D.E., Moonis, M., Levine, R., Holzer, C. and Cain, V.A. (2003) 'Racial differences in the diagnosis of dementia and in its effects on the use and costs of health care services', *Psychiatric Services*, 54 (1): 92–6.

Ikels, C. (2002) 'Constructing and deconstructing the self: dementia in China', *Journal of Cross-cultural Gerontology*, 17 (3): 233–51.

Iliffe, S. and Manthorpe, J. (2004) 'The debate on ethnicity and dementia: from category fallacy to person-centred care?', *Aging and Mental Health*, 8 (4): 283–92.

Iliffe, S., De Lepeliere, J., Hout, H., van Kenny, G., Lewis, A. and Vernooij-Dassen, M.J.F.J. and the DIADEM Group (2005) 'Understanding obstacles to the recognition of and response to dementia in different European countries: a modified focus group approach using multi-national, multi-disciplinary expert groups', *Aging and Mental Health*, 9 (1): 1–6.

Ineichen, B. (1998) 'Responding to dementia in east Asia: developments in Japan, China, Taiwan and South Korea', *Aging and Mental Health*, 2 (4): 279–85.

Innes, A. (1997) 'Towards an understanding of care assistants' constructions of residents as "difficult"', MSc thesis, University of Stirling.

Innes, A. (2000) *Training and Development for Dementia Care Workers*. London: Jessica Kingsley.

Innes, A. (2001) 'Student-centred learning and person-centred dementia care', *Education and Ageing*, 16 (2): 229–52.

Innes, A. (ed.) (2003a) *Dementia Care Mapping: Applications Across Cultures.* Baltimore, MD: Health Professions Press.

Innes, A. (2003b) 'Dementia care mapping data for care planning purposes', in A. Innes, (ed.), *Dementia Care Mapping: Applications Across Cultures.* Baltimore, MD: Health Professions Press. pp. 71 –80.

Innes, A. (2003c) 'Developing ethnically sensitive and appropriate dementia care practice', in T. Adams and J. Manthorpe (eds), *Dementia Care*. London: Arnold. pp. 202–12.

Innes, A., Archibald, C. and Murphy, C. (eds) (2004) *Dementia and Social Inclusion: Marginalised Groups and Marginalised Areas of Dementia Research, Care and Practice.* London: Jessica Kingsley.

Innes, A., Blackstock, K., Mason, A., Smith, A. and Cox, S. (2005) 'Dementia care provision in rural Scotland: service users' and carers' experiences', *Health and Social Care in the Community*, 13 (4): 354–65.

Innes, A. and Capstick, A. (2001) 'Communication and personhood', in C. Cantley (ed.), *A Handbook of Dementia Care*. Buckingham: Open University Press. pp. 135–45.

Innes, A. and Kelly, F. (2007) 'Evaluating long-stay settings: reflections on the process with particular reference to dementia care mapping', in A. Innes and L. McCabe (eds), *Evaluation in Dementia Care*. London: Jessica Kingsley.

Innes, A. and Surr, C. (2001) 'Measuring the well-being of people with dementia living in formal care settings: the use of Dementia Care Mapping', *Aging and Mental Health*, 5 (3): 258–68.

Innes, A., Macpherson, S. and McCabe, L. (2006a) *Promoting Person-Centred Care at the Front line.* York: Joseph Rowntree Foundation: <http://www.jrf.org.uk/ bookshop/details.asp?pubID=782> [accessed 12 December 2006].

Innes, A., Cox, S., Smith, A. and Mason, A. (2006b) 'Service provision for people with dementia in rural Scotland: difficulties and innovations', *Dementia*, 5 (2): 249–70.

Jacob, S., Bourke, L. and Luloff, A. (1997) 'Rural community stress, distress and well-being in Pennsylvania', *Journal of Rural Studies*, 13 (2): 275–88.

Jacques, I. and Innes, A. (1998) 'Who cares about care assistant work?', *Journal of Dementia Care*, 6 (6): 33–7.

Janevic, M.R. and Connell, C.M. (2001) 'Racial, ethnic and cultural differences in the dementia caregiving experience: recent findings', *Gerontologist*, 41 (3): 334–47.

Johnson, M.L. (2005) 'The social construction of old age as a social problem', in M.L. Johnson (ed.), *The Cambridge Handbook of Age and Ageing*. Cambridge: Cambridge University Press. pp. 563–71.

Jones, R.S., Chow, T.W. and Gatz, M. (2006) 'Asian-Americans and Alzheimer's disease: assimilation, culture and beliefs', *Journal of Aging Studies*, 20 (1): 11–25.

Jonsson, L. and Berr, C. (2005) 'Costs of dementia in Europe', *European Journal of Neurology*, 12 (1): 50–3.

Kalis, A., Schermer, M.H. and van Delden, J.J. (2003) Ideals regarding a good life for nursing home residents with dementia: views of professional caregivers, *Medical Health Care Philosophy*, 6 (1): 35–44.

Kasayka, R., Hatfield, K. and Innes, A. (2001) 'Conclusion', in A. Innes and K. Hatfield (eds), *Healing Arts Therapies and Person-Centred Dementia Care*. London: Jessica Kingsley. pp. 113–21.

Katz, S. (2006) 'From Chronology to functionality: critical reflections on the gerontology of the body', in J. Baars, D. Dannefer, C. Phillipson and A. Walker (eds), *Aging, Globalization and Inequality: The New Critical Gerontology*. Amityville, NY: Baywood Publishing Company. pp. 123–37.

Kaufman, S.R., Shim, J.K. and Russ, A.J. (2004) 'Revisiting the biomedicalization of aging: clinical trends and ethical challenges', *Gerontologist*, 44 (6): 731–8.

Keady, J. (1996) 'The experience of dementia: a review of the literature and implications for nursing practice', *Journal of Clinical Nursing*, 5 (5): 275–88.

Keen, J. (1993) 'Editorial – dementia: questions of cost and value', *International Journal of Geriatric Psychiatry*, 8 (5): 369–78.

Kelly, F. (2007) 'Well-being and expression of self in dementia: interactions in long-term wards and creative sessions'. PhD dissertation, University of Stirling.

Kelly, M.P. and Field, D. (1998) 'Conceptualising chronic illness', in D. Field and S. Taylor (eds), *Sociological Perspective on Health, Illness and Health Care*. Oxford: Blackwell Science. pp. 3–20.

Killick, J. and Allan, K. (2001) *Communication and the Care of People with Dementia*. Buckingham: Open University Press.

Kitwood, T. (1990) 'The dialectics of dementia: with particular reference to Alzheimer's disease', *Ageing and Society*, 10 (2): 177–96.

Kitwood, T. (1993) 'Towards a theory of dementia care: the interpersonal process', *Ageing and Society*, 13: 51–67.

Kitwood, T. (1996) 'A dialectical framework for dementia', in R.T. Woods (ed.), *Handbook of Clinical Psychology*. Chichester: Wiley.

Kitwood, T. (1997) *Dementia Reconsidered: The Person Comes First*. Buckingham: Open University Press.

Kitwood, T. (1998) 'Toward a theory of dementia care: ethics and interaction', *Journal of Clinical Ethics*, 9 (1): 23–34.

Kitwood, T. and Bredin, K. (1992a) 'Towards a theory of dementia care: personhood and well-being', *Ageing and Society*, 12 (3): 269–87.

Kitwood, T. and Bredin, K. (1992b) 'A new approach to the evaluation of dementia care', *Journal of Advances in Health and Nursing Care*, 1 (5): 41–60.

Knapp, M., Comas-Herrera, A., Somani, A. and Banerjee, S. (2007a) *Dementia: International Comparisons: Summary Report for the National Audit Office*. London: London School of Economics and Political Science; Personal Social Services Research Unit and King's College London; Insitute of Psychiatry, Section of Mental Health and Ageing: <www.nao.org.uk/publications/nao_reports/0607/0607604_International_Comparisons.pdf> [accessed 12 December 2006].

Knapp, M., Prince, M., Albanese, E., Banerjee, S., Dhanasiri S., Fernandez, J.L., Ferri, C., McCrone, P., Snell, R. and Stewart, R. (2007b) *Dementia UK: A Report to the Alzheimer's Society on the Prevalence and Economic Cost of*

Dementia in the UK Produced by King's College London and London School of Economics. London: Alzheimer's Society.

Knight, B.G., Robinson, G.S., Longmire, C.V.F., Chun, M., Nakao, K. and Kim, J.H. (2002) 'Cross-cultural issues in caregiving for persons with dementia: do familism values reduce burden and distress?', *Ageing International*, 27 (3): 70–94.

Kolb, D. (1984) *Experiential Learning*. Englewood Cliffs, NJ: Prentice Hall.

Kontos, P. (2006) 'Embodied selfhood: an ethnographic exploration of Alzheimer's disease', in A. Liebing and L. Cohen (eds), *Thinking about Dementia: Culture, Loss and the Anthropology of Senility*. New Brunswick: Rutgers University Press. pp. 195–217.

Kosloski, K., Schaefer, J.P., Allwardt, D., Montgomery, R.J.V. and Karner, T.X. (2002) 'The role of cultural factors on clients' attitudes toward caregiving, perceptions of service delivery and service utilization', *Home Health Care Services Quarterly*, 21 (3–4): 65–88.

Lampley-Dallas, V.T. (2002) 'Research issues for minority dementia patients and their caregivers: what are the gaps in our knowledge base?', *Alzheimer Disease and Associated Disorders*, 16 (2): S46–9.

Langa, K.M., Chernew, M.E., Kabeto, M.U., Herzog, A.R., Oftedal, M.B., Willis, R.J., Wallace, R.B., Mucha, L.M., Straus, W.L. and Fendrick, M.A. (2001) 'National estimates of the quantity and cost of informal caregiving for the elderly with dementia', *Journal of General Internal Medicine*, 16 (11): 770–8.

Langdon, S.A., Eagle, A. and Warner, J. (2007) 'Making sense of dementia in the social world: a qualitative study', *Social Science and Medicine*, 64 (4): 989–1000.

Lawton, J. (2000) *The Dying Process: Patients' Experience of Palliative Care*. London: Routledge.

Lawton, M.P. (1997) 'Assessing quality of life in Alzheimer Disease research', *Alzheimer Disease and Associated Disorders*, 11 (Suppl. 6): 91–9.

Layder, D. (1998) *Sociological Practice: Linking Theory and Social Research*. London: Sage.

Lechner, C. (2003) 'Social, political and economic considerations of dementia care mapping', in A. Innes (ed.), *Dementia Care Mapping: Applications Across Cultures* Baltimore, MD: Health Professions Press. pp. 123–34.

Lee, E. (1982) 'A social systems approach to assessment and treatment for Chinese-American families', in M. McGoldrick, J. Giordano, J.K. Pearce and J. Giordano (eds), *Ethnicity and Family Therapy*. New York: Guildford Press. pp. 527–51.

Lee-Treweek, G. (1997a) 'Emotion, work, order and emotional power in care assistant work', in N. James (ed.), *The Sociology of Health and the Emotions*. Oxford: Blackwell.

Lee-Treweek, G. (1997b) 'Women, resistance and care: an ethnographic study of nursing auxiliary work', *Work, Employment and Society*, 11 (1): 47–64.

Lee-Treweek, G. and Linkogle, S. (eds) (2000) *Danger in the Field: Risk and Ethics in Social Research*. London: Routledge.

Leibing, A. (2002) 'Flexible hips? On Alzheimer's disease and aging in Brazil', *Journal of Cross-Cultural Gerontology*, 17 (3): 213–32.

Leibing, A. (2006) 'Divided gazes: Alzheimer's disease, the person within and death in life', in A. Liebing and L. Cohen (eds), *Thinking about Dementia:*

Culture, Loss and the Anthropology of Senility. New Brunswick, NJ: Rutgers University Press. pp. 240–68.

Leichsenring, K. (2004) 'Providing integrated health and social care: a European overview', in K. Leichsenring and A.M. Alaszewski (eds), *Providing Integrated Health and Social Care for Older Persons: A European Overview of Issues at Stake.* Aldershot: Ashgate. pp. 9–52.

Levkoff, S., Levy, B. and Weitzman, P.F. (1999) 'The role of religion and ethnicity in the help seeking of family caregivers of elders with Alzheimer's disease and related disorders', *Journal of Cross-Cultural Gerontology,* 14 (4): 335–56.

Li, H. (2004) 'Barriers to and unmet needs for supportive services: experiences of Asian-American caregivers', *Journal of Cross-Cultural Gerontology,* 19: 241–60.

Lister, R. (1997) *Citizenship: Feminist Perspectives.* Basingstoke: Macmillan.

Longley, M. and Warner, M. (2002) 'The national policy context across Europe', in M. Warner, S. Furnish, M. Longley and B. Lawlor (eds), *Alzheimer's Disease: Policy and Practice across Europe.* Abingdon: Radcliffe Medical Press. pp. 11–26.

Lopez, A.D., Mathers, C.D., Ezzati, M., Jamison, D.T. and Murray, C.J.L. (eds) (2006) *Global Burden of Disease and Risk Factors.* Oxford University Press and The World Bank.

Lopez, S.H. (2006) 'Emotional labor and organized emotional care', *Work and Occupations,* 33 (2): 133–60.

Lowin, A., Knapp, M. and McCrone, P. (2001) 'Alzheimer's disease in the UK: comparative evidence on cost of illness and volume of health services research funding', *International Journal of Geriatric Psychiatry,* 16 (12): 1143–8.

Lutzky, S.M. and Knight, B.G. (1994) 'Explaining gender differences in caregiving distress: the roles of emotional attentiveness and coping styles', *Psychology and Aging,* 9 (4): 513–19.

Lyman, K.A. (1989) 'Bringing the social back in: a critique of the bio-medicalisation of dementia', *Gerontologist,* 29 (5): 597–604.

McCabe, L.F. (2006) 'The cultural and political context of the lives of people with dementia in Kerala, India', *Dementia,* 5 (1): 117–36.

McLean, A. and Perkinson, M. (1995) 'The head nurse as key informant: how beliefs and institutional pressures can structure dementia care', in N.J. Henderson and M.D. Vesperi (eds), *The Culture of Long-Term Care: Nursing-Home Ethnography.* London: Bergin and Garvey. pp. 127–48.

McColgan, G. (2001) *'They Come Here to Tangle': An Ethnographic Study of Relationships of People with Dementia.* PhD dissertation, University of Stirling.

McColgan, G. (2004) 'Images, constructs, theory and method: including the narrative of dementia', in A. Innes, C. Archibald and C. Murphy (eds), *Dementia and Social Inclusion: Marginalised Groups and Marginalised Areas of Dementia Research, Care and Practice.* London: Jessica Kingsley. pp. 169–83.

McCormack, B. (2003) 'Researching nursing practice: does person-centredness matter?', *Nursing Philosophy,* 4 (3): 79–88.

McCormack, B. (2004) 'Person-centredness in gerontological nursing: an overview of the literature', *Journal of Clinical Nursing,* 13 (s1): 31–8.

McElmurry, B.J., Solheim, K., Kishi, R., Coffia, M.A., Woith, W. and Janepanish, P. (2006) 'Ethical concerns in nurse migration', *Journal of Professional Nursing*, 22 (4): 226–35.

McGregor, J. (2007) '"Joining the BBC (British Bottom Cleaners)": Zimbabwean migrants and the UK care industry', *Journal of Ethnic and Migration Studies*, 33 (5): 801–24.

McHugh, K. (2003) 'Three faces of ageism: society, image and place', *Ageing and Society*, 23 (2): 165–85.

Mackenzie, J. (2006) 'Stigma and dementia: East European and South Asian family carers negotiating stigma in the UK', *Dementia*, 5 (2): 233–47.

McNamee, P., Bond, J. and Buck, D. (2001) 'Costs of dementia in England and Wales in the 21st century', *British Journal of Psychiatry*, 179: 261–6.

McPherson, C.J. and Addington-Hall, J.M. (2003) 'Judging the quality of care at the end of life: can proxies provide reliable information?', *Social Science and Medicine*, 56 (1): 95–109.

Mace, N.L. and Rabins, P.V. (2006) *The 36-Hour Day: A Family Guide to Caring for Persons With Alzheimer Disease, Related Dementing Illnesses, and Memory Loss in Later Life*. 4th edition. Baltimore: Johns Hopkins University Press.

MacRae, H. (1999) 'Managing courtesy stigma: the case of Alzheimer Disease', *Sociology of Health and Illness*, 21 (1): 54–70.

Mahoney, D.F., Cloutterbuck, J., Neary, S. and Zhan, L. (2005) 'African-American, Chinese and Latino family caregivers' impressions of the onset and diagnosis of dementia: cross-cultural similarities and differences', *Gerontologist*, 45 (6): 783–92.

Mannheim, K. (1936) *Ideology and Utopia*. New York: Harcart Brace.

Manthorpe, J. and Adams, T. (2003) 'Policy and practice in dementia care', in T. Adams and J. Manthorpe (eds), *Dementia Care,* London: Arnold. pp. 35–47.

Marshall, M. (1999) 'What do service planners and policy makers need from research?', *International Journal of Geriatric Psychiatry*, 14 (2): 86–96.

Maslow, K. and Whitehouse, P. (1997) 'Defining and measuring outcomes in Alzheimer Disease research: conference findings', *Alzheimer Disease and Associated Disorders*, 11 (Suppl. 6): 186–95.

Merton, R.K. (1937) 'The sociology of knowledge', *ISIS*, 27 (3): 493–503.

Mills, C. Wright (1959) *The Sociological Imagination*. Oxford: Oxford University Press.

Milne, A. and Chryssanthopoulou, C. (2005) 'Dementia care-giving in black and Asian populations: reviewing and refining the research agenda', *Journal of Community and Applied Social Psychology*, 15 (5): 319–37.

Minichiello, V., Browne, J. and Kendig, H. (2000) 'Perceptions and consequences of ageism: views of older people', *Ageing and Society,* 20 (3): 253–78.

Minkler, M. and Estes, C.L. (eds) (1991) *Critical Perspectives on Aging: The Political and Moral Economy of Growing Old*. Amityville, NY: Baywood Publishing Company.

Moise, P., Schwarzinger, M., Um, M.Y. and the Dementia Experts Group (2004) *Dementia Care in 9 OECD Countries. OECD Health Working Papers No.12.* Paris: OECD.

Moore, T.F. and Hollett, J. (2003) 'Giving voice to persons living with dementia: the researcher's opportunities and challenges', *Nursing Science Quarterly*, 16 (2): 163–7.

Morgan, D.G., Semchuk, K.M., Stewart, N.J. and D'Arcy, C. (2002) 'Rural families caring for a relative with dementia: barriers to use of formal services', *Social Science and Medicine*, 55 (7): 1129–49.

Morgan, D.G., Semchuk, K.M., Stewart, N.J. and D'Arcy, C. (2003) 'The physical and social environments of small nursing homes: assessing supportiveness for residents with dementia', *Canadian Journal on Aging*, 22 (3): 283–96.

Morris, J. (1993) *Independent Lives: Community Care and Disabled People*. Basingstoke: Palgrave Macmillan.

Morris, R.G., Woods, R.T., Davies, K.S. and Morris L.W. (1991) 'Gender differences in carers of dementia sufferers', *British Journal of Psychiatry*, 158 (Suppl. 10): 69–74.

Müller-Hergl, C. (2003) 'A critical reflection of dementia care mapping in Germany', in A. Innes (ed.), *Dementia Care Mapping: Applications Across Cultures*. Baltimore, MD: Health Professions Press. pp. 57–70.

Murman, D.L., Von Eye, A., Sherwood, P.R., Liang, J. and Colenda, C.C. (2007) 'Evaluated need, costs of care and payer perspective in degenerative dementia patients cared for in the United States', *Alzheimer Disease and Associated Disorders*, 21 (1): 39–48.

Navaie-Waliser, M., Feldman, P.H., Gould, D.D., Levince, C., Kuerbis, A.N. and Doelan, K. (2001) 'The experiences and challenges of informal caregivers: common themes and differences among whites, blacks and Hispanics', *Gerontologist*, 37 (1): 89–101.

Newcomer, R.J., Fox, P.J. and Harrington, C.A. (2001) 'Health and long-term care for people with Alzheimer's disease and related dementias: policy research issues', *Aging and Mental Health*, 5 (Suppl. 1): S124–37.

NICE-SCIE (2006) *Dementia: Supporting People with Dementia and their Carers in Health and Social Care. NICE Clinical Guideline 42*. London: National Institute for Health and Clinical Excellence and Social Care Institute for Excellence.

Nolan, M.R., Grant, G. and Keady, J. (1996) *Understanding Family Care*. Buckingham: Open University Press.

Nolan, M.R., Ryan, T., Enderby, P. and Reid, D. (2002) 'Towards a more inclusive vision of dementia care practice and research', *Dementia*, 1 (2): 193–211.

Nolan, M.R., Davies, S., Brown, J., Keady, J. and Nolan, J. (2004) 'Beyond "person-centred" care: a new vision for gerontological nursing', *Journal of Clinical Nursing*, 13 (3A): 45–53.

Nordeberg, G., Wimo, A., Jonsson, L., Kareholt, I., Sjolund, B.M., Largergren, M. and Von Strauss, E. (2007) 'Time use and costs of institutionalised elderly persons with or without dementia: results from the Nordanstig cohort in the Kungsholmen project – a population-based study in Sweden', *International Journal of Geriatric Psychiatry*, 22 (7): 639–48.

Nygard, L. (2006) 'How can we get access to the experiences of people with dementia? Suggestions and reflections', *Scandinavian Journal of Occupational Therapy*, 13 (2): 101–12.

O'Connor, D. (1993) 'The impact of dementia: a self psychological perspective', *Journal of Gerontological Social Work*, 20 (3–4): 113–28.

O'Connor, D., Phinney, A., Smith, A., Small, J., Purves, B., Perry, J., Drance, E., Donnelly, M., Chaudhury, H. and Beattie, L. (2007) 'Personhood in dementia care: developing a research agenda for broadening the vision', *Dementia*, 6 (1): 121–42.

O'Shea, E. (2004) *Policy and Practice for Dementia Care in Ireland.* Lampeter: Edwin Meller Press.

O'Shea, E. and O'Reilly, S. (2000) 'The economic and social cost of dementia in Ireland', *International Journal of Geriatric Psychiatry*, 15 (3): 208–18.

Oakley, A. (1999) 'People's ways of knowing', in S. Hood, B. Mayall and S. Oliver (eds), *Critical Issues in Social Research: Power and Prejudice.* Buckingham: Open University Press. pp. 154–70.

Oliver, M. (1996) *Understanding Disability: From Theory to Practice.* Basingstoke: Macmillan.

Oliver, M. (1998). 'Theories of disability in health practice and research', *British Medical Journal*, 317 (7170): 1446–9.

Oliver, M. and Barnes, C. (1998) *Disabled People and Social Policy.* London: Longman.

Papastavrou, E., Kalokerinou, A., Papacostas, S.S., Tsangari, H. and Sourtzi, P. (2007) 'Caring for a relative with dementia: family caregiver burden, *Journal of Advanced Nursing*, 58 (5): 446–57.

Parker, C. and Philp, I. (2004) 'Screening for cognitive impairment among older people in black and minority ethnic groups', *Age and Ageing*, 33 (5): 447–52.

Parker, J. (2001) 'Interrogating person-centred dementia care in social work and social care practice', *Journal of Social Work*, 1 (3): 329–45.

Parker, J. (2005) 'Constructing dementia and dementia care: daily practices in a day care setting, *Journal of Social Work*, 5 (3): 261–78.

Parsons, T. (1951) *The Social System.* London: Routledge & Kegan Paul.

Patel, N., Mirze, N.R., Lindblad, P., Amstrrup, K. and Samaoli, O. (1998) *Dementia and Minority Ethnic Older People: Managing Care in the UK, Denmark and France.* Lyme Regis: Russell House Publishing.

Perrin, T. (1997) 'The positive response schedule for severe dementia', *Aging and Mental Health*, 1 (2): 184–91.

Phillips, M.R. (1993) 'Strategies used by Chinese families coping with schizophrenia', in D. Davis and S. Harrell (eds), *Chinese Families and the Post-Mao Era.* Berkley, CA: University of California Press. pp. 277–306.

Phillipson, C. (2003) 'Globalisation and the future of ageing: developing a critical gerontology', *Sociological Research Online*, 8 (4): 1–12: <http://www.socresonline.org.uk/8/4/phillipson.html> [accessed 12 December 2006].

Phinney, A. (1998) 'Living with dementia from the patient's perspective', *Journal of Gerontological Nursing*, 24 (6): 8–15.

Pointon, B. and Keady, J. (2005) 'Comment – dementia and long-term care: costs and compassion', *British Journal of Nursing*, 14 (8): 426.

Post, S. (1995) *The Moral Challenge of Alzheimer Disease.* Baltimore, Maryland: Johns Hopkins University Press.

Post, S. (2000a) *The Moral Challenge of Alzheimer Disease*. 2nd edn. Baltimore, MD: Johns Hopkins University Press. (1st edn 1995)

Post, S. (2000b) 'The concept of Alzheimer Disease in a hypercognitive society', in P.J. Whitehouse, K. Maurer and J.F. Ballenger (eds), *Concepts of Alzheimer Disease: Biological, Clinical and Cultural Perspectives*. Baltimore, MD: Johns Hopkins University Press. pp. 245–56.

Post, S. (2001) 'Comments on research in the social sciences pertaining to Alzheimer's disease: a more humble approach', *Aging and Mental Health*, 5 (1): 107–19.

Poveda, A.M. (2003) 'An anthropological perspective of Alzheimer Disease', *Geriatric Nursing*, 24 (1): 26–31.

Powell, J.L. (2001) 'Theorizing gerontology: the case of old age, professional power, and social policy in the United Kingdom', *Journal of Aging and Identity*, 6 (3): 117–35.

Powell, J.L. and Biggs, S. (2003) 'Foucauldian gerontology: a methodology for understanding aging', *Electronic Journal of Sociology*, 17 (2): 1–10: <http://www.sociology. org/content/vol17.2/03_powel_biggs.html>

Powers, B.A. (2001) 'Ethnographic analysis of everyday ethics in the care of nursing home residents with dementia', *Nursing Research*, 50 (6): 332–9.

Preston, L., Marshall, A. and Bucks, R.S. (2007) 'Investigating the ways that older people cope with dementia: a qualitative study', *Aging and Mental Health*, 11 (2): 131–43.

Prior, L. (2003) 'Belief, knowledge and expertise: the emergence of the lay expert in medical sociology', *Sociology of Health and Illness*, 25: 41–57 Sp. Iss. SI.

Proctor, G. (2001) 'Listening to older women with dementia: relationships, voices and power', *Disability and Society*, 16 (3): 361–76.

Putney, N.M., Alley, D.E. and Bengston, V.L. (2005) 'Social gerontology as public sociology in action', *American Sociologist*, 36 (4): 88–104.

Rait, G. and Burns, A. (1997) 'Appreciating background and culture: the South Asian elderly and mental health', *International Journal of Geriatric Psychiatry*, 12 (10): 973–7.

Reed, J., Cantley, C., Clarke, C. and Stanley, D. (2002) 'Services for younger people with dementia', *Dementia*, 1 (1): 95–122.

Rimmer, E., Stave, C., Sganaga, A. and O'Connell, B. (2005) 'Implications of the Facing Dementia Survey for policy makers and third-party organizations across Europe', *International Journal of Clinical Practice*, 59 (Suppl. 146): 34–8.

Robertson, A. (1990) 'The politics of Alzheimer's Disease: a case study in apocalyptic demography', *International Journal of Health Services*, 20 (3): 429–42.

Robinson, A. and Cubit, K. (2007) 'Caring for older people with dementia in residential care: nursing students' experiences', *Journal of Advanced Nursing*, 59 (3): 255–63.

Robinson, E. (2002) 'Should people with Alzheimer's Disease take part in research?', in H. Wilkinson (ed.), *The Perspectives of People with Dementia: Research Methods and Motivations*. London: Jessica Kingsley. pp. 101–7.

Rosengard, A., Laing, I., Ridley, J. and Hunter, S. (2007) *A Literature Review on Multiple and Complex Needs*. Edinburgh: Scottish Executive. <http://www.scot

land.gov.uk/Publications/2007/01/18133419/0> [accessed 31 January 2008].

Royal College of Nursing (1995) *Nursing and Older People: Report of the RCN Taskforce on Nursing and Older People.* London: RCN.

Royal Commission on Long-Term Care (1999) *With Respect to Old Age: Long-Term Care – Rights and Responsibilities.* London: Stationery Office.

Ryan, T., Nolan, M., Enderby, P. and Reid, D. (2004) '"Part of the family": sources of job satisfaction amongst a group of community-based dementia care workers', *Health and Social Care in the Community,* 12 (2): 111–18.

Sabat, S.R. (1994) 'Excess disability and malignant social-psychology – A case study of Alzheimer's disease', *Journal of Community and Applied Social Psychology,* 4 (3): 157–66.

Sabat, S.R. (2001) *The Experience of Alzheimer's Disease: Life through a Tangled Veil.* Oxford: Blackwell.

Sabat, S.R. (2002) 'Surviving manifestations of selfhood in Alzheimer's disease: a case study', *Dementia,* 1 (1): 25–36.

Sabat, S.R. (2005) 'Capacity for decision-making in Alzheimer's disease: selfhood, positioning and semiotic people', *Australian and New Zealand Journal of Psychiatry,* 39 (11–12): 1030–5.

Sabat, S.R. (2006) 'Mind, meaning and personhood in dementia: the effects of positioning', in J.C. Hughes, S.J. Louw and S.R. Sabat (eds), *Dementia: Mind, Meaning and the Person.* Oxford: Oxford University Press. pp. 287–302.

Sabat, S.R. and Collins, M. (1999) 'Intact social, cognitive ability and selfhood: a case study of Alzheimer's disease', *American Journal of Alzheimer's Disease,* 14 (1): 11–19.

Sabat, S.R. and Harré, R. (1992) 'The construction and deconstruction of self in Alzheimer's Disease', *Ageing and Society,* 12 (4): 443–61.

Sabat, S.R., Fath, H., Moghaddam, F.M. and Harré, R. (1999) 'The maintenance of self-esteem: lessons from the culture of Alzheimer's sufferers', *Culture and Psychology,* 5 (1): 5–31.

Salguero, R.J., Kohn, R., Salguero, L.F. and Marotta, C.A. (1998) 'Caregivers of persons with Alzheimer's Disease: cultural differences in perceived caregiver burden in Guatemala and Rhode Island', *Journal of Cross-Cultural Gerontology,* 13 (3): 229–40.

Sands, L., Ferreira, P., Stewart, A., Brod, M. and Yaffe, K. (2004) 'What explains differences between dementia patients and their caregivers' rating of patients' quality of life?', *American Journal of Geriatric Psychiatry,* 12 (3): 272–80.

Sassi, F. and McDaid, D. (eds) (1999) *Transnational Analysis of the Socio-Economic Aspects of Alzheimer's Disease (AD) in the European Union.* London: London School of Economics and Political Science.

Schneider, J., Hallam, A., Kamrual Islam, M., Murray, J., Foley, B., Atkins, L., Banerjee, S. and Mann, A. (2003) 'Formal and informal care for people with dementia: variations in costs over time', *Ageing and Society,* 23 (3): 303–26.

Schulz, R. (2001) 'Some critical issues in caregiver intervention research', *Aging and Mental Health,* 5 (1): S112–15.

Schulz, R. and Williamson, G.M. (1997) 'The measurement of caregiver outcomes in Alzheimer disease research', *Alzheimer Disease and Associated Disorders,* 11 (6): 117–24.

Scottish Executive (2007) *Social Inclusion Research Bulletin No.: 16/2007*: <http://www.scotland.gov.uk/Resource/Doc/173580/0048431.pdf> [accessed 3 March 2008].

Scurfield-Walton, M. (2003) 'Dementia Care Mapping and Staff Development', in A. Innes (ed.), *Dementia Care Mapping: Applications Across Cultures*. Baltimore: Health Professions Press.

Selai, C. and Trimble, M.R. (1999) 'Assessing quality of life in dementia', *Aging and Mental Health*, 3 (2): 101–11.

Sidell, M. (1995) *Health in Old Age: Myth, Mystery and Management*. Buckingham: Open University Press.

Slocum, H.E. (1989) '"Not him again!": thoughts on coping with irritating elderly patients', *Geriatrics*, 44 (10): 75–84.

Smith, S.C., Murray, J., Banerjee, S., Foley, B., Cook, J.C., Lamping, D.L., Prince, M., Harwood, R.H., Levin, E. and Mann, A. (2005) 'What constitutes health-related quality of life in dementia? Development of a conceptual framework for people with dementia and their carers', *International Journal of Geriatric Psychiatry*, 20 (9): 889–95.

Social and Health Care Workforce Group (2002) *Independent Sector Workforce Survey 2001*. London: Employers' Organisation for Local Government.

Solari, C. (2006) 'Professionals and saints: how immigrant careworkers negotiate gender identities at work', *Gender and Society*, 20 (3): 301–31.

Steeman, E., De Casterle, B.D., Godderis, J. and Grypdonck, M. (2006) 'Living with early-stage dementia: a review of qualitative studies', *Integrative Literature Reviews and Meta-Analyses*, 54 (6): 722–38.

Steeman, E., Godderis, J., Grypdonck, M., Bal, N. and De Casterle, B.D. (2007) 'Living with dementia from the perspective of older people: is it a positive story?', *Aging and Mental Health*, 11 (2): 119–30.

Stehr, N. (2003) 'The social and political control of knowledge in modern societies', *International Social Science Journal*, 55 (178): 643–55.

Stommel, M., Collins, C.E. and Given, B.A. (1994) 'The costs of family contributions to the care of persons with dementia', *The Gerontologist*, 34 (2): 199–205.

Sutherland, S. (1999) *With Respect to Old Age: Long-Term Care – Rights and Responsibilities: A Report by the Royal Commission on Long-Term Care*. London: The Stationary Office: <http://www.archive.official-documents.co.uk/document/cm41/4192/4192.htm> [accessed 12 December 2006].

Sweeting, H. and Gilhooly, M. (1997) 'Dementia and the phenomenon of social death', *Sociology of Health and Illness*, 19 (1): 93–117.

Szasz, T. (1974) *The Myth of Mental Illness*. London: Harper and Row.

Tellis-Nayak, V. and Tellis-Nayak, M. (1989) 'Quality of care and the burden of two cultures: when the world of the nurse's aide enters the world of the nursing home', *Gerontologist*, 29 (3): 307–13.

Tester, S. (1999) 'Comparative approaches to long-term care for adults', in J. Clasen (ed.), *Comparative Social Policy: Concepts, Theories and Methods*. Oxford: Blackwell. pp. 136–58.

Thomas, W.H. (1996) *Life Worth Living: How Someone You Love Can Still Enjoy Life in a Nursing Home*. Acton, MA: VanderWyk and Burnham.

Thompson, L. and Kingston, P. (2004) 'Measures to assess the quality of life for people with advanced dementia: issues in measurement and conceptualisation', *Quality in Ageing*, 5 (4): 29–39.

Ticehurst, S. (2001) 'Is dementia a mental illness?', *Australian and New Zealand Journal of Psychiatry*, 35: 716–23.

Townsend, P. (1962) *The Last Refuge*. London: Routledege & Kegan Paul.

Townsend, P. (2006) 'Policies for the aged in the 21st century: more "structured dependency" or the realisation of human rights?', *Ageing and Society*, 26: 161–79.

Townsend, P. (2007) 'Using human rights to defeat ageism: dealing with policy-induced "structured dependency"', in M. Bernard and T. Scharf (eds), *Critical perspectives on Ageing Societies*. Bristol: Policy Press. pp. 27–44.

Tronto, J.C. (1993) *Moral Boundaries – A Political Argument for an Ethic of Care*. London: Routledge.

Turner, B.S. (1990) 'Outline of a theory of citizenship', *Sociology*, 24 (1): 89–217.

Turner, B.S. (2001) 'The erosion of citizenship', *British Journal of Sociology*, 52 (2): 189–210.

Ungerson, C. (1987) *Policy is Personal: Sex, Gender and Informal Care*. London: Tavistock.

Ungerson, C. (2005) 'Care, work and feeling', *Sociological Review*, 53 (Suppl. 2): 188–203.

Ungerson, C. and Yeandle, S. (2007) 'Conclusion: dilemmas, contradictions and change', in C. Ungerson and S. Yeandle (eds), *Cash for Care in Developed Welfare States*. Basingstoke: Palgrave Macmillan. pp. 187–206.

Vernooij-Dassen, M.J.F.J., Moniz-Cooke, E.D., Woods, R.T., De Lepeleire, J., Leuschner, A., Sanetti, O., De Rotrou, J., Kenny, G., Franco, M., Peters, V., Iliffe, S. and The INTERDEM Group (2005) 'Factors affecting timely recognition and diagnosis of dementia across Europe: from awareness to stigma', *International Journal of Geriatric Psychiatry*, 20 (4): 377–86.

Vesperi, M.D. and Henderson, J.N. (1995) 'Introduction', in N.J. Henderson and M.D. Vesperi (eds), *The Culture of Long-Term Care: Nursing Home Ethnography*. London: Bergin and Garvey. pp. 1–4.

Vincent, J. (2003) *Old Age*. London: Routledge.

Vincent, J. (2006a) 'Anti-ageing science and the future of old age', in J.A. Vincent, C.R. Phillipson and M. Downs. *The Futures of Old Age*. London: Sage. pp. 192–200.

Vincent, J. (2006b) 'Globalization and critical theory: political economy of world population issues', in J. Baars, D. Dannefer, C. Phillipson and A. Walker (eds), *Aging, Globalization and Inequality: The New Critical Gerontology*. Amityville, NY: Baywood Publishing Company. pp. 245–71.

Vittoria, A.K. (1998) 'Preserving selves: identity work and dementia', *Research on Aging*, 20 (1): 91–136.

Vittoria, A.K. (1999) '"Our own little language": naming and the social construction of Alzheimer's disease', *Symbolic Interaction*, 22 (4): 361–84.

Von Kondratowitz, H.J. (2003) 'The legacy of social constructionism for social gerontology', in S. Biggs, A. Lowenstein and J. Hendricks (eds) (2003) *The Need for Theory: Critical Approaches for Social Gerontology*. Amitville, NY: Baywood Publishing Company. pp. 45–62.

Voss, S.J. (1996) 'The church as an agent in rural mental health', *Journal of Psychology and Theology*, 24 (2): 114–23.

Waldemar, G., Phung, K.T.T., Burns, A., Georges, J., Hansen, F.R., Iliffe, S., Marking, C., Rikkert, M.O., Selmes, J., Stoppe, G. and Sartrius, N. (2007) 'Access to diagnostic evaluation and treatment for dementia in Europe', *International Journal of Geriatric Psychiatry*, 22 (1): 47–54.

Walker, A. (2006) 'Reexamining the Political Economy of Aging: Understanding the Structure/Agency Tension', in J. Baars, D. Dannefer, C. Phillipson and A. Walker (eds), *Aging, Gobalization and Inequality: The New Critical Gerontology*. Amityville, NY: Baywood Publishing Company.

Walker, A. and Phillipson, C. (1986) 'Introduction', in C. Phillipson and A. Walker (eds), *Ageing and Social Policy: A Critical Assessment*. Aldershot: Gower. pp. 1–12.

Wanless, D. (2006) *Securing Good Care for Older People: Taking a Long-Term View*. London: Kings Fund.

Ward-Griffin, C., Bol, N. and Oudshoorn, A. (2006) 'Perspectives of women with dementia receiving care from their adult daughters', *Canadian Journal of Nursing Research*, 38 (1): 120–46.

Warner, M. and Furnish, S. (2002) 'Towards coherent policy and practice in Alzheimer's disease across the EU', in M. Warner, S. Furnish, M. Longley and B. Lawlor (eds), *Alzheimer's Disease: Policy and Practice across Europe*. Abingdon: Radcliffe Medical Press. pp. 175–92.

Warnes, T. and Phillips, J. (2007) 'Progress in gerontology: where are we going now?', in M. Bernard and T. Scharf (eds), *Critical Perspectives on Ageing Societies*. Bristol: Policy Press. pp. 139–54.

Whitehouse, P. (1999) 'Conclusion: quality of life in Alzheimer's disease: future directions', *Journal of Mental Health and Aging*, 5 (1): 107–111.

Whitlatch, C.J., Judge, K., Zarit, S.H. and Femia, E. (2006) 'Dyadic intervention for family caregivers and care receivers in early-stage dementia', *Gerontologist*, 46: 688–94.

Wilkinson, D., Sganga, A., Stave, C. and O'Connell, B. (2005) 'Implications of the Facing Dementia Survey for health care professionals across Europe', *International Journal of Clinical Practice*, 59 (S146): 27–31.

Wilkinson, H. (ed.) (2002) *The Perspectives of People with Dementia: Research Methods and Motivations*. London: Jessica Kingsley.

Williams, J. and Rees, J. (1997) 'The use of "dementia care mapping" as a method of evaluating care received by patients with dementia: an initiative to improve quality of life', *Journal of Advanced Nursing*, 25: 316–23.

Wilson, G. (1995) *Community Care: Asking the Users*. London: Chapman and Hall.

Wilson, G. and Fearnley, K. (2007) *The Dementia Epidemic: Where Scotland is Now and the Challenge Ahead*. Edinburgh: Alzheimer Scotland.

Wimo, A., Jonsson, L. and Winblad, B. (2006) 'An estimate of the worldwide prevalence and direct costs of dementia in 2003', *Dementia and Geriatric Cognitive Disorders*, 21 (3): 175–81.

Winblad, B., Ljunggren, G., Karlsson, G. and Wimo, A. (1996) 'What are the costs to society and to individuals regarding diagnostic procedures and care of patients with dementia?', *Acta Neurologica Scandinavica*, Suppl. 168: 101–4.

Wittenberg, R., Sandhu, B. and Knapp, M. (2007) 'Funding long-term care: the public and private options', in E. Mossialos, A. Dixon, J. Figueras and J. Kutzin (eds), *Funding Health Care: Options for Europe*. New York: World Health Organization and Oxford University Press. pp. 226–49.

Wolstenholme, J., Fenn, P., Gray, A., Kenne, J., Jacoby, R. and Hope, T. (2002) 'Estimating the relationshop between disease progression and cost of care in dementia', *British Journal of Psychiatry*, 181: 36–42.

Woodrow, P. (1998) 'Interventions for confusion and dementia: changing cultures', *British Journal of Nursing*, 7 (21): 1329–31.

Woods, B., Keady, J. and Seddon, D. (2007) *Involving Families in Care Homes: A Relationship-Centred Approach to Dementia Care*. London: Jessica Kingsley. pp. 76–97.

Woods, R.T. (1989) *Alzheimer's Disease: Coping with a Living Death*. London: Souvenir.

World Health Organization [WHO] (2001) *Fact Sheet No. 265: Mental and Neurological Disorders*: <http://www.who.int/mediacentre/factsheets/fs265/en/> [accessed 12 December 2006].

World Health Organization [WHO] and World Psychiatric Association [WPA] (2002) *Reducing Stigma and Discrimination against Older People with Mental Disorders: A Technical Consensus Statement*. Geneva: WHO/MSD/MBD/02.3.

World Health Organization [WHO] (2006) 'Mental Health and Substance Abuse Facts and Figures: Alzheimer's Disease: The Brain Killer': <http://www.searo.who.int/en/Section1174/Section1199/Section1567/Section1823_8066.htm> [accessed 23 January 2008].

Writh, L. (1936) 'Preface', in K. Mannheim, *Ideology and Utopia: An Introduction to the Sociology of Knowledge*. Translated by L. Writh and W. Shils. New York: Harcourt Brace.

Yeo, G., Gallagher-Thompson, D. and Lieberman, M. (1996) 'Variations in dementia characteristics by ethnic category', in G. Yeo and D. Gallagher-Thompson (eds), *Ethnicity and the Dementias*. Washington, DC: Taylor & Francis. pp. 21–30.

Zarit, S.H., Gaugler, J.E. and Jarrott, S.E. (1999) 'Useful services for families: research findings and directions', *International Journal of Geriatric Psychiatry*, 14 (3): 165–77.

Zola, I.K. (1972) 'Medicine as an institution of social control', *Sociological Review*, 20 (4): 487–504.

INDEX

Adams, T. 29, 51
Adamson, J. 77–8
Adelman, R.C. 129
adult daughters, as carers 105–6
advanced dementia sufferers,
    research 124
African-American ethnic communities
    78, 79–80, 82, 88, 111
African/Caribbean ethnic
    communities 78
ageing
    biomedicalization of 21
    dementia as normal part of,
        assumption 8, 10
    normal 8, 21
    social-gerontological understandings
        of 19–22
ageism 98
Aggarwal, N. 124
Alzheimer, Alois 4, 5
Alzheimer's disease 8
    costs issues 33–4
    and demography 20
    histories of development 4–5, 134
    ignorance about in minority
        populations 80
    institutionalization, need for 54
    Malignant Social Psychology model
        applied to 14–15
    and public culture 9
Alzheimer's disease Movement
    6, 46–7, 131, 162
Alzheimer's Society, France 74
Alzheimer's Society, Netherlands 74
Alzheimer's Society, UK 28, 74
American Indian tribes 85
analysis levels 149, 161–2
Aneshensel, C.S. 162

anti-ageing science 22
anti-dementia drugs 6, 22
Antuono, P. 151
apocalyptic demography 20
Aranda, M.P. 84, 86, 111
Arkansas Delta, caregiving in 79–80
art therapy 13
Asian populations, caregiving in
    74, 78, 80
Asian-Americans 87
Askham, J. 56
asylums 42
attentiveness 53

Bamford, C. 127
Barnes, C. 155
Barnett, E. 107–8
Bartlett, R. 157
Beard, R.L. 124
Beattie, A.M. 78
Beck, C. 92, 117–18, 129
Becker, H.S. 2, 145, 152, 153
'bed and body' care 96
Bell, V. 18
Berghmans, R.L. 116, 117
Best Friends Approach to Dementia Care,
    The (Bell and Troxel) 18
Bettio, F. 59
Beyer, J. 151
Biggs, S. 142, 144, 145
Binney, E. A. 21
biomedical approaches/biomedicalization
    concept
    see also medical
        model/medicalization
        of dementia
    dominance of 144, 145
    medicalization of dementia 1, 5

biomedical approaches/biomedicalization concept *cont.*
  social-gerontological understandings of age 21, 22
  and stigma of dementia 76
black populations, caregiving in 80
Bond, J. 5, 126, 141–2, 143, 160
Boston, ethnic groups in 78
Bowes, A. 89, 158
Bradford Dementia Group 16
Brannelly, T. 50, 53, 157
Brazil, caregiving in 79
Bredin, K. 15, 16, 18, 51
Brooker, D. 17–18
Bruce, E. 127

Cantley, A. 158
Capstick, A. 16
care dyads 50
caregiver burden 105
caregiving 45–71
  see also person-centred care/personhood
  challenges 68
  dilemmas of caregivers 97
  expectations 46–54, 69
  faith, importance for caregivers 79
  ideals of 45, 47–8, 66, 68, 135
  implications for family care 60–2
  informal 40–1
  location of care 62–4
  moral practice 47
  paid care 41–3, 106–7
  providers of care 54–62
  student nurses, experiences of 94
  sufferers, as heterogenous group 64–71
  undervaluation of care work 70, 99
  unpaid family caregivers *see* family carers, unpaid
  'warehousing' model 100
  women as carers 48, 69
cash-for-care schemes 61
Certified Nursing Assistants (CNAs) 96
Chee, Y.K. 85
China
  cognitive impairment, attitudes to 84
  dementia care in 75
  filial piety 85

Chinese-American ethnic communities 77–9, 81, 82, 87, 89
chronic illness, dementia as 3
Chryssanthopoulou, C. 80–1
citizenship 154–62
Clare, L. 143
closure of long-stay wards 42
CNAs (Certified Nursing Assistants) 96
Cohen-Mansfield, J. 100
communication 50
competence 53
Connell, C.M. 79, 112
consent issues, research 115–18
constraints, physical or chemical 5
construction of dementia 7–11, 134
control issues 117–18
Cooke, D.D. 114
costs of dementia 28–9, 33–7, 61
Cotrell, V. 119
Cree society 82
critical gerontology 20, 22, 143, 161–2
Cubit, K. 94
cultural space of dementia 2
culture
  beliefs about 'other' cultures 78
  comparative study of countries 83–4
  cultural groupings, approach to caregiving 84–8
  ethnicity 76–83
  and ethnicity, caregiving examples 88–91
  and experience of dementia 75–91, 135
  health professionals' views of groupings 82
  service provision cultures 91–9
  traditions of family care 84
  understandings about dementia 72–3

Davis, D.H.J. 15, 16, 60
decision-making 117
definitions of dementia 4
demented role 9
Dementia Care Mapping 16–17
dementia epidemic 29, 33
dementia patients
  'early' and 'late' stage dementia 109
  as heterogenous group 64–8, 69

dementia patients *cont.*
  misunderstanding of 93
  passivity of 96
  subgroups 85–6
*Dementia Reconsidered: the Person
  Comes First* (Kitwood) 11
dementia-ism 17
demography 20, 28
developing countries, and lower
  dementia prevalence 28
deviance, medicalization of 5
Dewing, J. 117
Di Minno, M.D. 81
diagnosis of dementia
  early diagnosis requirement 32–3
  timing considerations 39
  under-diagnosis 32
dialectics of dementia 11
'difficult' patients 98
Dillman, R.J.M. 5
Dilworth-Anderson, P. 75–6
disability, and medical model 137
disability movement 61
disability research 155, 156
disease, dementia as 18
diversity of dementia sufferers
  ethnic 65–6
  geographical 66–71
Donovon, J. 77–8
Douthit, K. 44
Downs, M. 108
Dressel, P. 38, 39–40
drug treatment 6, 22
dying process 15

early diagnosis requirement 32–3
Eastern Europe, caregiving in 74
economic issues 33–7, 135
Edvardsson, D. 48–9
Elliott, K.S. 81
epistemology 143, 144, 145
Estes, C.L. 21, 144
ethic of care model 53
ethnic diversity of sufferers 65–6
ethnicity 76–83
  and culture, caregiving examples
    88–91
  ethnic diversity of sufferers 65–6

ethnicity *cont.*
  research, inclusion of ethnic groups
    in 110–11
European Union countries, convergence
  of dementia care policies 30
existing knowledge on dementia 1–26
  social construction 7–11, 134, 159–60
  social science 2–3, 22–5
expectations, dementia care 46–54, 69

faith, importance for caregiving 79
family carers, unpaid
  costs of care 35
  economic issues 34
  implications for care 60–2
  informal caregiving 40–1
  research 104–6
Featherstone, M. 21
feminism, and citizenship 155
Field, D. 142
'folk' beliefs 89–90
Fontana, A. 15
Forbat, L. 51, 81
Foucault, Michel 96
Fox, P. 6, 129, 162
France, Alzheimer's Society
  in 74
Fukushima, T. 97, 127
funding of care 36–7

Gaze, concept of 96
geographical diversity of sufferers
  66–71
Gerdner, L.A. 79–80
gerontological nursing,
  person-centred 17
Gibson, B.E. 75–6
Gibson, G.D. 79, 112
Global Burden of Disease (World
  Health Report) 35
Goffman, E. 42
Goldsmith, M. 107
Guangzhou region, China 84
Guatemala, caregiving in 86, 87
Gubrium, J.F.
  alternative explanations of 23
  on caregivers 54
  on 'cultural space' of dementia 2

Gubrium, J.F. *cont.*
  on medicalization of dementia 8
  on old age 9, 10
  on popularization of dementia 162
  and Vittoria 24

Hammersley, M. 147
Harding, N. 2, 10, 18, 19, 134
Hatfield, K. 13
head nurses 92–3
health and illness 142
  sociology of 3, 153
'health care triads' 50
Henderson, L.C. 84–5
Henderson, N.J. 83, 84–5, 96, 98–9
Hendrie, H.C. 28
Hepworth, M. 21
Hicks, M.H.R. 87
'high-income' countries 28
Hispanic communities 82, 111
Holst and Hallberg 123
Holstein 2, 4, 5
hooks, bell 159
Hulko, W. 86, 150
human rights 157

ideals of caregiving 45, 47–8, 66, 68, 135
Ikels, C. 84
Iliffe, S. 76
immigrants, as caregivers 57–9
inclusiveness 156–7
India 83, 85
individualistic analysis level 149, 163
informal care *see* family carers, unpaid
Innes, A. 13
institutional care 41–3
  effects on elderly people 42
  historical images of 41–2
  location of establishments 55
  order and control function 10–11
  social science 24
interactionist perspectives 3
interviews 122, 123
Irish-American ethnic communities 78, 79

Janevic, M. R. 79
Japanese caregiving 89, 97
Jewish people 57–8, 65

Johnson (2005) 20
Journal of Dementia Care 16, 96

Kalis, A. 48
Kasayka, R. 13
Katz, S. 22
Kaufman, S.R. 21, 22
Keen, J. 34
Kelly, F. 120
Kelly, M.P. 142
Kerala (India), lack of dementia
  awareness in 83–4
Kitwood, Tom 18
  carers on ideas of 16
  experience of dementia sufferers 107
  on Malignant Social Psychology 12,
    14–15, 23, 142
  on 'moral' challenge of dementia 24
  on 'new culture' of care 42
  on person-centred care *see*
    person-centred care/personhood
  on relationships, importance for
    dementia sufferers 40
  and Sabat 14–15
  on standard paradigm 148
Knapp, M. 28
Knight, B.G. 88–9
knowledgable patient 3
knowledge generation and development
  dementia studies model 133–64
  citizenship 154–62
  dementia, knowledge of 162–4
  social inclusion 155, 158
  social science perspective 136–43
  sociology of knowledge, application
    of ideas from 143–53
Kolb, D. 138
Kontos, P. 89
Korea, caregiving in 85, 87–8, 89
Kosloski, K. 90
Kraepelin 5

labelling of dementia
  see also stigma
  and institutionalization of sufferers 42
  and medicalization of dementia 4, 6
  and social contruction of
    dementia 8, 9
  social isolation, promoting 156

Lam, M.S.C. 87
Langdon, S.A. 122
Latino caregivers 80, 82
learning cycle 138, 139, 140
Lechner, C. 44
Lee-Treweek, G. 49, 62, 63
Leibing, A. 79, 96
Leichsenring, K. 156
Levkoff, S.E. 79, 82, 85
Li, H. 87
life history 55
location of caregiving 62–4, 69
Longley, M. 30
Lopez, S.H. 49
Lyman, K.A. 5, 7

MacRae, H. 74
Mahoney, D.F. 80, 82
Malignant Social Psychology (MSP)
    12, 14–15, 23, 142
managers of care settings, views 92–3
Mannheim, K. 149, 150
Manthorpe, J. 29, 76
marginalized groups 94, 110–14, 161
Marshall, M. 91
mask of ageing/dementia 21
McCabe, L.F. 83–4, 86
McColgan, G. 10, 42
McCormack, B. 17, 118
McElmurry, B.J. 56–7
McGregor, J. 58, 59, 60
McLean 92–3, 94
medical advances, and prolonging
    of life 21
medical model/medicalization of
    dementia 3, 4–7, 134
    and 'folk' beliefs 89–90
mental illness 162
Merton, R.K. 149
migrant workers, as carers 57–9
Milne, A. 80–1
minority groups see ethnicity
misdiagnosis 81
moral practice 47
MSP (Malignant Social Psychology)
    12, 14–15, 23, 142
Müller-Hergl, C. 16
multi-method research 124, 125
myths of old age 19

National Institute of Aging (US) 129
negativity and stigma 39–40
Netherlands
    Alzheimer's Society in 74
    family carers 61
neurobiology/neuropsychology 5
Nolan, M. 104, 160
normal ageing 8, 21
North America 84
nursing assistants, US 95
nursing homes 74, 92–3, 97
Nygard, L. 118

Oakley, A. 147–8
observation 124–5
O'Connor, D. 15, 109, 113, 157
OECD (Organization for Economic
    Cooperation and Development)
    31–2, 33, 35
old age, pathology and normalcy 5
Oliver, M. 155
ontology 145
oppressions, multiple 86
Organization for Economic
    Cooperation and Development
    (OECD) 31–2, 33, 35
O'Shea, E. 39
outreach services 86

PACE (Problem of All-Inclusive Care
    for the Elderly) 95
paid care 41–3, 106–7
Palfrey, C. 2, 10, 18, 19, 134
Parker, C. 77
Parkes 158–9
Parsons, T. 9
participatory research 117
Perkinson 92–3, 94
person-centred care/personhood
    117, 150, 159, 160
    challenges 98
    and institutional care 97
    and Kitwood 11–13, 49, 55, 92
    practical implications 15–18
    spatial and social context of
        individual 67
Philp, I. 77
Phinney, A. 124–5
politicization of dementia 27–33, 135

Portugal, stigma of dementia in 74
positive person work 13
Post, S.
  on care 47, 48, 55, 60–1
  on 'moral' challenge of dementia
    23, 24
  on research 127, 130
Powell, J. 142, 144, 145
Powers, B.A. 97
Preston, L. 123
prevalence of dementia, estimates
  27–8, 29
Prior, L. 7
privileges, multiple 86
Proctor, G. 120
psycho-social approaches 1
Puerto Rican ethnic communities 78, 79
Putney, N.M. 141

qualitative research 123
quality of life measures 127, 130

relationship-centred care 160
relationships, importance to dementia
  sufferers 40–1
research 102–31, 136, 153
  advanced dementia sufferers 124
  applied nature of 31
  conduct 114–15
  consent 115–18
  costs 121
  disseminating 128–31
  including dementia sufferers
    in 115–25
    practical issues 121–2
  methods of 122–5
  multi-method studies 124, 125
  non-therapeutic 116
  observation 124–5
  outcomes and measurement challenge
    125–8
  participatory 117
  quality of life measures 127, 130
  role of researcher in facilitating
    research process 118–22
  social 104–14
  success measures 127

responsibility 53
responsiveness 53
restraint culture, care homes 97
Rhode Island (US), caregiving in 86
Robinson, A. 94
rural areas, services in 67, 69
Russian Orthodox Christians, as caregivers
  57–8

Sabat, Steven 17, 18, 23
  and Kitwood 14–15
  and self 13–14, 19, 89, 143, 150
Sabat and Harré, experience of
  dementia sufferers 107
Salguero, R. J. 87
Schultz, R. 119
Scotland
  free personal care in 36
  South Asians in 89
  stigma of dementia in 73
screening, cognitive impairment 77
Scurfield-Walton, M. 16
SDAT (Senile Dementia of the
  Alzheimer's Type) 24–5
self
  and Dewing 117
  and Sabat 13–14, 19, 143, 150
senile dementia 8
Senile Dementia of the Alzheimer's
  Type (SDAT) 24–5
senility, and old age 8
service provision cultures 91–9
Shue, V. 117–18
sick role 9
slavery 79–80
Slocum, H.E. 98
Smith, R.W. 15
Smith, S.C. 126
social construction of dementia/social
  constructionism 7–11,
  134, 159–60
social context of dementia 37–40
  negativity and stigma 39–40
social gerontology 134, 159, 161
  understandings of ageing 19–22
social inclusion 108–9, 155, 158
social model of dementia 137–8

social psychology 1, 11–19, 134
  contribution to understandings/
    conceptualisations of dementia
    18–19
social research, focus of 104–14
  aspects of experience of dementia
    sufferer 107–10
  conduct of research 114–15
  marginalized groups, including
    110–14
  trends 103
  unpaid family caregivers 104–6
social science 2–3, 22–5
  knowledge generation and
    development dementia studies
    model 134, 136–43
sociology
  of dementia 2, 3, 141
  of health and illness 3
  of knowledge 143–53
socio-structural perspectives 3
Solari, C. 57–8, 59
somatic origin 5
South Asia, caregiving in 74, 78
South Asian communities, Scotland 89
stage theories 1
Steeman, E. 123–4
stigma 39–40, 73–5, 92
  see also labelling of dementia
student nurses, experiences of 94
subcultures, caregiving 95
support groups 82, 87
surrogate decision-making 117–18
surveillance culture, care homes 97
Sutherland Report 36
Sweden, qualitative research 123
symptoms of dementia 19
Szasz, T. 7

Tellis-Nayak, V. 42
Ter Meulen, R.H.J. 116, 117
Ticehurst, S. 6–7
Townsend, P. 36, 42, 154, 157
traditions of care 84
Tronto, J.C. 53

Troxel, D. 18
Turner, B.S. 158

under-diagnosis of dementia 32
undervaluation of care work 70
Ungerson, C. 50
United Kingdom
  Alzheimer's Society in 74
  family carers 61
  minority ethnic groupings, carers in 77
  prevalence of dementia in 28, 76
United States
  African-American ethnic
    communities 78, 79–80,
    82, 88, 111
  American Indian tribes 85
  Asian-Americans 87
  Boston, ethnic groups in 78
  Chinese-American ethnic
    communities 77–9, 81,
    82, 87, 89
  Irish-American ethnic communities
    78, 79
  Japanese caregivers 89
  nursing assistants 95
  Rhode Island, caregiving in 86
unmet needs 87
urban settings, care in 67
utopian ideals, caregiving 45, 47–8, 66,
  68, 135

Vincent, J. 22, 24, 26
Vittoria, A.K. 10

Wanless, D. 36
Ward-Griffin, C. 129
Warner, M. 30
well-being, notions of 15
Whitehouse, P. 130
Wilkinson, H. 89
With Respect to Old Age (Royal
  Commission) 63
Wittenberg, R. 43
women as carers 48, 69
World Health Organization (WHO) 46

Supporting researchers for more than forty years

Research methods have always been at the core of SAGE's publishing. Sara Miller McCune founded SAGE in 1965 and soon after, she published SAGE's first methods book, Public Policy Evaluation. A few years later, she launched the Quantitative Applications in the Social Sciences series – affectionately known as the "little green books".

Always at the forefront of developing and supporting new approaches in methods, SAGE published early groundbreaking texts and journals in the fields of qualitative methods and evaluation.

Today, more than forty years and two million little green books later, SAGE continues to push the boundaries with a growing list of more than 1,200 research methods books, journals, and reference works across the social, behavioral, and health sciences.

From qualitative, quantitative, mixed methods to evaluation, SAGE is the essential resource for academics and practitioners looking for the latest methods by leading scholars.

www.sagepublications.com

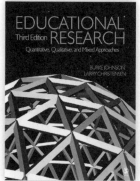

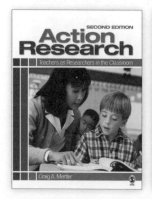

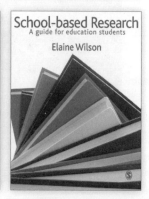

The Qualitative Research Kit

Edited by Uwe Flick

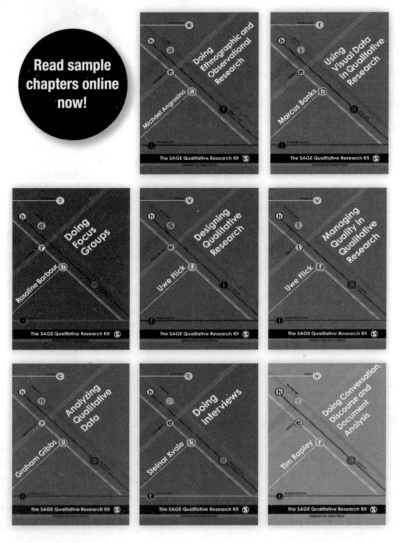

Read sample chapters online now!

Doing Ethnographic and Observational Research — Michael Angrosino — The SAGE Qualitative Research Kit — Edited by Uwe Flick

Using Visual Data in Qualitative Research — Marcus Banks — The SAGE Qualitative Research Kit — Edited by Uwe Flick

Doing Focus Groups — Rosaline Barbour — The SAGE Qualitative Research Kit — Edited by Uwe Flick

Designing Qualitative Research — Uwe Flick — The SAGE Qualitative Research Kit — Edited by Uwe Flick

Managing Quality in Qualitative Research — Uwe Flick — The SAGE Qualitative Research Kit — Edited by Uwe Flick

Analyzing Qualitative Data — Graham Gibbs — The SAGE Qualitative Research Kit — Edited by Uwe Flick

Doing Interviews — Steinar Kvale — The SAGE Qualitative Research Kit — Edited by Uwe Flick

Doing Conversation, Discourse and Document Analysis — Tim Rapley — The SAGE Qualitative Research Kit — Edited by Uwe Flick

www.sagepub.co.uk

SAGE